INDIA'S
SPIRITUAL RENAISSANCE

The life and times of Lord Chaitanya

bahu-koti chandra jini 'vadana ujjvala:
"The brilliance of Lord Chaitanya's face conquers millions of moons. . . ."

— Shrila Bhaktivinode Thakur

INDIA'S SPIRITUAL RENAISSANCE

The life and times of Lord Chaitanya

STEVEN ROSEN
FOREWORD BY SATSVARUPA DAS GOSWAMI

FOLK BOOKS

©1988 by Steven Rosen
All rights reserved.

No part of this book may be reproduced, stored in a retrieval system, or transmitted in any form, by any means, including mechanical, electronic, photocopying, recording, or otherwise, without the prior written permission of the publisher.

First FOLK Books Edition published in 1988

Library of Congress Cataloging-in-Publication Data

Rosen, Steven, 1955-
    The Life and Times of Lord Chaitanya
    Includes index.
    1. Lord Chaitanya—Biography. I. Title.
ISBN 0-9619763-0-6
Library of Congress Catalog Card Number: 87-83265

For information or correspondence with the author, please write to FOLK Books, P.O. Box 400716, Brooklyn, New York 11240-0716.

DEDICATION
To Shri Satyaraj Khan,
one of Lord Chaitanya's intimate associates.
By mercifully giving me the name Satyaraj Das
("Servant of the King of Truth"),
my spiritual master,
His Divine Grace A. C. Bhaktivedanta Swami Prabhupada,
saw fit to remind me
that I am eternally a servant of devotees
such as Shri Satyaraj Khan.

ACKNOWLEDGMENTS

The book you now hold in your hands is the collaborative effort of many individuals. The immediate followers of Lord Chaitanya, who scrupulously endeavored to fully document the Lord's activities, are perhaps the earliest and most important contributors to this work. More directly, many of Lord Chaitanya's most exalted present-day followers have enriched the manuscript in a number of ways. Satsvarupa Das Goswami, for instance, kindly contributed a gracious and encouraging foreword. Tamal Krishna Maharaj and Hridayananda Das Goswami have expressed their appreciation for the project, and they have supported my work by giving many helpful suggestions in regard to content and propriety. Jagat Guru Swami, a dear friend, financed a lengthy journey throughout the Indian subcontinent and personally took me to many of the sites that are directly connected to Lord Chaitanya's pastimes.

Several devotees with whom I had become very close and other good friends in the world of academia have thoughtfully read my text and provided a thorough critique of early drafts of the manuscript. Dr. O.B.L. Kapoor, Lakshmi Nrisinghadeva Das, Lochanananda Das, Mrigendra Das, Rupa Vilas Das, and Vaiyasaki Das were six of the devotees whose critiques benefited the book enormously. Nancy Terry did a first-rate copyediting job, and Per Sinclair offered valuable advice in terms of Sanskrit grammar and Bengali translations.

Dr. Anant S. Tiwari, Professor of Sanskrit at the University of Gorakhpur, India, was also helpful, for he advised me to use the phonetic spellings of Sanskrit and Bengali words that appear throughout the text. He felt that the traditional diacritical marks used by scholars would be inconvenient for readers who were not familiar with Indian theological literature.

I would also like to thank the Bhaktivedanta Book Trust for the use of their archives. And especially for supplying the slides taken by Yadubara Das. These exclusive pictures represent the terra-cotta murals that grace the Mayapur Chandrodaya Mandir, a huge temple complex recently built just under a mile from Lord Chaitanya's birthplace. The murals were sculpted by Uddhaya Baug and were painted by Dinesh C. Mandal. Other photos were supplied by Bhavananda Roy Maharaj, who was very helpful in offering his photographic skills.

Early issues of *Back To Godhead* were an invaluable asset. Parts of this book are based on articles from that magazine. Staff members Yamaraj Das (who gave technical advice in terms of the artwork) and Pranada Dasi (who did the typesetting) were particularly accommodating.

Nandini Dasi of *ISKCON World Review* took time out of her busy schedule to assist with this project. Her enthusiasm is always encouraging, and she readily supplied many of the photos depicting the Deity forms of Lord Chaitanya. In addition, she gave me free access to the IWR archives.

Finally, I would like to thank my wife Vrinda-devi, who worked diligently to manage our household affairs, giving me the necessary free time to complete the book. She also contributed directly by lending her artistic skills in terms of design and production. She is my partner, friend, and colleague, and I remain sincerely grateful.

CONTENTS

PREFACE .... *i*
    Who Is Lord Chaitanya? .... *ii*
    "The Life and Times of Lord Chaitanya" .... *iii*
    Methodology .... *vi*

FOREWORD
    by Satsvarupa Das Goswami .... *ix*

THE DISCIPLIC SUCCESSION .... *xii*

INTRODUCTION 1
    East Meets West 2
    Shrila Prabhupada 2
    Sanatan Dharma 3
    The Vedic Literature 3
    Vidyapati, Jayadeva, and Chandidas 5
    The Alvars 5
    Buddha and Shankara 7
    Ramanujacharya 7
    Madhvacharya 8
    Achintya-bhedabheda-tattva 9
    Hinduism 9
    Foreign Invaders 10
    Navadvip 11
    Spiritual Renaissance 12

CHAPTER ONE: *Birth and Divinity* 15
    Shri Nimai 16
    Bodily Symptoms 16
    Visual Description 17
    Authorized Biographies 17
    Scriptural Evidence 18

CHAPTER TWO: *Infancy and Youth* 23
    The Serpent 23
    Krishna! Krishna! 23
    Two Thieves 24
    Clay and Sweets 24
    Nimai and Krishna Are Nondifferent 25
    Ekadashi Day 26
    Naughty Nimai 26
    Lakshmidevi 27
    Nimai the Scholar 28
    Marriage 29
    Shri Ishvara Puri 29

CHAPTER THREE: *The Defeat of Keshava Kashmiri* 31
    Glorification of the Ganges 32
    Goddess Saraswati 33
    The Greatest Scholar 34
    Journey to Bangladesh 34
    Tapan Mishra 35
    The Passing of Lakshmidevi 35

CHAPTER FOUR: *Initiation in Gaya* 37
    Initiation 38
    Divine Madness 39
    Return Journey 40
    Total Absorption 40
    Electrical Devotion 41
    Nityananda Prabhu 41
    Adwaita Acharya 42
    Gadadhar Pandit 42
    Shrivas Thakur 43
    Haridas Thakur 43

CHAPTER FIVE: *The Hare Krishna Maha-Mantra* 45
    Maha-Mantra Defined 46

Krishna and His Name are One 46
Science of Sound 47
Inverted Mantra 48
The Name and the Shadow 48
Three Stages of Chanting 49
The Ten Offenses 49
Material Pleasure Insufficient 50
The Greatest Sacrifice 51
The Ultimate Goal 51

CHAPTER SIX: *Navadvip Pastimes* 53
Jagai and Madhai 54
Chand Kazi 55
Vegetarianism: The Religious Imperative 56
Change of Heart 57
Mahabhava Prakash 58

CHAPTER SEVEN: *Renunciation* 61
Why Keshava Bharati? 62
Sannyasa 63
Tricked by Nityananda 64
Breaking the Lord's Staff 65

CHAPTER EIGHT: *Jagannath Puri* 67
Sarvabhauma Bhattacharya 67
The Lord Tested 68
The Vedanta Sutra 69
"As It Is" 70
Atmarama Verse 71
The Conversion 72

CHAPTER NINE: *Ramananda Roy* 75
Miracles 76
Governor of Rajahmundry 78
Conversations 79
Varnashram Dharma 79
Higher Truth 80
The Ultimate End 81
Highest Rasa 82
Confidential Knowledge 83
Shrimati Radharani 83
The Delusions of Love 84

CHAPTER TEN: *Shri Rangam* 87
- Conversations with Vyenkata Bhatta 87
- Lord Chaitanya's Jagannath 88
- The Illiterate Brahmana 88
- Converting the Buddhists 90

CHAPTER ELEVEN: *King Prataparudra* 93
- Aversion to Opulence 93
- Petitioning the Lord 94
- The Lord's Garment 95
- Ramananda Roy 95
- The King's Determination 96
- The King's Son 97
- The King Sweeps the Road 98
- The King Sees the Lord 98
- Service to the Lord 99
- Dabhir Khas and Sakara Mallik 100

CHAPTER TWELVE: *Vrindavan* 103
- The Animals Chant and Dance 104
- Mathura 104
- Recognizing Mahaprabhu 105
- Holiest Places in the Universe 105
- Govardhan Hill 105
- Gopalaji 106
- Childhood Pastimes 106
- The Highest Paradise 107

CHAPTER THIRTEEN: *Rupa Goswami* 109
- Muslim Soldiers 109
- The Prayers of Rupa Goswami 110
- Journey of the Soul 111
- Devotional Service 112
- Devotional Sweetness 112
- "Rupanuga" 113

CHAPTER FOURTEEN: *Sanatan Goswami* 115
- Benares 115
- Shiva or Vishnu? 116
- Mahaprabhu In Benares 117
- Instructions to Sanatan Goswami 117
- Brahman 117

 Paramatma 118
 Bhagavan 119
 An Analogy 119
 Expansion of God 120
 Prakashananda Saraswati 122
 The Conversion 124
 Sankirtan In Benares 124
 Historical Controversy 125

CHAPTER FIFTEEN: *Return to Puri* 127
 Ballabhacharya 127
 Guru Nanak 128
 Devotees come to Puri 129
 The Perfect Example 129
 Kalidas 132
 Kavi Karnapur 132
 Haridas Thakur 133
 The Passing of Haridas Thakur 135
 Gambhira Lila 136
 The Shikshashtakam Prayers 138

CHAPTER SIXTEEN: *The Lord's Disappearance* 141
 Drowning at Sea 141
 A Natural Death 142
 Tota Gopinath 142
 The Jagannath Deity 143
 Mahaprabhu as God 144

AFTERWORD 147
 Patronage 148
 Devotees in Vrindavan 148
 Shyamananda and Baladev 148
 Every Town and Village 149

APPENDIX ONE: *The Festival of Lord Jagannath* 151
 Ratha-yatra and the British Imperialists 152
 Idol Worship 154
 The Story of Lord Jagannath 155
 Jagannath Puri 156
 Ratha-yatra 157

APPENDIX TWO: *Devotion and Reflection*
by William H. Deadwyler, Ph.D. 161

REFERENCES 173
INDEX 186

P R E F A C E

I first heard the name "Lord Chaitanya" in May 1973, during my second visit to the New York Hare Krishna temple. I had been invited to the temple a week earlier by a devotee, and I was unimpressed with my first visit. In fact, I had no intention of returning. Nonetheless, my devotee friend had insisted that I visit him one more time, for the following week his *guru* was scheduled to arrive from India.

"What was the point of seeing his teacher?" I asked myself. "What could the *guru* give me that the disciple could not?" I was soon to learn the answer, for somehow or other I decided to visit the temple one last time. Or so I thought.

His Divine Grace A. C. Bhaktivedanta Swami Prabhupada, the movement's founder and spiritual preceptor, was indeed in town that weekend lecturing on the teachings of Lord Chaitanya. As I sat in front of him, struggling to understand his words through his heavy Bengali accent, I found myself listening with rapt attention.

Although I had never met a genuine saint, I could immediately understand that Shrila Prabhupada definitely fit into that category. The contrast between Prabhupada and any other religious person I had ever met was more than glaring. I remember that I was amazed, in fact, at the confident and yet pure, humble and sincere manner in which he spoke. I was also moved by his complete dedication to his subject.

i

And his subject was God. This, too, was unique. Many religious leaders, it seemed to me, were often side-tracked by superficial rituals and mundane piety, neglecting to teach the masses about God and the essence of spiritual life. In their sermons, and even in their traditional scriptures, I could barely find answers to the basic questions of human life: Who am I? Why am I here? Who is God? Where is His Kingdom?

Years earlier, I had practically begged my rabbi to answer questions that Prabhupada was almost nonchalantly addressing in this lecture about Lord Chaitanya. My rabbi never answered those questions, and, for a time, I had given up the quest for spiritual knowledge. There were, I am sure, others who could have answered my questions, but my rabbi was not able to.

Yet Prabhupada's complete absorption in spiritual knowledge was obvious, and he was willing to share this knowledge with all who would listen. I, for one, was becoming more and more desirous of hearing Prabhupada speak about his method of attaining spiritual enlightenment—especially because he presented it not as *his* method but as the original method of saints and sages of the past. And he supported everything he said with authoritative quotes from scripture and personal realization. Here, I thought, is someone who takes religion seriously.

The more he spoke, the more my desire to adhere to his process increased. He repeatedly asserted that *Bhakti-yoga*, "devotional service to God," is the nonsectarian, spiritual path for which everyone was inwardly looking, the path that would fulfill the desires of anyone who traversed it. He said that the essence of this path can be found in the chanting of the *maha-mantra*: Hare Krishna, Hare Krishna, Krishna Krishna, Hare Hare/ Hare Rama, Hare Rama, Rama Rama, Hare Hare (pronounced Ha-ray, Krish-nah and Rah-mah). And he asked his listeners to read his book called *The Teachings of Lord Chaitanya*.

I took this book home with me and spent the entire night reading it. Soon after, I purchased Shrila Prabhupada's other books and gradually became convinced that there was great validity to his teachings. Remembering, however, that he had described *Bhakti-yoga* as an ancient path and not simply his own concoction, I decided to do some research on my own.

Who Is Lord Chaitanya?

Lord Chaitanya,[1] I discovered, was considered an especially confidential and esoteric incarnation of God by the orthodox Gaudiya Vaishnavas,

Preface

who base their conclusion on prophesies from the ancient Vedic scriptures. These scriptures foretold that God Himself would descend in the current age as a perfect devotee, and that He would start a movement based upon the chanting of the holy name of the Lord. The prediction, in fact, came to pass, for Lord Chaitanya spearheaded a spiritual renaissance in sixteenth-century India that had as its foundation the chanting of the Hare Krishna *maha-mantra*.

To be sure, there have been great religious reformations and spiritual uprisings in the Western world. But to my mind the depth and profundity of the tradition that was revitalized by Lord Chaitanya is incomparable to anything before or since. And Shrila Prabhupada represented the tenth generation of perfect masters in an esoteric line of disciplic succession (*parampara*) from the Lord Himself.[2] (See chart on page *xii*.) Enthusiastic if also unqualified to become part of that prestigious disciplic chain, I was initiated by Shrila Prabhupada in July 1975.

As I continued my research, I found that Lord Chaitanya's achievements were not simply abstract or philosophical. Five hundred years before Gandhi, this remarkable personality inaugurated a massive nonviolent civil-disobedience movement against the Islamic occupational government in India. He swept aside many of the stifling restrictions of the hereditary caste system and made it possible for all people to transcend social barriers and achieve the highest platform of spiritual enlightenment.

In doing so, He freed India's religious life from the stranglehold of a proud, intellectual elite. Superceding popular but outmoded rituals and superficial formulas, He introduced a revolutionary spiritual movement based on the world's oldest and most comprehensive religious scriptures, the *Vedas*. This movement, He taught, would have universal appeal because it was based upon the Absolute Truth, which transcends sectarian notions of race or creed. Lord Chaitanya's theory has today been proven; His movement has been spread to every nation of the world by Shrila Prabhupada and his International Society for Krishna Consciousness (ISKCON).

"The Life and Times of Lord Chaitanya"

In October 1984, while in India, I visited Dr. O.B.L. Kapoor, a distinguished scholar and the author of a book on Lord Chaitanya. Dr. Kapoor is also a disciple of Prabhupada's *guru*, Shrila Bhaktisiddhanta Saraswati

Thakur, and consequently he is Shrila Prabhupada's "Godbrother." I was thus anxious to benefit from his association.

Knowing that I was a writer, Dr. Kapoor asked me on our first meeting to write a book about Lord Chaitanya's life and times. "Your movement has a book about the *teachings* of Lord Chaitanya," he said, "but you do not have a biographical account, and that is a misfortune for the world." As he spoke, he seemed tired, as if he needed to rest. Although retired from a half-century teaching profession, he had just returned from a lecture tour. I asked him if I should leave, for I was unsure as to whether he was able to continue the discussion. But he was determined to make his point. "This book on the life of Lord Chaitanya would be a very important contribution," he said.

I had to be frank with him. Shrila Prabhupada had already given the world a book about the life of Lord Chaitanya. "Shrila Prabhupada has translated the *Chaitanya Charitamrita*," I said to him, "and this gives many details about the Lord's life and times."

He considered my response. His seventy-some-odd years gave him a depth and wisdom that I admired. "The *Chaitanya Charitamrita* is seventeen volumes long," he said impatiently, "and there are some who would find it intimidating. In addition, it is just as much philosophy as it is His life story."

He had my interest and he knew it. "Shrila Prabhupada's *Chaitanya Charitamrita* is a masterpiece," he continued with renewed enthusiasm, "but I am speaking about a single-volume account of the Lord's travels—who He met, where He went, what He said. The philosophy would come through, but it would be incidental. The Lord's life, in and of itself, is instructive. Such a book would be invaluable, and since you are already a writer, you should do it."

As I walked away that evening, I was overcome by a sense of trepidation. "How can I even consider this project?" I thought. "One has to be pure to write about the pastimes of the Lord. I could only do it an injustice."

Still, O.B.L. Kapoor was Prabhupada's Godbrother, and I took his arguments very seriously. After all, the Vedic scriptures teach that one should respect the spiritual master's Godbrothers in the same way that one respects the spiritual master. Shrila Prabhupada, in fact, is emphatic about this point in his own *Chaitanya Charitamrita*.[3]

It is, I must admit, difficult to accept *anybody* in the way that I accept Prabhupada. Nonetheless, I considered Dr. Kapoor's words carefully and thought about them for the next several weeks. When I returned to America, I discussed the subject with many of my senior Godbrothers. To my surprise, they encouraged me to undertake the project. Quoting *Bhagavad-gita* (9.22), one devotee said that "Krishna will carry what you lack and preserve what you have." Another said, "Lord Chaitanya is merciful; He will give you the necessary ability to write the book." These words and blessings from my Godbrothers gave me confidence.

Despite all encouragement, however, I knew that I was unqualified for the task. Yet more and more it was becoming an obsession. Although I was unsure whether or not I should attempt the work, I continually studied the life of Lord Chaitanya as presented in Shrila Krishnadas Kaviraj Goswami's authorized biography, *Shri Chaitanya Charitamrita*. In this way I had hoped to find the necessary inspiration to at least begin this ambitious project.

While reading, I came upon one particular passage that seemed to speak directly to me: "I wish the grace of Lord Chaitanya Mahaprabhu, by whose mercy even one who is fallen can describe the pastimes of the Lord."[4]

In Shrila Prabhupada's explanation of this verse, he elaborates: "To describe Shri Chaitanya Mahaprabhu or Lord Shri Krishna, one needs supernatural power, which is the grace and mercy of the Lord. Without this grace and mercy, one cannot compose transcendental literature. By dint of the grace of the Lord, however, *even one who is unfit for a literary career can describe wonderful transcendental topics*."[5] [italics added]

There is a similar verse wherein Kaviraj Goswami again expresses his apparent inadequacy in writing about Lord Chaitanya: "It is by the mercy of all the Vaishnavas and *gurus* that I attempt to write about the pastimes and qualities of Lord Chaitanya Mahaprabhu. Whether I know or know not, it is for self-purification that I write this book."[6] For Kaviraj Goswami, who is a perfectly liberated soul, such statements are little more than a manifestation of his superlative humility. But in regard to my own work, it is quite accurate that I require divine mercy. Furthermore, I am in need of the realization, so eloquently expressed by the Goswami, that this book is being written primarily for self-purification, not for publication.

Shrila Prabhupada had many times asked his followers to write about spiritual topics, and as long as they had remained faithful to the conclusions of the scriptures and the previous sages, he said, their work would be successful. Therein, I knew, lay the resolution to my dilemma. And this gave me the necessary impetus to begin writing about Lord Chaitanya, for total fidelity to tradition would certainly be a great challenge.

As quoted in the verse by Krishnadas Kaviraj Goswami, "One who is unfit for a literary career" certainly applied to me, especially in regard to transcendental literature. But if I could somehow convey the truths of the Vedic literatures and the sages of the past, avoiding concoction and novel interpretations, then such allegiance would assure the book's success. Perhaps it would even evoke the grace of the Lord.

Before embarking on the project, however, I felt the need to pray for purification before the three manifestations of the Lord that had played a special role in my own devotional life. Shri-Shri Radha Damodar, Shri-Shri Kishor-Kishori, and especially Shri-Shri Radha Govinda. So I traveled to Pennsylvania, Chicago, and back to New York, where these three sets of Radha-Krishna Deities respectively reside, and I begged Them for the necessary sincerity and intelligence to properly represent Lord Chaitanya.

Shri-Shri Radha Damodar had initially inspired me and watched me grow in devotional life as I traveled with Them throughout the United States. Shri-Shri Kishor-Kishori had presided, along with Shrila Prabhupada, over my initiation in 1975. And Shri-Shri Radha Govinda I continue to serve to this day, the following pages being nothing more than a humble offering at Their lotus feet. I pray that Shrila Prabhupada and the above manifestations of Krishna will be pleased by the endeavor.

Actually, if this work has any merit it is because it is based upon the Vedic conclusion as presented by Shrila Prabhupada. Although the moon is naturally dark and cold, it is illuminated by the reflection of the sun, which emits a vast amount of heat and light. Similarly, this biographical account may suffer some deficit in that I am the author. But if it can properly reflect the teachings of His Divine Grace A. C. Bhaktivedanta Swami Prabhupada, then it will shine brightly for all to see.

Methodology

My chief source for this work is Krishnadas Kaviraj Goswami's *Chaitanya Charitamrita*, as translated and explained by His Divine Grace A. C. Bhaktivedanta Swami Prabhupada. Other primary sources include Shrila Prabhupada's numerous magazine articles, recorded lectures, and personal letters to friends and disciples. Where other scholarly and academic sources deviate from Shrila Prabhupada's, I have explained why they do so. And after considering the relative authenticity and accuracy of such deviant texts, I have given an honest account of where they fall short. In all cases, thorough, scholarly research tends to support Shrila Prabhupada's presentation, and this will be proven throughout by reason and logic as well as by reference to literature written by Lord Chaitanya's contemporaries.

For this purpose, I have also consulted many historical and archaeological documents, and I have extensively referenced my statements. I have found the Archaeological Survey of India particularly helpful in this regard, since at the Survey I discovered the necessary reference materials needed to authenticate my arguments. In addition, to be as thorough as possible, I toured the Indian subcontinent just before I began this work. Visiting many of the places directly associated with Lord Chaitanya's pastimes served as a personal inspiration. Moreover, at these holy places I was able to secure many facts and heard about oral traditions that I would otherwise not have been able to obtain.

I have also used translations of early Bengali literature and scholarly studies of the Gaudiya tradition. Shrila Krishnadas Kaviraj himself used eyewitness accounts, such as the notes prepared by Murari Gupta (to retell the Lord's early pastimes) and the records kept by Swarup Damodar, the Lord's secretary (in order to document His later pastimes). Similarly relying on the work of my predecessors, I pray that my presentation is historically accurate and at the same time spiritually beneficial for all who read it.

I know, too, that this work will be full of faults, especially in terms of spiritual content. I ask my readers to forgive these errors. As it is said in *Shrimad Bhagavatam* (a spiritual treatise which is considered the essence of Vedic knowledge): "That literature which is full of descriptions of the transcendental glories of the name, fame, form, and pastimes of the unlimited Supreme Lord is a transcendental creation meant to bring about a revolution in the impious life of a misdirected civilization. Such transcendental literatures, even if imperfectly composed, are heard, sung and accepted by purified persons who are thoroughly honest." (S.B. 1.5.11) This work is only successful in as much as it is used to glorify Lord Chaitanya, the Supreme Personality of Godhead. And since I am unqualified to engage in such glorification, I fervently pray that the Lord will agree to communicate through this book, allowing me, the writer, to serve Him if only as an instrument.

Although the idea of God working through an ordinary living being may seem pretentious and even pompous, the Lord is ultimately "the Doer" of *all* activities, and I am simply asking for His *special* mercy in order to compensate for my own inadequacy. If that divine Player agrees to do this, then rather than being "imperfectly composed" this work will naturally reflect His own perfect nature and melodiously convey the glories of Lord Chaitanya. Then all of its readers will chant and dance in ecstasy.

FOREWORD

by Satsvarupa Das Goswami

Although many biographies of Lord Chaitanya Mahaprabhu have been written in the 500 years since His appearance, this book is the first one-volume life written by a direct disciple of His Divine Grace A. C. Bhaktivedanta Swami Prabhupada. It fulfills a distinct purpose, condensing the biographical information from the authoritative seventeen-volume rendering of Krishnadas Kaviraj Goswami's *Chaitanya Charitamrita* by Shrila Prabhupada into an easily readable and authorized form.

Steven Rosen's book is a faithful rendering of the gist of *Chaitanya Charitamrita*, to which he has added historical facts gathered from research into the life and times of Lord Chaitanya. The historical facts occur like tasty spicing or chutney added to a meal. But the main fare is the telling of the glorious activities of Lord Chaitanya, from the spiritual, *parampara* point of view.

The synopsis form adopted here is fundamental, but its value should not be minimized. Mr. Rosen writes as a patient, humble worker, carefully following the accounts given by Krishnadas Kaviraj and His Divine Grace A. C. Bhaktivedanta Swami Prabhupada, and therein lies the book's greatest asset. When describing activities of the Supreme Lord, concoctive interpretations are like deadly poison. The important quality of the spiritual biography is the author's depth of realization and his faithfulness to the disciplic succession. Thus Shrila Prabhupada writes in the introduction to his own translation and commentary on *Chaitanya Charitamrita*:

> This edition of *Shri Chaitanya Charitamrita* is presented for the study of sincere scholars who are really seeking the Absolute Truth. It is not the arrogant scholarship of the mental speculator but a sincere effort to serve the order of a superior authority whose service is the life and soul of this humble effort. It does not deviate even slightly from the revealed scriptures, and therefore anyone who follows in the disciplic line will be able to realize the essence of this book simply by the method of aural reception.

Mr. Rosen follows on this path. He also points out in several places how academic and nondevotional biographers have interpreted aspects of Lord Chaitanya's life in a mundane way, in some cases even falsifying the authentic records of His magnanimous deeds. Mr. Rosen analyzes these deviant theories, and gives evidence why we should accept only the accounts of the authoritative biographers.

It is a boon to get so much in such a small volume. *India's Spiritual Renaissance* is thus a good introduction for those who have not yet read the life of Lord Chaitanya, and it will also serve as a convenient reference for those who have already read the *Chaitanya Charitamrita*, who will relish hearing the pastimes (*lila*) of Lord Chaitanya in brief.

Krishnadas Kaviraj, the author of *Chaitanya Charitamrita*, suggests that there is a great joy awaiting one who makes a serious study of Lord Chaitanya's life: "If you are indeed interested in logic and argument, kindly apply it to the mercy of Shri Chaitanya Mahaprabhu. If you do so, you will find it to be strikingly wonderful." By an impartial study into Lord Chaitanya's contribution to humanity, one will conclude that He is the most magnanimous of all teachers and welfare workers. Most educators and philanthropists perform their activities in connection with the body, whereas Lord Chaitanya's activities are performed in connection with the eternal soul. Without neglecting the necessities of the body, Lord Chaitanya imparted the science of spiritual advancement for purifying the troubled condition of humanity. He distributed love of Godhead freely and taught spiritual truths that were never revealed by previous masters or incarnations.

Without interrupting the flow of the biographical narrative, Mr. Rosen gives ample evidence of the sublime teachings of Lord Chaitanya. The reader will especially benefit from the account about the chanting of the holy names of God, as taught by Lord Chaitanya. According to the Vedic

Foreword

scriptures, spiritual disciplines that were possible in former ages cannot be successfully practiced by people in today's fallen age of quarrel and hypocrisy (Kali Yuga). Only the chanting of the holy name is effective, and it can be adopted very easily. How Lord Chaitanya taught this process of chanting, and how it has come down in disciplic succession today, is one of the most important episodes conveyed in this book.

I will not delay the reader any longer, but I encourage you to now directly relish the pastimes of Lord Chaitanya.

एवं परम्पराप्राप्तमिमं राजर्षयो विदुः ।

THE DISCIPLIC SUCCESSION
Brahma-Madhva-Gaudiya Sampradaya

Bhagavan Shri Krishna
Brahma
Narada
Vyasadev
Madhvacharya
Padmanabha
Nrihari
Madhava
Akshobhya
Jayatirtha
Gyanasindhu
Dayanidhi
Vidyanidhi
Rajendra
Jayadharma
Purushottama
Brahmanyatirtha
Vyasatirtha
Lakshmipati
Madhavendra Puri
Ishvara Puri (Nityananda, Adwaita)
Shri Krishna Chaitanya Mahaprabhu
Rupa Goswami (Swarup Damodar, Sanatan Goswami)
Raghunath das Goswami, Jiva Goswami
Krishnadas Kaviraj Goswami
Narottam das Thakur
Vishvanath Chakravarti Thakur
(Baladev Vidyabhushan) Jagannath das Babaji
Bhaktivinode Thakur
Gaurakishor das Babaji
Bhaktisiddhanta Saraswati Thakur
His Divine Grace A. C. Bhaktivedanta Swami Prabhupada

INTRODUCTION

To understand the life and times of Lord Chaitanya (1486-1534), it is necessary to have background information about the fifteenth-century period in which He appeared, to know the historical setting and philosophical climate of the day. In Europe, at that time, culture and learning were undergoing rebirth, so to speak. This epoch in world history was subsequently dubbed the *Renaissance*, which in fact literally means "rebirth" or "renewal." For many, this period evokes a brilliantly colored picture of an age when all life was a work of art, an age of versatile craftsmen and cultured princes. One naturally thinks of Leonardo da Vinci or Michelangelo, or other divinely inspired painters and sculptors.

This unique time in the life of European culture also gave birth to religious upheaval, with Martin Luther's reformation of Christianity in Germany and, much earlier, St. Francis' move toward pantheism in Italy. But while the Renaissance undoubtedly produced individuals who were fascinated, and even obsessed, with God, it is more commonly remembered for its almost Aristotelian perception of the world. Renaissance philosophers, in particular, elucidated upon this materialistic world view. The works of Machiavelli, Bohme, Erasmus, Descartes, and Montaigne moved toward a philosophy of humanism in which emphasis shifted from God to man. According to many historians, it was the Renaissance that ushered in the scientific age—man became self-sufficient and had little need for a transcendent "God."

Because the Renaissance effected such a drastic change in man's attitude toward himself and the world around him, it has been widely accepted as one of the most noteworthy movements in European history. Indeed, this short time period, from the late 1400s to the early 1600s, changed the entire Western world, and its influence continues to affect our lives.

In India, too, this period was one of great renewal. But the Eastern flow moved in the opposite direction, and the resurgence of a deeply spiritual tradition inundated the Asian subcontinent. At the heart of this devotional renaissance was Lord Chaitanya Mahaprabhu, believed by His followers to be the Supreme Lord Shri Krishna in the guise of His own devotee. So intense was the movement inaugurated by Lord Chaitanya and His followers that the reverberations are still heard and felt around the world.

East Meets West

Lord Chaitanya's teaching reached Western shores by the grace of Shrila Bhaktivinode Thakur (1838-1914), a pure devotee of the Lord who was the first to express Mahaprabhu's teaching in English. He wrote many books that he mailed to academicians and scholarly institutions in both the United States and Europe. His son, Shrila Bhaktisiddhanta Saraswati (1874-1936), was a pure devotee as well, and he was to become widely known as the greatest authority on Lord Chaitanya's teachings since the time of the Lord's immediate disciples.

Shrila Prabhupada

It was Shrila Bhaktisiddhanta, in fact, who encouraged his foremost disciple, His Divine Grace A. C. Bhaktivedanta Swami Prabhupada (1896-1977), to personally come west and fulfill Lord Chaitanya's prophecy: "In every town and village of the world, My name will be sung, and the chanting of Hare Krishna, Hare Krishna, Krishna Krishna, Hare Hare/ Hare Rama, Hare Rama, Rama Rama, Hare Hare will permeate the globe."

This could only have been accomplished by Shrila Prabhupada, a pure devotee of Krishna, a scholar, and a religious leader of unassailable character and integrity. In 1965, at the age of sixty-nine, Shrila Prabhupada sailed alone and penniless from India to the United States and, after a year of great personal struggle and sacrifice, founded and incorporated the International Society for Krishna Consciousness (ISKCON) in New York City. His movement then expanded rapidly throughout the United States and the rest of the world.

By the time Shrila Prabhupada passed away in 1977, he had established more than one hundred Krishna conscious temples, *ashramas*, farms, and schools worldwide, and the public chanting of Hare Krishna, inaugurated by Lord Chaitanya, had become a colorful, familiar sight on the streets of most major cities. To date, the movement has distributed well over one hundred million copies of the sacred literatures of India (based on Lord Chaitanya's teachings) in some thirty languages.

Sanatan Dharma

The tradition represented by Shrila Prabhupada did not begin with Lord Chaitanya's spiritual renaissance, although it was certainly revitalized at that time. As the word "renaissance" implies, Lord Chaitanya reestablished and expanded upon a much older spiritual heritage. Gaudiya Vaishnavism, or Lord Chaitanya's Bengali ("Gauda-desh") devotional tradition, can be traced back to the prehistoric Brahma-Madhva Sampradaya (lineage), which has its roots in *sanatan dharma*, the "eternal function of the soul." The esoteric truths at the basis of this profound theological system are to be found in the Sanskrit Vedic literatures. Having an oral tradition dating back to antiquity, they are considered the world's most time-honored and comprehensive scriptural texts. They were put into written form some 5,000 years ago.

The Vedic Literature

According to an essential Vedic text, *Bhagavad-gita* (15.15), the original compiler of the *Vedas* is the Supreme Lord Himself. All religious traditions claim that their scriptures are divinely inspired. But only the Vedic tradition claims that its scriptures are actually *compiled* by God. Consequently, as one might suspect, the Vedic scriptural tradition is in a class of its own. A comparative study of the world's great religions reveals quite clearly the distinctive, all-inclusive nature of the Vedic revelation.

This is not merely a subjective view, but it is brought out in the traditions themselves. Jesus Christ, for example, admits the limitations of the Bible:

"There is much I have to say unto you, but your ears cannot bear it yet" (John, 16.12). And in the popular *Hadith*, the prophet Mohammed acknowledges a similar truth about Islam: "I have only spoken to men according to their relative mental capacities."[7] In sharp contrast to these two confessions, however, Lord Krishna says in *Bhagavad-gita* (7.2), "I shall now declare unto you in full this knowledge both phenomenal and noumenal, by knowing which there shall remain nothing further to be known." While Mahaprabhu recognized the importance and authenticity of all the major world religions, it was this all-inclusive Vedic tradition that He based His teachings upon.

This tradition is carefully passed down, from master to disciple, by highly qualified scholars and pure devotees of the Lord. In this way, the Vedic prophets sought to maintain the initial purity of their scriptural tradition. When properly received in disciplic succession, the *Vedas* are indeed devoid of the defects invariably associated with mundane literature, such as imperfection, interpolation, and irrelevancy. In this sense, too, the *Vedas* stand apart from other religious literature.

Further, the Vedic literatures contain information on everything from medicine and farming to a detailed explanation of time sequences on upper and lower planets; from techniques of *yoga* and meditation to household hints and recipes for tasty vegetarian dishes; from detailed explanations of governmental organization to masterful directions on constructing and decorating a temple or residential building. The verses in each of the thousands of Vedic texts conform to strict rules of poetry and meter. The *Vedas* contain drama, history, and complex philosophy, as well as simple lessons of etiquette. Military protocol, use of musical instruments, biographies of great saints and sages of the past—these are but a few of the subjects covered by the *Vedas*.

Most important for Lord Chaitanya, however, was the fact that the Vedic literature explained both *rasa* (relationship with God) and *bhakti* (devotional love) in minute detail, as a science. Lord Chaitanya based his movement on these texts, especially the *Bhagavad-gita*, *Shrimad Bhagavatam*, and the other *Puranas*. In addition, Mahaprabhu discovered the *Brahma-samhita* at the Adi Keshava temple (Trivandrum District, South India), and, when He traveled further south, He came upon Bilvamangal Thakur's *Krishna Karnamrita*; Mahaprabhu incorporated both of these works into His Gaudiya Vaishnava theology.

Vidyapati, Jayadeva, and Chandidas

Lord Chaitanya particularly relished the highly esoteric works of Vidyapati, Jayadeva Goswami and Chandidas, primarily because they elucidated upon the essence of spiritual life—the intimate pastimes of Radha and Krishna. Vidyapati was a famous composer of songs about these pastimes. He was born in a priestly family, in Mithila, and it is calculated that he composed his songs during the reign of King Shivasimha and Queen Lachimadevi in the beginning of the fourteenth century, almost one hundred years before the appearance of Lord Chaitanya Mahaprabhu. Vidyapati's songs about the pastimes of Shri Krishna express intense feelings of love for God, and Lord Chaitanya relished all those songs in His ecstasy of divine separation from Krishna.[8]

Jayadeva Goswami was born during the reign of Maharaja Lakshman Sen of Bengal in the eleventh or twelfth century. His father was Bhojadev, and his mother was Vamadevi. Most authorities acknowledge the village of Kendubilva in the Birbhum district of Bengal as his birthplace. Others, however, claim that he was born in Orissa, and still others say that he was born in South India. Nonetheless, it is certain that he lived in Navadvip for many years and that he passed the last days of his life in Jagannath Puri. One of his famous books is *Gita-govinda*, which is full of transcendental feelings of love for Krishna. The *gopis* (village cowherd girls who are considered the most intimate devotees of Lord Krishna) felt divine separation from Krishna before the *rasa* dance, as mentioned in the *Shrimad Bhagavatam*, and the *Gita-govinda* expresses such confidential, spiritual feelings. There are many important commentaries on the *Gita-govinda*.[9]

Chandidas was born in the village of Nannura, which is also in the Birbhum district of Bengal. He was born of a priestly family in the beginning of the fourteenth century. It has been suggested that Chandidas and Vidyapati were great friends because the writings of both express the transcendental feelings of love for Krishna in a similar way. The feelings of ecstasy described by Chandidas and Vidyapati were actually exhibited by Lord Chaitanya Mahaprabhu.[10]

The Alvars

There were many other important precursors to the Chaitanyite legacy.

For instance, the medieval *bhakti* movement flourished in South India with the Alvars, Yamunacharya, and his immediate follower, Ramanuja, the great sage from the Shri Sampradaya.[11] *Alvar* literally means "absorbed in meditation," and the saints and sages of the medieval *bhakti* movement were indeed absorbed in love of God. The following twelve Alvars, especially, were important promulgators of the *bhakti* religion later perfected by Lord Chaitanya: Poygai or Poykai Alvar; Bhutattar Alvar; Pey Alvar; Tirumalisai Alvar; Namm-Alvar of Satakopa; Madhurkavi Alvar; Kulashekhar Alvar; Periy-Alvar or Vishnuchitta; Andal Alvar; Tondaradippodi Alvar; Tiruppana Alvar; and Tirumangai Alvar.[12]

According to most scholars of Indian religion, all the Alvars lived before the ninth century. But according to the prominent historian, R. G. Bhandarkar, Kulashekhar probably lived in the first half of the twelfth century, while the earliest of the Alvars may be placed at about the fifth or the sixth century.[13] The Alvars composed the *Prabandham*, a collection of four thousand devotional songs in the language of Tamil. This work was regarded as very sacred and for some time was worshiped as the *Vaishnava Veda*. The special feature of the *bhakti* religion as preached by the Alvars was its accessibility to people of high and low castes, men and women, rich and poor, wise and ignorant, pious and impious alike. Among the Alvars themselves, Andal was a woman; Tiruppana belonged to the lower class; Kulashekhar was a king; and Tondaradippodi was a reformed sinner. The only thing necessary for realization, according to the Alvars, was *prapatti*, or self-surrender.

The songs of the Alvars have been a great source of inspiration to Vaishnavas throughout South India. According to some scholars, these songs may have influenced Vaishnavism in the North as well, since they taught the basic premise of *rasa* (relationship with God), soon to be developed into a science by the followers of Lord Chaitanya. While the Alvars emphasized the *rasas* of *dasya* (servant's love for his master), *sakhya* (friendly love), and *vatsalya* (parental love), Lord Chaitanya brought out the special nectar of the *madhurya* (conjugal) *rasa*. This "*rasa*" concept has been identified with both southern and northern Vaishnavism.

Whether in the South or the North, however, the great monotheistic tradition of Vaishnava (Vedic) philosophy in general was in a terrible slump during the medieval period. Despite the noble attempt of great devotees, such as the Alvars, India had long since become spiritually side-tracked by the teachings of Buddha and Shankara.

His Divine Grace A. C. Bhaktivedanta Swami Prabhupada, who brought Lord Chaitanya's teachings to every nation of the world. (pp. 2-3)

Shrila Bhaktisiddhanta Saraswati Thakur, foremost authority on the teachings of Lord Chaitanya and Shrila Prabhupada's spiritual master. (p. 2)

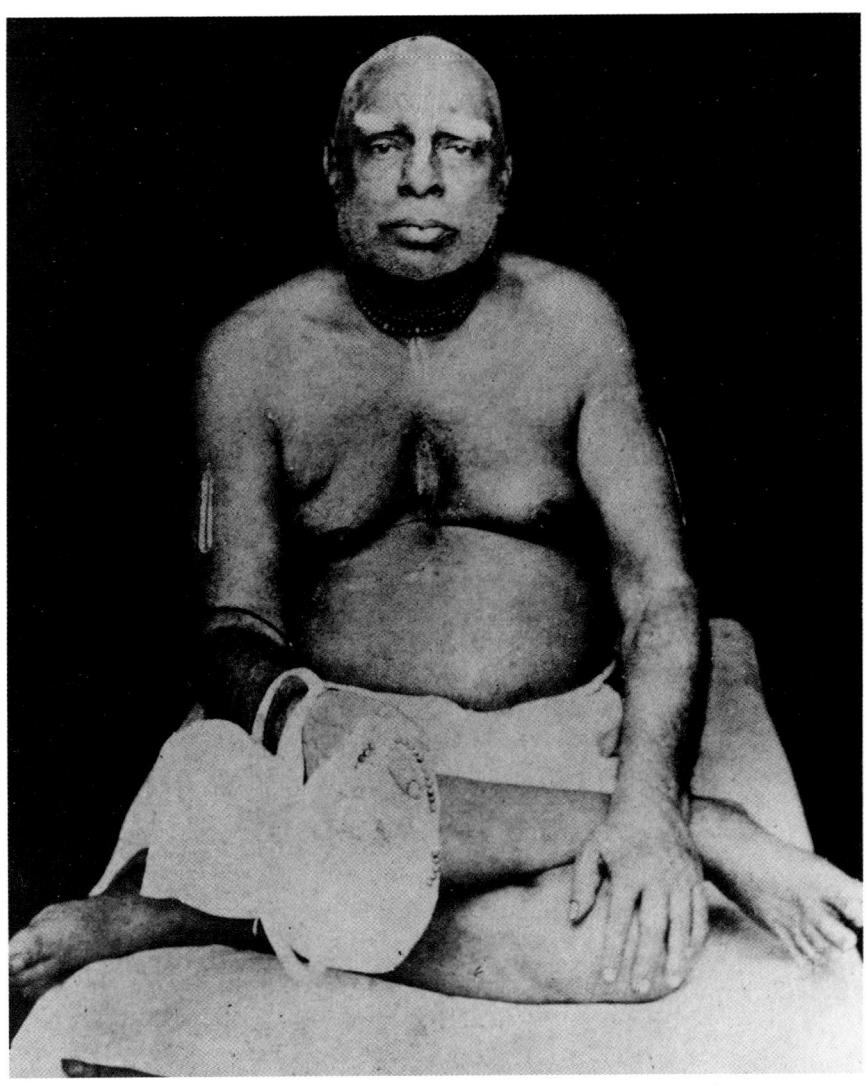

Shrila Bhaktivinode Thakur, the first to express Lord Chaitanya's teachings in English. (p. 2)

Deities of the Pancha-tattwa (from LEFT to RIGHT): Adwaita Acharya, Nityananda Prabhu, Lord Chaitanya, Gadadhar Pandit, Shrivas Thakur. (p. 51) The *neem* tree and reconstructed house commemorating Mahaprabhu's birthplace. (p. 16)

Detail of Deities in reconstructed house: Jagannath Mishra (the Lord's father) and Sachidevi, holding her divine child.

Shad-bhuj-murti, Lord Chaitanya's mystical six-armed form. (p. 72)

Shri Shri Radha-Govinda, the Divine Couple as they are lovingly worshiped by Chaitanya Mahaprabhu. (p. *vi*)

Lord Jagannath and His attendants, as they prepare for Puri's Ratha-yatra festival. (pp. 151–59)

The Festival of the Chariots, millions of pilgrims come to Jagannath Puri to see the parade of Lord Jagannath. (pp. 151-159)

Chaitanya Mahaprabhu was captivated by the majestic beauty of Shri Rangam. (p. 87)

Ranganath Swami (TOP), Shri Rangam's presiding Deity of Vishnu (Krishna). (p. 88) Deities of (LEFT to RIGHT) Baladev, Subhadra, and Jagannath (BOTTOM). (p. 68)

The same three Jagannath Deities as fashioned by Lord Chaitanya's own hands. (p. 88)

Lord Chaitanya's room (Gambhira). On the wall is an Orissan bas-relief of Lord Chaitanya—with Swarup Damodar on His right andRamananda Roy on His left. Below, His servant Govinda holds His waterpot. In the forefront are the Lord's quilt and shoes, preserved to this day. (p. 136)

Deity of Tota Gopinath, into whom the Lord amalgamated Himself. (pp. 142–43)

(TOP LEFT) Commemorative stamp issued by the Indian government in 1986, the Lord's 500th anniversary. (TOP RIGHT) India's former Prime Minister, Indhira Gandhi, offering *puja* (worship) to Lord Chaitanya. (BOTTOM) Gaudiya Vaishnavas engaging in *nagara-sankirtan*.

A terracotta bas-relief of the Lord revealing the secrets of Krishna consciousness.

Buddha and Shankara

As history relates, during the time of Buddha (500 B.C.) the Vedic religion had become somewhat debased. Followers of the *Vedas* were slaughtering animals in the name of Vedic sacrifice. Eventually, Buddha incarnated to condemn such hypocrisy. And, in so doing, he had to repudiate the *Vedas* altogether. He did, indeed, amass a large following.

But when Shankara later appeared in the eighth century, he reestablished the Vedic scriptures, albeit in perverted form. Shankara taught, in effect, that the *Vedas* were accurate and divinely inspired but were to be interpreted in an impersonalistic way. In other words, for Shankara, God was an abstract force, and any personal reference to God was to be taken metaphorically.

Ramanujacharya

The teachings of Shankara were challenged by the great devotional preaching of the Alvars, which culminated in the appearance of Ramanujacharya (1017-1137). He took the Vedic restoration one step further. Whereas Buddha had stopped the blatant hypocrisy of the ill-informed Vedic followers by denying the scriptures, and Shankara reinstated the Vedic scriptures by allowing his followers to misinterpret the contents, Ramanuja moved closer to the original monotheism of the *Vedas* by formulating his *Vishishtadvaita* philosophy—a sort of qualified monism.

We are the same as God, Ramanuja taught, but we are different as well. Superficially, it seemed that Ramanuja accentuated the similarity rather than the difference. Thus, according to his critics, his philosophy allowed less of an aptitude for devotional service, for if one is the same as God then such "service" loses meaning. "If both God and the living being are one," it might be asked, "then who is serving whom?"

The doctrine that espouses the oneness between God and the living being is more characteristic of Shankara's philosophy, and Ramanuja's system, in reality, comes closer than either Buddha or Shankara to the actual Vedic *siddhanta* (conclusion). This is so because Ramanuja ultimately acknowledged the distinction between the living entity and God.

This distinction was emphasized even further by Madhvacharya.

Madhvacharya

Approximately one hundred years after the time of Ramanuja, Madhvacharya (1239-1319) was to preach his doctrine of *dvaita*, clearly accentuating the dual nature of reality. Historically, Indian philosophical literature has largely been an ongoing exposition of the differences between Madhva's school of pure dualism and the monistic school of Shankaracharya. Shankaracharya's ideology was in fact taken a step further by Ballabha (Lord Chaitanya's contemporary), for he in some ways complemented Shankara with his *shuddhadvaita*, or "pure non-dualism."[14] Madhvacharya, Ramanuja, and even Ballabha recognized the oneness and difference between God and the living entity. Shankara only recognized the oneness.

According to Vedic theology, Madhva and Ramanuja especially stand out as the most authentically Vaishnava of all Indian philosophers because they emphasized the difference between God and the living entity (as opposed to the similarity). Still, it might be noted here that the Tattvavadis (a particular school of Madhvacharya's followers) were less in line with the teachings of Lord Chaitanya than were the followers of Ramanuja, who, in some ways, were very close to Lord Chaitanya.

Overall, Mahaprabhu promoted the view that God and the living being are one and different at the same time, although like Madhva and Ramanuja the Lord preferred to accentuate the difference. Consequently, Lord Chaitanya aligned himself with the Madhva Sampradaya and befriended many members of the Ramanuja (Shri) Sampradaya. It is also said that he gradually converted Ballabha, although the latter eventually founded his own school of thought.

But Lord Chaitanya was to further modify these philosophical systems. His teaching became known as *achintya-bhedabheda-tattva*, or the inconceivable and simultaneous oneness with and difference from God. We are one with God in *quality*, Mahaprabhu taught, but not in *quantity*. A drop of water and an entire ocean, chemically analyzed, are exactly the same. But one is small and the other is great. Similarly, God is full of all opulences, such as beauty, wealth, fame, knowledge, strength, and renunciation. As His parts and parcels, we have these qualities as well, but in minute proportion. Therefore, we are not supreme. Rather, being subservient, we are meant to serve the Supreme.

Achintya-bhedabheda-tattva

According to the Vedic literatures, God is the ultimate source of multifarious kinds of energy. In this way He resembles the sun, which gives off energy in the form of heat and light. And just as the sun is inseparable from its rays, God is inseparable from His energies. God and His energies are therefore nondifferent.

Yet simultaneously God and His energies are distinct. Although the sun and its rays are one, they are different as well: while we on earth enjoy the rays of the sun, the fiery sun itself is millions of miles away. Similarly, although God is present everywhere by the manifestations of His energy, He simultaneously maintains His distinct personal identity, with His own name, form, qualities, abode, pastimes, and entourage. Since all living beings are manifestations of God's energy, God and the living beings are simultaneously different (*bheda*) and nondifferent (*abheda*). For the conditioned mind this truth (*tattva*) is held to be inconceivable (*achintya*). This is consistent with the original Vedic *siddhanta*, and so with the appearance of Lord Chaitanya, the Vedic restoration was complete.

Hinduism

When we speak of Lord Chaitanya's philosophy, or Krishna consciousness, we should not confuse it with Hinduism. Krishna consciousness originates in the ancient Vedic literatures; Hinduism is not mentioned in the *Vedas* at all. Furthermore, the current popular usage of the term Hinduism does not correspond to its original meaning. When Alexander the Great invaded India around 325 B.C., he crossed the River Sindhu and renamed it Indus, which was easier for the Greek tongue to pronounce. Alexander's Macedonian forces called the land east of this river "India".[15]

Later, the Muslim invaders called the Sindhu River the Hindu River because in their language, Parsee, the Sanskrit sound "s" converts to "h." Thus, for the Persians, "Sindhu" became "Hindu," and the land east of that river became known as Hindustan.

In more recent times, the land was again called India, but during the British regime, politicians frequently used the words "Hindu," or "Hinduism," emphasizing the alien overtones of these words. This was done to differentiate the Hindus from the Muslims, thus aiding the British policy of "divide and rule." Western writers then adopted these terms for the sake of convenience, and Eastern writers conformed to the norms set by those in power.[16]

Confusion spread as the word Hinduism increasingly came to be used to designate the so-called religion of the Indian people. In actuality, however, it is more appropriately used to describe the entire culture of a geographic region that, though quite diverse in many ways, holds just as many underlying traits in common. The misconceptions surrounding the term Hinduism now make it a virtually useless word. Its usage is roughly analogous to the hypothetical case of invaders occupying the United States and referring to the native way of life as "Yankee-ism" and then purporting this to be the "American religion."[17]

In India, no religion called Hinduism ever existed, and even today the learned and well-informed spiritual and religious leaders do not use this term. Instead, they refer to *sanatan-dharma*, which means "eternal law," and it is *this* that is described in ancient India's Vedic literatures, not "Hinduism," which is simply an expurgated derivative. Lord Chaitanya's Vedic philosophy is based on this pre-Hindu, nonsectarian, and universal teaching, and its principles can be applied by followers of all spiritual paths.

Foreign Invaders

The centuries immediately preceding the advent of Lord Chaitanya marked a confused period in the history of India. Wave after wave of alien hordes had come from across the Hindukush mountains, and, after an orgy of pillaging, raping and slaying, made themselves masters of the country.[18]

But their appetites were never appeased. Their swords remained drawn. When they were not fighting against those indigenous to the land, they were fighting among themselves. The peace of the countryside was shattered by the cries of war. In Bengal itself, where Lord Chaitanya was soon to appear, Vedic rule came to an end toward the close of the twelfth century, with the defeat of the native ruler Lakshman Sen at the hands of the Turks.[19] Bengal became part of the Islamic empire.

A general decline of traditional Indian life and culture naturally led to the disappearance, with only some very rare exceptions, of Vedic civilization. People became aliens in their own homes, to their own heritage. Their persons, properties, and now distorted beliefs were secure only on suffer-

Introduction

ance. A feeling of defeatism prevailed. Faith drooped. "Hinduism" (if not Islam itself) replaced Vaishnavism, the original Vedic religion.

Navadvip

This was especially the case in Navadvip, which was then the capital of Bengal. According to the scriptures, Navadvip, being the birthplace of Lord Chaitanya, is nondifferent from Vrindavan, the birthplace of Lord Krishna—both are considered manifestations of the spiritual world.

One may wonder, then, why the Lord would have allowed Navadvip to fall into such a seemingly irreligious state. In fact, the pastime of war and its mundane conquerors paved the way for the great spiritual renaissance under discussion. Vaishnava scriptures tell us that the Lord uses His camouflaged kingdoms on earth to enact His pastimes for the pleasure of His devotees. And no matter how difficult things seem to get at times, He always emerges victorious. Thus His abode, of which Navadvip is a primary manifestation, is glorified more than any other place. Ultimately, it is here that the Lord enacts His pastime of saving religion, destroying the demonic mentality and securing the righteous.

Navadvip can be found at the confluence of the Ganges and Jalangi Rivers, on the western bank of the Ganges. About sixty-five miles north of Calcutta, to which it is connected by road, river, and rail, Navadvip is a large trading center and is today of regional importance to the handloom cloth industry.[20] But no one would deny that Navadvip's greatest assets are still spiritual.

Historically, Navadvip was supposedly an area of nine islands. Hence the derivation of its name: *nava* (nine), *dvip* (islands). Many believe "the nine islands" refer to nine *spiritual* islands, to be perceived only by those who have attained the topmost realization.

Founded by the Sen Dynasty of Hindu rulers in A.D. 1063, Navadvip became the capital of Bengal under Lakshman Sen.[21] But it was soon conquered and destroyed by Muhammed Bakhtiar Khilji in 1202. It was at this time that Bengal passed under Islamic rule.[22]

Still, Hindus and Muslims lived there together, and Navadvip became the scholarly center of *navya-nyaya*, even at that time. *Navya-nyaya* is an elaborate system of logic and polemics, and its greatest literature was composed in Sanskrit. Thus Navadvip became famous as a seat of medieval Sanskrit learning, which resulted in its becoming a stronghold of orthodox brahmanism and scriptural debate.[23] As India's spiritual renaissance developed around the personality of Lord Chaitanya, the world of the intellect came to be counterbalanced by the world of devotion.

Spiritual Renaissance

Eloquently describing the period of Indian history that preceded Lord Chaitanya, Ravindra Swarup Das, a modern scholar and practitioner of Lord Chaitanya's teachings, writes:

> It was into this setting that Lord Chaitanya inaugurated a *bhakti* renaissance and turned people's vision to God at the same time that the Renaissance in Europe turned people's vision to man and the world. Men like da Vinci, fascinated by the marvelous and cunning complexities of material nature, began to delve into her secrets with an insatiable curiosity and were rewarded with discovery. At the same time, as if in counterbalance, Lord Chaitanya, through the renaissance of *bhakti*, gave to the world an unprecedented view into the inner dynamics of infinite love in the all-attractive Supreme Personality of Godhead. Just as men of the Renaissance tried to open up the world and unlock the secrets of nature, Lord Chaitanya and His associates opened up the kingdom of God and unlocked the secrets of love of God.
>
> To the people of the Renaissance, the world and man seemed imbued with limitless possibility and promise. Western civilization to the present day has been following up on that vision, and it becomes more and more apparent that the world and man have not lived up to their promise. The Renaissance shift of vision from God to man and matter has cut people off from any transcendent source of meaning and value, and the resultant relativism and nihilism—the ripened fruit of the Renaissance—have released demonic energies that have devastated the earth in our time. And there is more to come.
>
> Therefore, Lord Chaitanya's appearance was most timely. The civilization born in Europe during the Renaissance has grown to straddle the earth. But there has been a most fortunate counterflux, as the *sankirtan* movement of Lord Chaitanya has also spread over the globe, in fulfillment of Lord Chaitanya's own prophecy. By showing how Krishna is supremely loving and all-attractive, and by making Krishna easily accessible through the chanting of His names, Lord Chaitanya has made it possible for us to shift our vision back to God once more. This is necessary. Man and the world cannot answer to the demand we have placed upon them. Only Krishna and His transcendental kingdom, where He eternally revels in pastimes of love, can

do that. This alone is the realm that is rich with infinite promise, beckoning to us with limitless possibilities.[24]

THE LIFE AND TIMES OF LORD CHAITANYA

INDIA/INSET NAVADVIP

With the exception of a short journey to East Bengal and another to Gaya, Lord Chaitanya spent the first twenty-four years of His life in Navadvip.

CHAPTER ONE

birth and divinity

Lord Chaitanya Mahaprabhu was born in Navadvip,[25] West Bengal, on Friday, February 18, 1486,[26] just as the full moon in eclipse was rising over the holy River Ganges. This scenario was poetically described by one of Lord Chaitanya's followers: "Nature joined with man and the gods to pay homage to the Moon of Navadvip (Chaitanya). On the appearance day of this 'perfect moon,' which is absolutely free from all blemishes, the spotted lunar disc hid its face in shame under the excuse of eclipse." Pious men and women took the opportunity to bathe in the cleansing water of the sacred river. As was the custom during an eclipse, they bathed in the holy name of the Lord, too, which served to further brighten their lives. It was this bathing in the holy name that Lord Chaitanya was soon to develop into a science, teaching it to all of Navadvip and to the rest of the world.

Jagannath (Purandara) Mishra—Lord Chaitanya's father—was a pure devotee of the Lord who settled in Navadvip[27] to study under Nilambar Chakravarti, a famous astrologer and astronomer. It was Chakravarti's chaste and religious daughter, Sachidevi, who became Jagannath Mishra's bride and eventually the mother of Lord Chaitanya.

Jagannath Mishra and Sachidevi were not given the opportunity to raise their first eight children, all daughters, for the girls died in their infancy. And their ninth child, a boy named Vishvarup, left home at a young age to become a wandering ascetic (*sannyasi*). Soon after being given the *sannyasa* name, Shankararanya Puri, Vishvarup died as well.

Vishvambar (literally, "One who sustains the universe") Mishra—later to be known as Lord Chaitanya—was their tenth and most dear child. And considering the fate of their eight daughters, Jagannath and Sachidevi were quite protective of little Vishvambar.

Shri Nimai

Sita Thakurani, wife of the great sage Adwaita Acharya, nicknamed the boy "Nimai," not only because He was born under a *neem* tree,[28] but because *neem* was known to have antiseptic properties and a bitter taste as well. In other words, the well-wishers of the child prayed that the cleansing, antiseptic nature of *neem* would keep the god of death away, and that the parents would not taste the bitter sorrow they had encountered with the first eight children.

Nimai was also known as "Gauranga" (literally, "the Golden one") by the neighboring ladies and friends of the family, for His bodily complexion was like that of molten gold. Nilambar, Nimai's grandfather and the family astrologer, could understand another way in which the boy was golden—his bodily limbs and zodiacal signs all indicated that he was no ordinary being. It was Nilambar Chakravarti, in fact, who named the extraordinary child "Vishvambar," indicating the boy's divinity.

Bodily Symptoms

According to Nilambar, Nimai was born at the most favorable moment of planetary conjunctions. His horoscope indicated that He would be an intellectual genius, a savior of the world, a unique preacher of religion and would declare the dispensation for the present age (chanting the Lord's name).[29] The astrologer recognized on His person all the signs of an *avatar* ("the descent of God"), both from the calculation of the constellations and from the auspicious marks on His limbs. For instance, His feet were marked with the flag, thunderbolt, conch, and fish, indicating, according to Vedic astrology, that He was undeniably an incarnation of the Supreme Lord.[30]

Shri Nimai is said to have possessed the thirty-two marks of divinity incarnate (*maho purusha lakshanas*).[31] These marks are as follows: the nose, arms, chin, eyes, and knees are large; the skin, fingertips, teeth, and the hairs of the body and head are fine; the corners of the eyes, the soles, palms, palate, lips, and nails are of crimson complexion; the chest, shoulders, nails, nose, waist, and mouth are raised; the neck, thighs, and organ of generation are short; the waist is thin and yet broad, as is the forehead and chest; and the navel, voice, and mind are deep.[32]

Visual Description

All biographers present Him as statuesque in presence, even from the mundane point of view, with broad forehead and long eyebrows, large eyes like the petals of a lotus, a long and aquiline nose like the beak of an elegant bird, lips like a ripe Bimba fruit, and teeth like pomegranate seeds. His throat, they say, was marked with three lines like a conch, His chest was broad and waist thin, like that of a lion. His thighs looked like the stalk of a banana tree and His knees like the proboscis of an elephant. He was over seven feet tall, and yet His imposing stature was fully surpassed by His graceful elegance.

Shrila Vrindavandas Thakur, describing Shri Nimai in the opening verses of his biographical account, *Chaitanya Bhagavat*, says that He could touch His knees with either hand without bending. In His later years, He was tall, exceptionally handsome and very distinguished in appearance, with His brilliant ultra-fair complexion for which He was given the name "Gaura" (golden). He was sometimes called "the Golden Avatar."

Apart from the miraculous traits assigned to Him by His biographers, there remain many qualities of head and heart, which were decidedly above average. He was to be a supremely gifted prodigy and a shining gem in the intellectual crest of Bengal.

Authorized Biographies

All of Lord Chaitanya's earliest biographers recognize not only His superlative characteristics, but also His complete divinity as a dual incarnation of Radha and Krishna. The earliest extant biographical account with this perspective is Murari Gupta's Sanskrit work *Shri Krishna Chaitanya-charitamrita*, which was completed within a decade of Lord Chaitanya's disappearance. Sometimes known as *Kadacha*, or "a brief biographical account," many later biographical works were based on this book. Kavi

Karnapur's life of Lord Chaitanya is one example, as is his ten-act drama, *Shri Chaitanya-chandrodaya*.

The earliest Bengali biography, *Chaitanya Bhagavat*, which was written by the great Vaishnava teacher, Vrindavandas Thakur, affirms Lord Chaitanya's divinity using historical accounts, logic and reason. Two other important biographers are Jayananda and Lochandas, who both give convincing evidence in their biographical works, which share the title, *Chaitanya Mangala*. These two "mangalas," however, have been somewhat interpolated and are now considered questionable by scholars of Gaudiya Vaishnavism. Nonetheless, Lochandas' book has been redeemed by modern academicians because the misinformation found in his work occurs in the spurious pages of only one particular edition.[33] His contemporaries have also attested to his impeccable character.

Of all the biographies, the most devotional as well as the most accurate and extensively researched is Shrila Krishnadas Kaviraj Goswami's *Shri Chaitanya Charitamrita*, which was written during the first quarter of the seventeenth century.

It is stated therein that Lord Chaitanya remained in His mother's womb for a full twelve months and that the conception was untainted, without any seminal discharge.[34] To an ordinary soul, such things are beyond the scope of possibility. But for the followers of Lord Chaitanya, these things confirmed His divinity. After all, Vedic culture had supplied for them a sort of fool-proof system, whereby one could know if a given personality is indeed an incarnation of God. Such a divinity is ascertained, according to Vedic teachings, by His bodily symptoms (which in relation to Lord Chaitanya have already been described), extraordinary activities, and by predictions in the scriptures. As the balance of the present work describes the Lord's extraordinary activities, what is described here are some of the many scriptural predictions.

Scriptural Evidence

According to certain misled scholars and followers of the Vedic scriptures, the Lord incarnates in only three out of the four ages, and since He has already appeared in Satya, Treta, and Dwapara *yugas*, He could not have appeared in Kali, the final age, as Lord Chaitanya. But this conclusion has a faulty basis.

Carefully examined, *Shrimad Bhagavatam* (10.8.13) reveals that in the

Birth and Divinity

four *yugas* the Lord descends in four different bodily colors—white, red, black, and yellow—to teach the path for each age. The Lord is indeed called *tri-yuga*, or "one who appears in three ages," but this is also explained in the *Bhagavatam* (7.9.38): He is known as *tri-yuga* because in the Kali-yuga He is covered; that is, He does not assert Himself as the Supreme Personality of Godhead. And this was the special feature of Lord Chaitanya, for He appeared in the role of a devotee. Not as the Supreme Lord.

The white, red, and black incarnations appeared in previous ages. So from these verses we see that the Lord descends in Kali-yuga in a yellowish color, as the *yuga-avatar*, to spread the *yuga-dharma*, or the chanting of the Lord's glories. These are all features of Chaitanya Mahaprabhu.

Great Vedic authorities, such as Shrila Rupa Goswami, Shri Sanatan Goswami, and Shri Jiva Goswami have all accepted Lord Chaitanya as Krishna Himself because the scriptures describe His personal features and His activities. In the *Shrimad Bhagavatam* (11.5.32), for instance, the great sage Karabhajana Muni explains all about the various *yuga-avatars* to Maharaj Nimi, and he describes the *yuga-avatar* for the present age as follows:

> *krishna-varnam tvishakrishnam*
> *sangopangastra-parshadam*
> *yagyaih sankirtan-prayair*
> *yajanti hi sumedhasah*

"In the age of Kali, intelligent persons perform congregational chanting to worship the incarnation of Godhead who constantly sings the names of Krishna. Although His complexion is not blackish, He is Krishna Himself. He is accompanied by His associates, servants, weapons [i.e. the Hare Krishna *mantra*], and confidential companions."

It has thus been predicted that in the Kali-yuga, the present age, the Lord teaches the *yuga-dharma* of *sankirtan*, the congregational chanting of the holy name. *Krishna-varnam* means both that He is Krishna Himself and that He is repeating the syllables *krish-na*. Yet His radiance or luster (*tvisha*) is not black (*akrishna*); it is golden.

There are many other scriptural texts that clearly predict Lord Chaitanya Mahaprabhu. For example, Lord Krishna Himself declares in the *Vayu Purana*: "In the Age of Kali when the *sankirtan* movement is inaugurated, I shall descend as the son of Sachidevi."

And from the *Brahma-yamala*:

> *athavaham dharadhame*
> *bhutva mad-bhakta-rupa-dhrik*
> *mayayam cha bhavishyami*
> *kalau sankirtanagame*

"Sometimes I personally appear on the surface of the world in the garb of a devotee. Specifically, I appear in the Kali-yuga to start the *sankirtan* movement." There are similar statements in the *Krishna-yamala* and the *Ananta-samhita* that predict the incarnation who will inaugurate a movement based upon the congregational chanting of God's holy name (*sankirtan*). Historically, only Lord Chaitanya is credited with having begun this movement.

The "Thousand Names of Lord Vishnu" (*Vishnusahasranam Stotram*, 75) section of the *Mahabharata*[35] also predicts that the Lord will have a golden complexion and inaugurate the *sankirtan* movement. In addition, the verse refers to Him as Sannyaskrita, indicating that He will appear as a *sannyasi*. Lord Chaitanya was the only incarnation of the Lord to accept the renounced order of life.

So there is no lack of Vedic authority for saying that Mahaprabhu is Krishna Himself, descended in the Kali-yuga to teach the world the process of salvation through the chanting of the holy names. Our readers are invited to study *Shri Chaitanya Charitamrita* by Krishnadas Kaviraj Gosvami, which has been translated into English from the Bengali, with commentary (seventeen volumes), by His Divine Grace A. C. Bhaktivedanta Swami Prabhupada. These books clearly establish the position of Chaitanya Mahaprabhu as the Supreme Personality of Godhead, and they historically show how He began the *sankirtan* movement that now claims followers all over the world.

In conclusion, someone may perform extraordinary activities, or may even possess the standard bodily symptoms of a divine being. But it would certainly be difficult to find someone who possessed both these characteristics and was predicted in the scriptures as well. Lord Chaitanya exhibited all three qualifications and was therefore accepted by thousands of followers as God incarnate, both in His lifetime[36] and down to the present day. Among His contemporary worshippers were men and women of the highest learning and intelligence, and He revealed to many of them the secret of His esoteric identity as the Supreme Lord.[37]

Despite the scriptural evidence and extraordinary pastimes, readers will naturally be skeptical and doubt Lord Chaitanya's divinity. It is important

Birth and Divinity

to note, however, that the acceptance of Mahaprabhu's divinity is not necessarily prerequisite to accepting the validity of His teaching. Echoing the words of Bhaktivinode Thakur:

> We leave it to our readers to decide how to deal with Mahaprabhu. The Vaishnavas have accepted Him as the great Lord, Shri Krishna, Himself. . . . Those who are not prepared to accept this perspective may think of Lord Chaitanya as a noble and holy teacher. That is all we want our readers to believe. . . . We make no objection if the reader does not believe His miracles, as miracles alone never demonstrate Godhead. Demons like Ravana and others have also worked miracles and these do not prove that they were gods. It is unlimited love and its overwhelming influence that would be seen in none but God Himself.[38]

CHAPTER TWO

infancy and youth

There is an age-old tradition in India that tests a newborn child's future predilections: various articles are set before the infant, such as gold, silver, food, and religious books, and that for which the child reaches first is said to indicate his future inclination. When this custom was employed by Lord Chaitanya Mahaprabhu's family, little Nimai immediately reached for the scripture, *Shrimad Bhagavatam*, indicating a major part of His life's mission.

The Serpent

As the divine child began to crawl about in the yard, He became the darling of all neighboring families. And when He once grabbed hold of a large hooded serpent, lying down on it without any worry, everyone screamed in fear, as if for their own lives. The serpent quickly disappeared, but the Lord's biographers inform us that it was actually Seshadev himself, the serpent-like carrier of Lord Vishnu, coming to once again carry his Lord.

Krishna! Krishna!

From morning until evening, the house of Sachi-Jagannath echoed the transcendental sound of the Lord's name ("Krishna"), because the child wept when such chanting could not be heard. As Nimai learned to walk, He would dance with what was considered a bewitching gait, especially when He heard the chanting of the holy name. The ladies of the neighborhood, in fact, would purposely chant just to see this singularly most beautiful child smile, laugh, and dance. In this way, Nimai kept them always chanting the holy name of the Lord.

Two Thieves

On one occasion, while playing outside the compound of His house, the Lord was abducted by two thieves who intended to rob Him of His golden ornaments, given by His parents and well-wishers. The thieves carried Him on their shoulders for several miles. But by a curious display of the Lord's mystic powers, they mistakenly carried the divine child back to His own home, thinking it was their hideout. Meanwhile, Sachi and Jagannath were quite alarmed to find their child missing and were vigorously searching for Him throughout the neighborhood. Suddenly, the thieves, detecting their own blunder, put the child down and proceeded to escape.

Although like the two thieves many try to exploit the Lord, He sometimes shows mercy to such would-be exploiters and allows them entrance into His eternal pastimes (*lila*). Letting the thieves give Him a ride marked the perfection of their relationship (*rasa*) with Him. While acting as thieves, then, they were actually His eternal associates relishing a transcendental pastime.

Clay and Sweets

Shri Nimai discussed philosophy with His mother when He was barely five or six years old. On one occasion, the child was given a meal of deliciously prepared rice with sweets, but He instead began eating clay. Mother Sachi saw this and naturally snatched the clay away from His mouth.

When asked why He preferred clay to the nice sweets set before Him, Nimai replied, "Why Mother, I see no distinction between clay and sweets, as one is merely a transformation of the other. In this way, all matter is related."

"Who taught You this bogus philosophy, my naughty child?" asked Sachidevi with unmixed astonishment. "Don't You see the difference?" she continued. "Boiled rice and sweets, though a transformation of clay, nourish the body, while moist clay undermines the health. A dry pot can hold water; soft clay cannot."

"How could I have known the difference?" Lord Chaitanya then asked His mother, "You had never explained this to me. I will never eat clay again." In this way, Lord Chaitanya indirectly encouraged His mother to defeat the monistic impersonal philosophers, who claim that everything is ultimately the same—even clay and sweets.

In the eighth century, Shripad Shankaracharya had indeed formulated the questionable clay/pot philosophy in his classic work, *Vivekachudamani*:

> A pot, through a modification of clay, is not different [from it]; because [the pot] is everywhere essentially clay . . . [similarly], the whole [world], as a modification of spirit, is nothing but spirit itself, it is all one . . .

Nimai and Krishna Are Nondifferent

As Nimai grew into boyhood, His divinity became apparent, and He soon began to reveal His identity and mission to His confidential followers. Once, a *brahmana* (priestly) pilgrim arrived at the house of Jagannath Mishra as a beggar asking for shelter. As was his custom, Jagannath paid special attention to his pious guest. The *brahmana*, according to his daily routine, cooked a meal and sat down to meditate in perfect tranquility, offering his food to the Deity of Krishna. Just then, Shri Nimai appeared, ate a morsel of the offering, and quickly ran away.

When Jagannath Mishra discovered what had transpired, he was terribly embarrassed, and, assuring his guest that this would not happen again, he requested that the *brahmana* be tolerant and cook for a second time.

Reluctantly, the *brahmana* agreed, but only because Nimai was this time kept under strict vigilance. But to the utter chagrin of the family, the same problem occurred a second time. The *brahmana* was encouraged to cook once more. And this time Nimai was kept in a locked room, with the doors bolted from outside. At midnight, while the Lord's entire family was asleep, the *brahmana* made one last effort to offer a meal to his Deity of Krishna. Shri Nimai mysteriously appeared again, however, and the pious *brahmana* now became totally vexed.

Just then, Nimai said: "O saintly priest! You call Me by purely chanting the appropriate prayers for offering your food. And then, when I come to partake of that which you offer Me, you become alarmed. Why do you engage in this contradictory behavior?" With this, the Lord revealed His manifestation as a divinity. He then explained to the *brahmana* the purpose behind His current appearance as Lord Chaitanya and asked him not to divulge this secret to others. The *brahmana* soon became a resident of Navadvip, regularly visiting Jagannath Mishra's house just to offer his obeisances to Nimai.

Ekadashi Day

On the Ekadashi Day, which occurs twice every month, followers of the *Vedas* fast from grains and beans in an attempt to cleanse the body. On this day, too, there is a special effort to cleanse the soul and to focus on the Absolute Truth. Nonetheless, the Lord's daily offerings should go on as usual, the Vaishnava scriptures say, and while the devotee must fast, the Lord Himself is offered His usual fare, including grains and beans.

Once, on Ekadashi, Hiranya and Jagadish, who lived some two miles away from the Mishra home, were preparing a special feast for the pleasure of their Deity. Nimai, pretending to be ill, insisted that His father take Him to the home of these two devotees, for a wonderful offering was taking place there. Jagannath, who just wanted to pacify his child, brought little Nimai to the home of Hiranya and Jagadish.

Much to Jagannath Mishra's surprise, there was indeed an offering being made. "How did my Nimai know this?" he thought.

Nimai, not surprised, went over and feasted upon the offering, along with the preparation that contained grains and beans. Temporarily, all three men understood that they were in the presence of the Supreme Lord Himself, who is not subject to the religious law of fasting on Ekadashi.

It should be noted, however, that Nimai strongly upheld the importance of Ekadashi for others. And, in general, He strictly observed it Himself. During His entire manifest pastimes, He only asked His mother to do one thing: "I know you would do anything for Me," He once told Sachidevi, "but all I ask is that you strictly observe the Ekadashi Day."[39]

Naughty Nimai

As usual for small children, He began to play, and with His playmates He went to the houses of neighboring friends. There, He would sometimes steal food and drink, and would fight with the boys who were His own age.

Many neighbors lodged complaints with Sachidevi about the Lord's stealing and fighting. As a result, she sometimes chastised or rebuked little Nimai. In this way, Mahaprabhu relished the pastimes of a seemingly ordinary mother to son relationship.

Sachidevi said: "Why do You steal others' things? Why do You beat the other children? And why do You go inside others' houses? What do You not have in Your own house?" She spoke like this, of course, as an enactment of the divine play (*lila*), for the Lord puts His intimate devotees into *yogamaya*, a divine counterpart to *mahamaya* ("the illusory energy"), so they can temporarily forget His Lordship and relish an intimate relationship with Him.

Once, Nimai chastised His mother with His little hand, waving it in front of her to show His anger. Sachidevi pretended to faint, as if in fear. Seeing this, the Lord became frightened and began to cry out of deep affection for His mother.

The neighboring ladies told Him, "Dear child, please bring a coconut from somewhere—only this will cure Your mother." Nimai immediately ran out and soon came back with two coconuts. All the ladies laughed because they were happy to see such endearing activities.

Lakshmidevi

Sometimes the Lord and His friends bathed in the Ganges. The neighboring girls went there as well, not only to bathe but to perform religious activities and pray for good husbands (as is the Vedic custom). Addressing the girls, the Lord said, "Worship Me and I will give you good husbands and all benedictions. The Ganges and goddess Durga are My maidservants. Lord Shiva and all the other demigods are simply My servants as well."

The girls then brought edible offerings as well as flowers for the Lord, who ate the food, enjoyed the aroma of the flowers, and blessed the girls to their satisfaction. Even though the inhabitants of Navadvip learned of Nimai's cunning behavior, they did not become disturbed. Rather, everyone enjoyed a special happiness in these transcendental dealings.

One day, a girl named Lakshmi, the daughter of Ballabha,[40] came to the bank of the Ganges for the same purpose as the other children. This

Lakshmi, however, was no ordinary girl. In Her previous life, She was Rukmini, Lord Krishna's wife in Dvaraka. And before that, She was Sita, the wife of Lord Ramachandra. In other words, Lakshmi was the Lord's eternal consort, who came to once again engage in His divine pastimes.

Seeing Lakshmi on the bank of the Ganges, the Lord was naturally attracted to Her. Their eternal love for one another was reawakened, although it was covered by childhood emotions. Lord Chaitanya and Lakshmidevi, in fact, are eternally husband and wife. But as They enacted Their childhood pastimes, They knew, it would take some time before They could manifest Their marriage. Consequently, They took the opportunity to relish the special taste of childlike activities.

Nimai the Scholar

Mahaprabhu's childhood was not simply spent in casual play. Before He was ten years old, He became a noted scholar. In fact, it is said that study of the scriptures, philosophical hermeneutics, Sanskrit, and *nyaya* (logic and polemics) was His chief occupation.

Shrila Bhaktivinode Thakur says that the Lord was given lessons first by a teacher named Vishnu and then by another named Sudarshan.[41] Later, when He was eight years old, He accepted Gangadas Pandit as His teacher[42] and learned grammar of a higher order. Serious study of Sanskrit necessitates learning such grammar, which takes at least twelve years to master. But if one does become an accomplished Sanskritist, he will then have easier access to the secrets of the Vedic scriptures. Nimai *Pandit* ("scholar"), as Mahaprabhu was now called, was quickly becoming such a master.

Fearing that Nimai might follow the example of His elder brother, who, by such study, understood the shallowness of materialistic life and thus renounced the world to become a wandering mendicant, Jagannath Mishra thought it prudent to temporarily put a stop to His son's studies. This he did, but it simply made Nimai more wild and restless than before.

One day, in fact, Nimai took refuge on a pile of black earthen cooking pots, which had been thrown into a ditch as refuse. Sachi begged Nimai to come down off the filthy pile of garbage, but the Lord, without moving an inch, began to philosophize with her: "How could pots used for cooking offerings to God be considered unclean or filthy? And even if they *were* filthy, do they not become pure once I touch them? The idea of clean and

Infancy and Youth

dirty—holy and unholy—is a mental delusion and has nothing to do with spiritual reality." Sachidevi considered the impractical words of her divine child, but in any case she immediately took Him to bathe in the Ganges.

Actually, by this incident Lord Chaitanya had hoped to coerce His mother into allowing Him to return to school. "How would I know these conclusions," the Lord said, "I am uneducated and need proper schooling."

Marriage

After some time, Jagannath Mishra passed away and attained the kingdom of God. Both Shri Nimai and Sachidevi were aggrieved in their hearts, for they would no longer have his loving and gentle association. Friends and relatives came to pacify both the Lord and His mother. Mahaprabhu's biographers state that He performed Vedic rituals for a deceased parent, as was the custom.

The Lord began to consider: "I have not taken *sannyasa*, as my brother has done. Rather, I am remaining at home. Thus, I should act as an ideal *grihasta*, a responsible family man." With this in mind, He thought of Lakshmidevi. "Without a wife," Lord Chaitanya considered, "there is no meaning to family life." Now fourteen years old, He married Lakshmidevi.[43]

Shri Ishvara Puri

Several years earlier, when He was only eleven, Shri Nimai Pandit began teaching students. By that age, He had become the greatest scholar of Sanskrit grammatical literature and the premier academician in the *nyaya* system of philosophy; He was widely known to be proficient in the scriptures as well.

At this point, Lord Chaitanya was, to all appearances, more intellectual than religious. And it was during His intellectual supremacy in the learning center of Navadvip that He first met Ishvara Puri (famed disciple of Madhavendra Puri and soon to become Nimai's spiritual master in disciplic succession),[44] who was visiting Gopinath Acharya, a great Vaishnava of Navadvip.

Ishvara Puri left a deep impression on Lord Chaitanya, who met with him every day to discuss religious matters. Once, Ishvara Puri requested that the Lord polish the language and correct the grammatical errors, if any, of his *Krishna Lilamrita* (a devotional work about the love of Radha and Krishna). Mahaprabhu responded that there could be no defect in the inspired writings of a great devotee such as he, and that any criticism of his devotional lyrics by the worldly-minded should be considered sacrilegious. Soon after relishing these exchanges, Ishvara Puri left Navadvip.

CHAPTER THREE

the defeat of Keshava Kashmiri

Lord Chaitanya often sat on the bank of the Ganges with His students discussing literature, rhetoric and the Vedic scriptures. One evening a great scholar named Keshava Kashmiri approached the Lord and His followers. Kashmiri, as his name indicates, was originally from Kashmir, but he had been traveling to centers of learning all over India, debating the Sanskrit Vedic literature with scholars.

Sanskrit debate is an extremely rigorous science. All subjects are broken down into five categories: the original purpose of a given text; reason and logic; examples and analogies given in terms of various facts; whether or not a new and clearer understanding of the subject is being presented; and support by authoritative quotations from scripture. A man of vast learning, Keshava Kashmiri was undefeated in this kind of debate. He was thus awarded the title Digvijaiyi, which means "one who has conquered everyone in all directions." Naturally, the champion debater came to Navadvip, for this was at the time India's greatest center of learning.

Formerly, such debates were more than academic exercises. In fact, the loser was obliged to become the disciple of the person by whom he was defeated. This fact was disconcerting to the scholars of Navadvip, so they wanted first to have the visiting scholar debate with young Nimai. If Nimai were to lose, they thought, they would be given another chance by the

Digvijaiyi. After all, Nimai was only a young boy. But if their young prodigy was to emerge victorious, then the name and fame of Navadvip would rise to greater heights than ever before.

Keshava Kashmiri knew of Shri Nimai's reputation as a scholar of Sanskrit grammar, but Kashmiri's years of learning evoked a sense of pride that was difficult to overcome. Thus, when they met on the bank of the Ganges, Keshava Kashmiri spoke rudely to the Lord. Very cleverly, he criticized Mahaprabhu, implying that the "grammatical jugglery" the Lord taught His students did not require great expertise. Lord Chaitanya, Who acts in many inconceivable ways to benefit the conditioned souls, replied to the scholar in a way that was meant to increase his arrogance. The Lord then presented Himself in a subordinate position and requested the scholar to demonstrate his poetic skill by composing verses in glorification of the Ganges.

Glorification of the Ganges

Keshava Kashmiri was a devotee of Saraswati, the goddess of learning, who bestowed upon him the blessing to always remain undefeated. In fact, the goddess told him, if he ever was to know defeat, it could only be at the hands of the Supreme Lord Himself. Naturally, then, the Digvijaiyi was confident of his intellectual abilities. And so upon Nimai Pandit's request, he immediately composed one hundred verses glorifying the Ganges.

After hearing Keshava Kashmiri's scholarly presentation, Mahaprabhu spoke in such a way as to curb the pride He had previously inflated. Sarcastically praising the poetry, the Lord, who had spontaneously memorized all one hundred verses, repeated the sixty-fourth verse and asked Keshava Kashmiri to explain it.

The Digvijaiyi, although astonished that Lord Chaitanya had memorized even one of the rapidly recited verses, explained the meaning of the verse. Mahaprabhu then asked him to explain the assets and faults of the verse.

The proud scholar became restless. "You are an ordinary student of grammar," he said. "What do You know about literary embellishments? You cannot review this poetry because you do not know anything about poetic science." Lord Chaitanya once again humbly submitted Himself before Keshava Kashmiri and replied, "Certainly I have not studied the art of literary embellishments. But I have heard about it from higher circles, and thus I can review this verse and find in it many faults and many good qualities as well. Let Me speak, and please hear Me without becoming angry."

Lord Chaitanya then fully explained five literary ornaments and five faults in the verse. The faults involved its improper composition, contradictory meanings, and redundancy. The Lord's praise of the verse centered around its beautiful alliteration, analogy, and purpose. The Lord concluded, "I have merely given an analysis of the verse in terms of the obvious faults and embellishments, but if we consider it in fine detail we will find unlimited faults." Lord Chaitanya's explanations were so thorough, even though he had heard the verse only once, that Keshava Kashmiri could not help but be impressed. And it was not easy to impress the Digvijaiyi.

When he attempted to reply to the Lord's comments, he could find no words to express himself. His confidence and intellect were baffled. His ill-begotten pride was now replaced with insecurity.

Keshava Kashmiri had become very proud, thinking himself undefeatable because of his magnificent scholarship. In reality, however, his pride had simply bewildered him. The actual position of the living being is one of dependence upon the Supreme Lord. In the Vedic literatures, the Supreme Personality of Godhead explains that all knowledge, remembrance, and forgetfulness come from Him. Keshava Kashmiri's pride made him ignorant of this truth, but Lord Chaitanya mercifully reminded him by curbing his pride which, in turn, would allow him to genuinely pursue transcendental knowledge.

Goddess Saraswati

Keshava Kashmiri soon called upon his worshipable deity, the goddess Saraswati, desiring to understand how he had displeased her and had thus been defeated by a young boy. That night mother Saraswati appeared to him in a dream and revealed to him that Lord Chaitanya—young Nimai—was actually the Supreme Personality of Godhead. From that moment, Keshava Kashmiri understood his subordinate position as the eternal servant of Lord Chaitanya. The next morning, in fact, he went to see the Lord and fully surrendered unto Him. Thereafter, Keshava Kashmiri gave up the profession of winning academic championships and became a great devotee of the Lord.

Shrila Vrindavandas Thakur summarizes Lord Chaitanya's lesson to the Digvijaiyi in his *Chaitanya Bhagavat*: "To conquer the universe is not the aim of learning, which is only valuable if service to God is achieved. When one leaves the body, one cannot take his wealth with him, not even his academic career. For this reason, great souls renounce the world. Therefore, one should worship the Lord with whatever one has, especially the intellect; this is the perfection of renunciation and the attainment of real wealth."

The Greatest Scholar

After this incident, Lord Chaitanya was unanimously proclaimed Navadvip's greatest scholar. He was called "Badi-singha," which meant that He was like a lion to His opponents. Soon he began to debate and defeat many "Keshava Kashmiris" and, in so doing, explained to them the Vedic conclusion. But because His conquests were loving, no one went away unhappy.

By age sixteen, the Lord was operating His own school. Befitting His mission as the incarnation for this age, the Lord taught Sanskrit grammar through Krishna conscious philosophy. He explained all the rules and definitions by ingeniously relating them to Krishna, thus inducing His students to chant the holy name of the Lord. In this way, He taught that there is ultimately nothing except Krishna. His teaching embodied a perpetual challenge for mundane wranglers, such as Keshava Kashmiri.

Journey to Bangladesh

Chaitanya Bhagavat, incidentally, states that Lord Chaitanya defeated Keshava Kashmiri before He left for East Bengal (now Bangladesh). Shrila Krishnadas Kaviraj Goswami, however, in his *Shri Chaitanya Charitamrita*, states that Lord Chaitanya's triumph occurred after His return from East Bengal.[45] Shrila Bhaktivinode Thakur concurs with Shrila Kaviraj Goswami.[46]

In either case, it was during this general period that Lord Chaitanya traveled to East Bengal, ostensibly to earn money for His household and academy; He also went to teach and bless those souls who flocked to see Him. According to historical records of the district, on His outward journey the Lord visited the parents of Lokanath (at Talkhadi in the Jessore district) and He also went to see His grandmother (Upendra Mishra, His grandfather, had already passed away), who lived nearby. The most authoritative biographers, however, do not mention the places He visited by name. Murari Gupta and the other biographers merely say that He lived on the banks of the River Padma.

The news of His arrival in East Bengal traveled quickly, and hundreds of students approached Him, hoping He would be their teacher. Not only was He a famous scholar, but by this time He had published an important book on Sanskrit grammar. He was thus met with a cordial reception, and the wealthy, pious *brahmanas* of East Bengal supported Him in every possible way.

Tapan Mishra

One resident of East Bengal, Tapan Mishra (father of the great saint Raghunath Bhatta Goswami), had a dream in which he was told to approach Shri Nimai for advice on a problem that had been bothering him for some time. He in fact did approach Mahaprabhu and asked his question, which involved some confusion in relation to spiritual methodology and the objects of devotion. Shri Nimai told him that *sankirtan*, or the congregational chanting of God's names, was the only method and the only object of devotion in this age. Tapan Mishra greatly appreciated the Lord's advice and could understand His mission. Mahaprabhu then asked Mishra to go to Benares, where he would soon be an important instrument in the spreading of the *sankirtan* movement.

The Passing of Lakshmidevi

While the Lord was in East Bengal, His wife, Lakshmidevi, was living with Mother Sachi in Navadvip. The separation from Her divine husband was more than She could endure. Consequently, She soon passed on to the transcendental aspect of Navadvip in the spiritual sky, for Mahaprabhu's biographers tell us that She died of a snake bite while the Lord was away. Some say it was the "snake bite" of separation that caused Her death.

Vaishnava commentators assert that Shri Nimai, being omniscient, knew of His wife's death and therefore quickly returned to Navadvip. Still, He expressed shock upon returning and could not believe that the love of His life had departed from the world. According to His mother's request, however, He soon remarried. Shri Vishnupriya Devi, daughter of Navadvip's court *pandit*, Sanatan Mishra, was the blessed woman, and

She was indeed an expansion of Lakshmidevi. All Vaishnava writers have described Vishnupriya Devi as the embodiment of selfless devotion, and this trait has made Her a central figure in the Vedic conception of ideal womanhood.

    Shri Nimai soon settled into a steady teaching profession in Navadvip and, in fact, conducted His academy with new vigor and enthusiasm. His scholarship did not affect His character, for He always remained humble and pure. Increasingly, He manifested an interest in the observance of Vedic rituals and the religious way of life.

CHAPTER FOUR

initiation in Gaya

In the year 1502, when Shri Nimai was sixteen years old, He went on a pilgrimage to Gaya.⁴⁷ Here He would perform *pinda-dan*, also called *shraddha*, a ceremony for the benefit of a deceased relative. In Lord Chaitanya's case, *pinda-dan* was performed for His father, a pure devotee of the Lord who had passed away one year earlier.

The Lord was accompanied to Gaya by Chandrashekhara Acharya (His wife's sister's husband) and a large number of His pupils. To arrive in the Gaya province, He apparently passed through the districts of Burdwan, Birbhum, and Bhagalpur before He reached the Mandara Hill across the River Sira, which is some 175 miles from Navadvip in a northwest direction.⁴⁸ When the Lord reached Mandara Hill (in the Bhagalpur district), He went to see the holy, prehistoric Deity of Shri Madhusudana. Although the temple that houses this Deity has subsequently been taken over by members of the Jain community, and the Deity has since been moved to another temple, the Lord's historic visit was recorded for all posterity by Shrila Bhaktisiddhanta Saraswati, who established the worship of the Lord's footprints there on October 13, 1929.⁴⁹

En route to Gaya, the Lord next visited Poona-Poon, across the River Falgu, some eighty miles from Mandara.⁵⁰ At that time the Lord is said to have undergone illness, and He was cured only when His followers brought Him several cups of water that had been used to wash the feet of the local *brahmanas*. In this way, He sought to show His pupils the importance of the priestly class.

Traveling with His followers for some time, He then finally arrived at Gaya, where He conducted the *pinda-dan* ceremony in honor of His father at the Brahma-kunda and at Chakra-vede. Afterwards, He went to Chakrabane to see the footprints of Lord Krishna in the temple of Gadadhar. As the Lord fixed His gaze upon the holy footprints, the temple *brahmanas* sang praises of love of God. It was at this time, His biographers tell us, that He first exhibited ecstatic symptoms for all to see. His hair stood on end, tears flowed from His eyes in a continuous stream, and His whole body trembled.

Initiation

It was during this period that Lord Chaitanya experienced the most important turning point in His manifest pastimes. He met with Ishvara Puri, the great sage He had previously encountered in Navadvip, and took initiation from him into the chanting of the holy name of Krishna. The Lord's initiation marked a period of vital transformation—He exhibited complete love for God in every activity.

According to Shrila Vrindavandas Thakur, the *pinda-dan* ceremony was only the external reason for Lord Chaitanya's journey to Gaya. His real objective, says the biographer, was to meet with and take intiation from Ishvara Puri. Since Gaya, at that time, was a meeting place for the followers of Madhvacharya, Lord Chaitanya knew that Ishvara Puri's presence there was probable.[51] And upon seeing Ishvara Puri, Mahaprabhu Himself revealed the internal reason for His trip to Gaya: "Now that I have seen your holy feet," the Lord said to Ishvara Puri, "I regard my pilgrimage to Gaya as successful."[52]

Lord Chaitanya taught the world two important lessons by taking initiation. In the first place, as the Supreme Personality of Godhead, He certainly did not require a *guru* in disciplic succession. His mission was not to act as the Lord, however, but rather as the Lord's perfect devotee. By His own example He demonstrated that the true devotee undergoes initiation according to the rules and regulations of scripture. Consequently, through Ishvara Puri, He aligned Himself with the prestigious and ancient Brahma-Madhva Sampradaya and thus set the perfect example by becoming formally initiated into the chanting of the holy name of the Lord.

Shri Nimai (Lord Chaitanya) began to debate with His mother while taking refuge atop a pile of dirty, earthen cooking pots. (pp. 28-29)

Chaitanya Mahaprabhu accepts initiation from Ishvara Puri. (pp. 38–39)

Nityananda Prabhu stops Lord Chaitanya from punishing Jagai and Madhai. (p. 54)

After Chand Kazi offers respects to the Lord, they began to discuss the Koran and vegetarianism. (p. 56)

While being worshiped by His intimate followers, the Lord revealed His own divinity and Krishna's pastimes to all who were present. (pp. 58-59)

At His *sannyasa* initiation, His head was shaved and He was given the staff of renunciation. (p. 63)

By embracing Vasudev, the leper, Lord Chaitanya miraculously healed him. (p. 76)

To Ramananda Roy, Chaitanya Mahaprabhu reveals His ontological nature as a dual incarnation of Radha and Krishna. (p. 85)

When the Buddhists tried to defame the Lord, providence acted quickly, and the Buddhists became the victims of their own plan. (pp. 90-91)

As He danced and chanted on the way to Vrindavan, the animals of the forest were induced to follow suit. (p. 104)

While in the forests of Vrindavan, all the animals recognized their dark-colored Lord Krishna, even though He now appeared as the Golden Avatar. (p. 105)

In great ecstasy, Chaitanya Mahaprabhu nearly toppled the boat with His singing and dancing. (p. 107)

The Muslim soldiers (Pathans) mistook Lord Chaitanya's followers for a band of dacoits. (pp. 109–110)

Just before leaving his body, Haridas Thakur placed the Lord's feet on his chest. (p. 135)

Chaitanya Mahaprabhu dances with unabashed bliss at the Ratha-yatra festival of Lord Jagannath. (pp. 151–59)

Lord Chaitanya came to teach the meditative process for the current age: congregational chanting and dancing (*sankirtan*).

The second important lesson of Lord Chaitanya's initiation is related to the first. One must be properly initiated to receive the full benefit of chanting the holy name. Scripturally, this is considered essential: "Whatever *mantra* one may be chanting is rendered useless by not taking initiation into one of the genuine disciplic successions."[53] Lord Chaitanya was surrounded by the chanting of God's names for His entire early life. By the Lord's own arrangement, however, it was not until initiation that these names actually took their full effect, making Him completely intoxicated with the divine nectar that is concealed within their sound.

Divine Madness

Soon after initiation, Lord Chaitanya's *guru*, Ishvara Puri, told Him that simply by chanting the holy name of Krishna one can obtain freedom from material existence and enjoy genuine spiritual life. "Indeed," Mahaprabhu's *guru* said, "simply by chanting the Hare Krishna *mantra* one will be able to see the lotus feet of the Supreme Lord."

After describing the potency of the Hare Krishna *mantra* in this way, Ishvara Puri taught the Lord a special verse from the *Brihan-naradiya Purana*, and he told Him to always keep this verse and the name of God upon His tongue. The verse that Ishvara Puri gave the Lord is as follows: "In this age of Kali, there is no alternative, there is no alternative, there is no alternative for spiritual progress than the holy name, the holy name, the holy name of the Lord."

Years later, when Mahaprabhu had recounted the story of His initiation for a large group of scholars and renunciants, He said, "Since I received this order from My spiritual master, I always chant the holy name. But I think that by chanting incessantly I have become bewildered. While chanting the holy name of the Lord, I lose Myself, and thus I laugh, cry, dance, and sing just like a madman."

Lord Chaitanya had even brought the matter before His *guru*: "My dear spiritual master," He said, "what kind of *mantra* have you given Me? I have become mad simply by chanting this *maha-mantra*!"

After hearing these words from the mouth of the Lord, Ishvara Puri smilingly replied: "It is the nature of the Hare Krishna *maha-mantra* that it evokes ecstasy in anyone who chants it. Ordinary religiosity, economic development, sense gratification, and liberation are known as the four goals of life, but before love of Godhead, the fifth and highest goal, these appear as insignificant as straw in the street. This love of God is easily available for one who purely chants the Hare Krishna *maha-mantra*." These were some of the truths that Ishvara Puri revealed to the Lord just after the initiation ceremony.

Return Journey

As the Lord began His return journey to Navadvip, He passed through Monghyr and Bhagalpur, and soon He reached the village of Kanair Natshala, which is about five miles from Rajmahal (Dumka district) in the present state of Bihar.[54] At the temple of Kanai (Krishna), Mahaprabhu is said to have experienced the beatific vision of Nava-Kishor Krishna (the Lord in His original form as a divine youth playing on His flute) as a consummation of His spiritual initiation by Ishvara Puri. To perpetuate the memory of this historic visit to Kanair Natshala, Shrila Bhaktisiddhanta Saraswati has installed the Lord's footprints at a nearby temple on October 15, 1929.[55]

The temple of Kanai was at least 170 miles from Gaya, and Lord Chaitanya, being anxious to return to Navadvip, did not stay there very long. Without much delay, then, He and His followers took a southern route from Kanair Natshala. Passing through the district of Murshidabad, They at long last reached Navadvip.

Total Absorption

According to His biographers, Lord Chaitanya was now thoroughly given to the devotional and mystical aspects of reality. His love knew no boundaries, and His every word reflected an intense relationship with the Supreme Personality of Godhead. In actuality, of course, Lord Chaitanya did not change in the slightest. As the Absolute Truth, He is always perfect and changeless. But to manifest His *lila*, He rightly exhibited the full symptoms of love for God *after* His initiation. Love of God, according to the Vedic scriptures, appears in one's heart by the grace of the *guru*, and so the Lord manifested His devotional sentiments accordingly, after receiving the mercy of Ishvara Puri. It should also be remembered that the Lord's special mission was not to appear as God but as a devotee, and thus the Lord showed gradual and progressive levels of spiritual advancement as if He were an ordinary soul.

Mahaprabhu's return to Navadvip was accepted with mixed feelings. Some found that they could not relate to His newly found devotionalism. They were accustomed to Nimai Pandit, the great scholar and debater. But Shri Nimai was no longer interested in grammar and polemics. He was now completely mad with love for Krishna, and even many of His pupils, who previously appreciated His connecting everything with Krishna consciousness by using the rules of grammar, could no longer understand His transcendental jargon. It had become too esoteric, as He sometimes chanted "*gopi . . . gopi . . . gopi . . .*" for no apparent reason. He now wept when reminded of Krishna (and this occurred frequently), and He swooned or went into trance upon hearing Krishna's pastimes. This state of affairs had become so severe that whenever He discoursed—on any subject whatsoever—the topic invariably turned into an exposition on Krishna's holy names. Within several months of this fervent and obsessive display of spirituality, His school had to be closed down.

This marked the beginning of His *sankirtan* movement, the professed mission of His incarnation. For despite the feelings of those who could not understand, there were many great souls who were simply waiting for Shri Nimai's transition. Aware of His superior intellect and sensitivity, they knew that He would one day take up the mission He was destined to fulfill.

Shri Nimai was soon acknowledged as the leader of the Vaishnavas, and Navadvip now became the nucleus for more than just academic study—it was a haven for devotees of God.

Electrical Devotion

But Mahaprabhu's love for Krishna was contagious, and so even sinners were converted into saints. He was like a live wire charged with the current of divine love, and anyone fortunate enough to contact Him was similarly charged with His electrical devotion (*bhakti*).

Mahaprabhu's most important followers at this time were Nityananda Prabhu, Adwaita Acharya, Gadadhar, Shrivas, and Haridas Thakur. Their significance in Lord Chaitanya's pastimes is incalculable.

Nityananda Prabhu

Nityananda Prabhu is accepted as a manifestation of Balaram, Lord Krishna's elder brother. As such, Mahaprabhu, Who is nondifferent from

Lord Krishna, would refer to Him as *borodada*, which means "elder brother." He was several years older than Lord Chaitanya, as was Vishvarup, who was Mahaprabhu's elder brother during Their manifest Navadvip pastimes and who was also an incarnation of Lord Balaram. In fact, according to the *Gaur-chandrodaya*, after Vishvarup's early death, He remained mixed within the form of Nityananda Prabhu.[56]

Born in the village of Ekachakra (Birbhum district), Nityananda Prabhu was the divine son of Hadai Pandit and Padmavati. When He was a young boy, a *sannyasi* came to His house and asked His father if the child could travel as the ascetic's assistant. Hadai Pandit immediately agreed, because he knew that this was the boy's destiny, but the shock of separation inevitably killed Nityananda Prabhu's father.

The boy traveled extensively with the *sannyasi*, and then they settled for some time in Mathura, where they heard of Lord Chaitanya's wonderful pastimes in Navadvip. Nityananda Prabhu could not contain Himself and soon left for Bengal to be reunited with His spiritual brother.[57]

Adwaita Acharya

Adwaita Acharya is an incarnation of Mahavishnu (an expansion of the Supreme Lord), and is sometimes known as Sadashiva, the personified procreative force of the universe. He was originally from Laur, in Sylhet, Bangladesh, where Lord Chaitanya's grandparents had resided. Some fifty years older than Mahaprabhu, Adwaita Acharya was known throughout Bengal as a senior and extremely pious Vaishnava.

Just prior to Lord Chaitanya's appearance, Navadvip was suffering at the hands of the irreligious, and Adwaita Acharya could not sit back idly and ignore the sad condition He saw surround Him. Instead, He sat on the banks of the Ganges, fervently praying for the Lord's descent. He could not tolerate the lack of genuine spirituality that pervaded not only Navadvip but all of India. It was due to His sincere prayers, Lord Chaitanya later revealed, that the Lord descended to manifest His pastimes.[58]

Gadadhar Pandit

Not much is known about the early life of Shri Gadadhar Pandit. He came from Sylhet, not far from the home of Adwaita Acharya, and He was the only son of Madhava Mishra. Eventually, He became the head priest at the

Tota Gopinath temple in Puri, and He was often glorified for His life-long celibacy.

Ontologically, He is a manifestation of Radharani, Lord Krishna's internal potency and eternal consort, and was thus very dear to Lord Chaitanya Mahaprabhu. Shri Gadadhar was initiated by Pundarik Vidyanidhi, an incarnation of King Brishabhanu, who was the father of Radharani in Krishna *lila*. This is significant because it shows how Shrimati Radharani manifested Her eternal relationship with Her father in Chaitanya *lila*. The *guru* is like the father of the disciple. Thus Pundarik Vidyanidhi acted as the spiritual father of Shri Gadadhar Pandit.

Shrivas Thakur

Shrivas Thakur was a *brahmana* who traveled to Navadvip from Sylhet with Adwaita Acharya. He was also advanced in years when Shri Nimai was born. In fact, he and his wife, Malini, were present at Shri Nimai's birth ceremony. He was known as an exceptional singer and was considered the incarnation of the ideal devotee, Narada Muni.[59]

The above four personalities are glorified, along with Chaitanya Mahaprabhu, as the Pancha-tattva. *Pancha* means "five," and *tattva* means "truth." Whenever the Lord descends into this world, He manifests as these five Truths: His own personality, His expansion, His incarnation, His energetic potency and His devotee.

Haridas Thakur

And whenever the Lord descends in this way, many eternally liberated souls also come into this world just to relish His manifest pastimes. Haridas Thakur is one such soul. Considered a dual incarnation of Lord Brahma (king of the demigods) and Prahlad Maharaj (foremost of the devotees), Shrila Haridas was a Muslim convert to the eternal religion of Lord Chaitanya. He was born in Budan (Jessore district of Bangladesh) in 1464. His father, Malai Kazi, was a magistrate, but Haridas was not interested in worldly affairs.[60] He was influenced by Adwaita Acharya at a young age and, although there was opposition from the less intelligent, he was accepted as a Vaishnava by those who understood that spiritual elevation is not dependent upon external considerations, such as race, creed and religion. Gradually, however, the entire Vaishnava community accepted Haridas for his superlative example of devotion and spirituality. He was awarded the title *Namacharya*, or "teacher of the divine name," because he chanted incessantly and purely. Vaishnava historians say that he chanted Krishna's name 300,000 times daily.

CHAPTER FIVE

the Hare Krishna maha-mantra

The devotees of Navadvip, headed by Lord Chaitanya, began the ecstatic congregational chanting of the holy name just after the Lord's return from Gaya. Hundreds of enthusiastic Vaishnavas would meet in the house of Shrivas Thakur for such chanting. This has been documented by an eyewitness, Murari Gupta, who explained that the devotees of Navadvip engaged in nocturnal *kirtans* at the Thakur's home and exhibited symptoms of divine love as they chanted.

The *kirtans* consisted of genuine hymns from the Vedic literature and songs of devotion composed by Lord Chaitanya's followers. The main prayer was the Hare Krishna *maha-mantra*: Hare Krishna, Hare Krishna, Krishna Krishna, Hare Hare/ Hare Rama, Hare Rama, Rama Rama, Hare Hare.

It might also be mentioned that the Hare Krishna *maha-mantra* can actually be expressed in two distinct ways. The most significant and well-known version consists of the names as previously described. The other way of chanting the *mantra* is elucidated upon in the *Chaitanya Charitamrita* (*Madhya* 9, pp. 331–32): *Haraye nama krishna yadavayah namaha/ gopal govinda rama shri madhusudan;* "I offer my respectful obeisances unto the Supreme Personality of Godhead, Krishna. He is the descendant of the Yadu dynasty. Let me offer my respectful obeisances unto Gopal, Govinda, Rama, and Shri Madhusudan, for these are all names of the same Supreme Lord."

Lord Chaitanya emphasized both versions of the *maha-mantra*, but while in Navadvip it is sometimes said that He especially taught the "*Haraye nama krishna*" version. However, it is the chanting of Hare Krishna, Hare Krishna, Krishna Krishna, Hare Hare/ Hare Rama, Hare Rama, Rama Rama, Hare Hare that the Vedic literature particularly recommends for the current age. Documentation for this many be found in the *Brahmanda Purana* (*Uttara-khanda*, 6.55), the *Kalisantarana Upanishad*, and in many other Vedic texts as well. Mahaprabhu accepted these scriptures implicitly.

Maha-Mantra Defined

The word *Hare* refers to "Lord Hari," a name for Krishna[61] that indicates His ability to remove obstacles from His devotees' path. But in a higher sense, the word "Hare" refers to the vocative form of "Mother Hara," who is none other than Shrimati Radharani, the Lord's devotional energy. *Krishna* is the name of the Supreme Personality of Godhead in His original form. It means the "All-Attractive One."

Etymologically, the word *krish* indicates "the attractive feature of the Lord's existence," and *na* means "spiritual pleasure." Further, when the verb *krish* is added to the affix *na*, it becomes *krishna*, which indicates the Absolute Truth. According to ancient Sanskrit semantic derivation (*nirukti*), it is also understood that *na* refers to the Lord's ability to stop the repetition of birth and death. And *krish* is another way of saying *sattartha*, or "existential totality." This, then, implies that Krishna is the whole of existence.

Rama refers to both Balaram (Krishna's elder brother) and Lord Ramachandra, a prominent incarnation of the Lord. It is also said, however, that "Rama" refers to *Radha Raman Rama*, which is another name for Krishna, meaning "one who brings pleasure to Shrimati Radharani." Thus the *maha-mantra* embodies the essence of Krishna consciousness, and it is solely composed of the Lord's most confidential names. As a prayer, the *mantra* is translated in the following way: "O Lord, O divine energy of the Lord (Shrimati Radharani). Please engage me in Your service."

Krishna and His Name are One

Lord Chaitanya taught that Krishna and His name are nondifferent. This teaching is based on Vedic authority. The *Padma Purana* states, "There is no difference between the holy name of the Lord and the Lord Himself. As such the holy name is as perfect as the Lord Himself in fullness, purity and eternity. The holy name is no material sound vibration, nor has it any material contamination." Also, Shrila Rupa Goswami says in his *Padyavali* (verse 24), "The holy name of Krishna and Krishna Himself are identical."

In the relative material world, according to Lord Chaitanya, a word and the object it represents are totally different. The word "water," for instance, cannot quench one's thirst; only the liquid itself can do this. However, in the absolute, spiritual world, which is the exact opposite of the material world, a word and that which it represents are absolutely the same. In this way, Lord Chaitanya taught the absolute similarity of Krishna and His name based on Vedic authority and logic.

Science of Sound

Modern science has explained that certain sounds are perceivable by individuals according to physical and environmental laws. As human beings, for instance, we are unable to perceive certain portions of the known vibratory spectrum. While we are extremely sensitive to sound waves of about 1,000 to 4,000 cycles per second (cps), we are completely deaf to sounds above 20,000 cycles per second. Dogs and cats, on the other hand, can hear up to 60,000 cps, while mice, bats, whales and dolphins can emit and receive sounds well over 100,000 cps. Thus, our senses are imperfect and limited, and we cannot calculate the various categories of sound beyond our sense perception.

According to Lord Chaitanya's Vedic philosophy, there are a number of sounds that can awaken one from one's materialistic slumber. Such sounds are called *shabda brahman*, or "spiritual sound vibration." These sounds may be emitted and received only by those who are adept in the process of *bhakti-yoga*, devotional service to the Supreme Lord. These sounds may be given to the common, "sleeping" man by one who is awake and fully cognizant. Such an initiator into the truths of spiritual sound is called *guru*, or spiritual master. After Lord Chaitanya's initiation, for instance, He taught and practiced this chanting without cessation. And He especially emphasized the Hare Krishna *maha-mantra*, which He described as the nonpareil of all spiritual sound vibrations.

Inverted Mantra

In Uttar Pradesh, various scholars of the Gaudiya tradition declare that the *mantra* appears in the original *Vedas* with the "Hare Rama" part first. But since Vedic *mantras* were forbidden to the lower classes, they say, Mahaprabhu switched the order, using the "Hare Krishna" part first. In this way He enabled everyone to take advantage of the holy name. It should be noted that Vedic *mantras* are not to be altered for any reason. Only the Lord Himself has the right to change such prayers for His own divine purposes.

The *maha-mantra*, however, is eternal, and the liberties taken by Lord Chaitanya should be understood in that context. If, as the story goes, the Lord did indeed change the sequence of the *mantra*, He did so to bring out the special nectar that was concealed in the Vedic texts from time immemorial. The sequence of the words actually end up the same in any case, for as one continually chants, the order becomes indistinguishable. Moreover, the spiritual essence is in the three divine names: "Hare," "Krishna" and "Rama."

In early manuscripts of the *Kalisantarana Upanishad* there is a verse that includes the *maha-mantra*, and in this verse the "Hare Rama" part comes first. But there are other editions of this same scripture that are just as early, and in their renditions of this verse it begins with "Hare Krishna." Consequently, the confusion in regard to sequence is only resolved by learning the *mantra* in disciplic succession. And according to this traditional method of receiving knowledge, the "Hare Krishna" part should certainly precede the other. In either case, however, the scriptures fully encourage the chanting of the *maha-mantra* for purification:

> hare krishna, hare krishna, krishna krishna, hare hare
> hare rama, hare rama, rama rama, hare hare
> iti shodashakam namnam kali-kalmasha-nashanam
> natak parataropayak sarva-vedeshu drishyate

"These sixteen names composed of thirty-two syllables are the only means to counteract the evil effects of Kali-yuga. In all the *Vedas* it is seen that to cross the ocean of nescience there is no alternative to the chanting of the holy name."

The Name and the Shadow

But the *mantra* must be chanted purely under the direction of a pure spiritual master. Otherwise, it may not actually be Krishna's name, but rather a material facsimile, a mere shadow of the divine sound. For example, if one were shown two white pills—one arsenic and the other aspirin—it might be difficult to discern one from the other. It then becomes essential to approach an authority, not a quack, who might suggest that one ingest the arsenic. Although both pills are white, it is invaluable to know the difference between the two. Therefore, one should approach a trained chemist or a qualified doctor.

Similarly, one must receive the chanting of the holy name from a pure doctor of the soul (the spiritual master in disciplic succession). Otherwise, the chanting will be like milk touched by the lips of a serpent. Milk is initially pure and healthful. But a serpent's venom can change its very constitution, making it a fatal poison.

Three Stages of Chanting

If one does indeed receive the holy name from a bona fide spiritual master, one very quickly advances from the impure, offensive stage of chanting to the "clearing" stage and finally to the offenseless, pure stage. Having achieved this position, one's chanting blossoms into the flower of love of God. But before any of this can occur, one must approach a genuine *guru*. Such a teacher in disciplic succession guides his disciple in the intricate chanting process, encouraging him to be sincere and attentive while reciting the holy name. In addition, the bona fide *guru* helps his disciple avoid the ten offenses that tend to beleaguer the inexperienced chanter.

The Ten Offenses

These offenses are summarized as follows: (1) The first offense is to blaspheme the devotees who have dedicated their lives to propagating the holy name. It must always be remembered that the holy name comes in disciplic succession. And if the great souls who come in this succession of teachers to bring us the name are ungratefully disparaged, it is an unfortunate reflection upon our view of the name itself. (2) It is also an offense to consider mundane personalities, however great they may be, to be on an equal level with the Lord. All greatness is dependent upon Him, for He is the source of all that is. (3) To disobey the orders of the spiritual master. Without the grace of the *guru*, one cannot make any advancement in spiritual life, and the holy name would be unavailable. (4) It is an offense to ridicule the Vedic scriptures or any other traditional literature that glorifies the Supreme Lord. Such holy books, like the *guru* himself, serve to guide the spiritual aspirant on the path back to Godhead. (5) To consider the glories of the holy name a figment of the imagination. Without complete faith in the name, one will give up one's chanting while still in the neophyte stage of spiritual life. Thus, one forfeits the opportunity to truly taste the nectar concealed within. (6) It is an offense to rationalize or interpret the name according to one's limited and concoctive reasoning. The real meaning and purpose of the name is explained in the scriptures and by realized teachers—there is no need to invent something new. (7) To commit sinful activities on the strength of the name. The Sunday confession syndrome will render one's chanting useless. It betrays an insincere heart to chant the Lord's name for one moment and sin in the next. (8) It is an offense to think of the name as an auspicious, ritualistic conveyance or to use it as a vehicle for pursuing fruitive actions. The holy name should be chanted with the desire to perform devotional service and develop love for God. (9) One should not instruct a faithless person about the glories of the holy name, for they may become blasphemous. In addition, there are many sincere souls who are willing to hear. (10) Finally, it is an offense not to have complete faith in the name and to maintain material attachments even after understanding the futility of materialistic life. The devotee should understand that the name alone is his eternal shelter, and that material life, although it may temporarily have some attraction, is ultimately retrogressive (in that all activities will end with the body).

Carefully avoiding these offenses under the direction of a bona fide spiritual master, one learns to purely chant Hare Krishna, Hare Krishna, Krishna Krishna, Hare Hare/ Hare Rama, Hare Rama, Rama Rama, Hare Hare, and this chant disseminates transcendental knowledge into the heart like moonlight disseminates cooling rays. Lord Chaitanya taught that when the *mantra* is properly chanted, it increases our internal, spiritual ecstasy at every moment.

Material Pleasure Insufficient

In material pleasures, the feeling of ecstasy gradually decreases. If one gets pleasure from eating a piece of sweet candy, for instance, before long one will need two or three pieces to get the same pleasure. According to Lord

Chaitanya, spiritual pleasure is just the opposite. It is *abhinanda*, or "ever-increasing." It does not diminish in the way that material pleasure does. Rather, one becomes thoroughly ecstatic and cleansed of all material inebrieties. One's entire being becomes submerged in transcendental bliss. *Atma*, the Sanskrit word for "self," refers to body, mind, intelligence, endeavor, soul, and Krishna. Chaitanya Mahaprabhu explained that the entire *atma* becomes satisfied and purified by properly chanting the holy name of the Lord. This means that the mind, the intelligence, the soul—all aspects of the living being—become satisfied when one chants "Hare Krishna." And Krishna also becomes happy when we chant.

The Greatest Sacrifice

According to all religious scriptures of the world, living entities in this age are encouraged to make sacrificial offerings to God. Sometimes there have been animal sacrifices. Other times fruits and flowers are recommended. Life means sacrifice. And if one does not sacrifice for God, one will make sacrifices for living beings who are less worthy than God. Although *yagya*, or sacrifice, must be performed to engage in proper religious actions, in this age of Kali the recommended sacrifice is *sankirtan-yagya*. Those who are intelligent, explain the Vedic scriptures, will perform this chanting of the holy names and thereby follow the teachings of Lord Chaitanya Mahaprabhu.

The Ultimate Goal

Mahaprabhu is the goal of the devotees. He is the object of their meditation and worship, and He also teaches the method for attaining Himself. In short, for the Vaishnava, He is everything, for He broke open the storehouse of love of God and freely distributed the contents to all who were fortunate enough to take. Further, He taught the science of worshipping Radha and Krishna through spontaneous devotion, their loving service (*prema-seva*) being the highest end.

Thus, as a tribute to Mahaprabhu and His intimate associates, Gaudiya Vaishnavas preface their daily chanting of the *maha-mantra* with the "Pancha-tattwa" *maha-mantra*: Jai Shri Krishna Chaitanya, Prabhu Nityananda, Shri Adwaita, Gadadhar, Shrivas, Adi Gaura Bhakta Vrinda. The mercy evoked by chanting this *mantra* is said to aid in the pure chanting of "Hare Krishna."

Another traditional *mantra*, composed by one of the Lord's intimate followers, Rupa Goswami, is also very pure and is said to reveal the true position of Lord Chaitanya.

> *namo maha-vadanyaya krishna-prema-pradaya te*
> *krishnaya krishna-chaitanya-namne gaura-tvishe namaha*

"I offer my respectful obeisances unto the Supreme Lord Shri Krishna Chaitanya who is more magnanimous than any other *avatar*, even Krishna Himself, because He is bestowing freely what no one else has ever given—pure love of Krishna."

Unlike incarnations of the Lord that descended prior to His appearance, Lord Chaitanya came with no weapons. Lord Ramachandra carries a bow and arrow for killing the demons; Parashuram carries an axe; even Lord Krishna appeared with His lethal disc. But Chaitanya Mahaprabhu is empty-handed. His only accoutrements are His associates. His only weapon is love.

Instead of killing the demons and thereby giving them liberation, He transformed them into devotees and conquered them by His devotion. Through little more than the chanting process, Mahaprabhu was able to liberate all who ventured within His path. According to His teachings and the example of His followers, we need only adopt the method.

CHAPTER SIX

Navadvip pastimes

Although the holy name of Krishna was now a household word in Navadvip, many of the *kirtans* were still held in secret places, such as the house of Shrivas Thakur. The devotees had decided that the ecstasy evoked by chanting the holy name was too confidential for those who were not predisposed to take part in it. In addition, Muslim rule deprecated the holy name as a "Hindu" phenomenon, and this also led the devotees to chant behind closed doors.

At that time, in the late fifteenth century, the Nawab Hussain Shah, whose full name was Ala Uddina Saiyada Husena Sa Seripha Makka, had occupied the throne of Bengal for nearly twenty-three years. He was formerly the servant of Mujahphara Khan, the cruel Nawab of the Habsi dynasty. Through some sort of intrigue, however, he had assassinated his master and become King. His rule was treacherous, and those who did not adhere to his own religion, Islam, were kept under strict vigilance, although they were allowed some token religious freedom. Maulana Sirajuddin Khan, also known as Chand Kazi, was the governor of Navadvip at that time, and it was he who enforced the laws of Nawab Hussain Shah.

It was into this setting that Lord Chaitanya inaugurated His *sankirtan* movement. Naturally, the Lord had many difficulties with which to contend. Antagonists and vandals ran amok. When Mahaprabhu would sometimes take His chanting party outdoors, it was not uncommon for Him to be confronted by bigots and religious fanatics. He and His followers, however, always remained undisturbed in the bliss of the holy name.

Jagai and Madhai

Nityananda Prabhu and Haridas Thakur especially pleased the Lord with their preaching spirit. While chanting, they would often go door to door, begging others to chant along with them. On one such occasion, they noticed a large crowd gathering around two unruly drunkards who were making a spectacle of themselves in the street. Jagai and Madhai,[62] the two drunkards, were brothers. And although they were the sons of a *brahmana*, they had become addicted to all kinds of abhorrent behavior. They were known throughout the town of Navadvip, in fact, for their women hunting, meat-eating, and intoxication. While these activities are commonplace today, they were frowned upon in Navadvip, where both pious Hindus and devout Muslims maintained a high standard of spirituality.

If these two debauchees could be delivered by the mercy of the holy name, reasoned Nityananda Prabhu and Haridas, then Mahaprabhu's mission would be enhanced and His reputation would be increased. But when the two saints begged the fallen brothers to rectify their behavior by chanting the holy name, the brothers threatened them and chased them down the road.

The next day, Lord Chaitanya asked Nityananda Prabhu and Haridas to return to the scene of the incident. This they did. Upon their arrival, however, more than just idle threats were thrown, for Madhai threw a piece of earthen pot at Nityananda Prabhu. This drew blood from His forehead.

When Chaitanya Mahaprabhu heard what had transpired, He immediately went to personally chastise the demonic brothers. Summoning His divine disc, Lord Krishna's spiritual weapon, Mahaprabhu was ready to kill Jagai and Madhai. He could not tolerate any offense directed toward other devotees, even though He was extremely tolerant when the irreligious attempted to offend Him.

Nityananda Prabhu pleaded that the brothers be spared. He reminded the Lord that He was *patita-pavan*, the deliverer of the most fallen, and thus should show mercy to Jagai and Madhai. If He were to kill these two brothers, Nityananda Prabhu reasoned, He would also have to kill a large percentage of the population, who were equally degraded. Knowing that

Navadvip Pastimes

Nityananda Prabhu was correct, the Lord relented.

Seeing Nityananda Prabhu's compassion, Jagai and Madhai repented, realizing the extremely elevated position of the *sankirtan* movement. They were deeply touched by Nityananda Prabhu's love and kindness and could understand that by the process of *bhakti-yoga*, as taught by Lord Chaitanya, they too might develop similar qualities. The two brothers thus fully surrendered to Lord Chaitanya's mission and received the names Jagannath and Madhava. With this, the Lord embraced them, and by His divine touch He freed them from the reactions to their previous sins and their sinful mentality. The brothers agreed to chant the holy name 100,000 times daily and to end their sinful activities. By doing so they gradually became exalted devotees of the Lord. According to Vaishnava tradition, after several years in the Lord's service, the two brothers resumed their heavenly posts in the kingdom of God. Their tombs are today found in the village of Ghoshahat, sometimes called Madhaitala-gram, which is about one mile south of Katwa. Devotees of the Lord regularly visit this place on pilgrimage.[63]

Chand Kazi

The grace of Lord Chaitanya led to the complete redemption of Jagai and Madhai. Because of Islamic rule, however, such spiritual conquests were played down by Navadvip's political leaders, but sometimes sent the Muslim fundamentalists into a rage. Complaints were often lodged with Chand Kazi, the city magistrate, whose men, on one occasion, stormed into Shrivas Thakur's house and disrupted the *kirtan*. The Kazi threatened the devotees that if they continued to chant the names of God, he would confiscate all their property and force them to convert to Islam. To show his seriousness, the Kazi had his men smash the devotees' *mridanga*, a two-headed drum used in *kirtan*.

Lord Chaitanya's response to the Kazi's hostility was vehement and fearless: "Go perform *sankirtan*," He told His followers, "and do not be afraid!"

The Lord then organized a massive nonviolent civil disobedience movement by gathering 100,000 torch-bearing followers to march on the house of the Kazi. They began their procession by performing *kirtan* in all nine districts of Navadvip. Each *kirtan* party was led by a group composed of twenty-one members, with singers and loud cymbals resounding in time to the beat of the *mridangas*. By the time they had reached the Kazi's home, the sound of the chanting had become tumultuous.

At Lord Chaitanya's request, the Kazi was asked to come out of his house to engage in a friendly conversation. When the Kazi complied, the Lord offered him a nice seat and then began to discuss philosophy with him.

Vegetarianism: The Religious Imperative

The first point of discussion was the Muslim practice of eating meat. "You drink cow's milk," the Lord said, "therefore the cow is your mother. And the bull produces grains for your maintenance; therefore he is your father. Since the cow and bull are your mother and father, how can you kill and eat them? What kind of religious principle is this? On what strength are you so daring that you could commit such sinful activities?"

According to Vedic texts, the first sub-religious principle is vegetarianism, for unless one abandons the cruel act of killing other creatures, one cannot progress in spiritual life. Therefore, Mahaprabhu began with this argument.[64]

A scholar of the Koran, Chand Kazi was considered a great spiritual leader among his peers. His knowledge of the Vedic literature, however, was faulty, and therefore he replied to Lord Chaitanya as follows: "In Your scriptures, as in our Holy Koran, there is an injunction for killing the cow, and thus great sages previously performed sacrifices involving cow killing."

The Kazi was referring to portions of the Vedic literature that were meant for a previous era. If he were more familiar with Vedic texts, however, the Kazi would have known that such sacrifices were forbidden in the current age. The *Vedas* explain that powerful *brahmanas* were once able to rejuvenate old animals by reciting mystic incantations and performing elaborate fire sacrifices. According to ancient Vedic texts, these *brahmanas* were actually able to send an old animal into a sacrificial fire and bring it back to life by the power of their chanting. However, this was meant for the benefit of the animal and to show the potency of *mantras* that were properly chanted. Such animal sacrifices were never meant for the wholesale slaughter of animals.[65]

The Lord thus strongly disagreed with the magistrate's statement: "The *Vedas* clearly enjoin that cows should *not* be killed, and followers of the Vedic literature, whoever they may be, do not indulge in cow killing." The Kazi could not refute this point, for he knew many followers of the *Vedas*, and they were all vegetarian.

Lord Chaitanya then warned the Kazi, "Cow killers are condemned to rot in hell for as many thousands of years as there are hairs on the body of the cow."[66] Mahaprabhu was not simply giving His opinion or making idle threats: these were the words of the *Vedas*. It gradually became clear to the Kazi that Lord Chaitanya was not propounding a sectarian view, but was actually endorsing eternal religious principles.

Change of Heart

The Kazi agreed that the Koran, as commonly interpreted, did not propound the highest spiritual truth, and that its followers tended toward sectarianism. While Islam, which means "submission to the will of God," is at the basis of all true religions, the universality of this truth can elude neophyte believers. In addition, the Kazi confessed, the Koran had only recently been written, and so instructions in regard to concepts such as vegetarianism and compassion for animals had not sufficiently been melded into the mainstay of Islamic theology.

He also explained how local opposition, both from Muslims and Hindus, had influenced him to harrass the *sankirtan* movement. The Muslims, headed by Nawab Hussain Shah, actually feared the mystic potency of the *maha-mantra*, for once, when the local Muslim leaders offensively mocked the holy name by mimicking the Hindus' chanting, they could not desist from uttering the name, as if by force. Fearful, they had demanded that Mahaprabhu and His *mantra* be driven out of town.

On the other hand, the Hindus, who were ill-informed about the power of the Hare Krishna *mantra*, had also lodged a complaint with the Kazi. They insisted that lower-class men should not be allowed to chant the holy name of God, for it was their misguided belief that such chanting was reducing the potency of the *mantra*. Thus, they were also against Mahaprabhu.

The Kazi, confiding in Lord Chaitanya, also told Him about a dream that he had had on the night that the *mridanga* drum was destroyed. In his dream, the Kazi saw a ferocious entity that was half man and half lion (who devotees know to be an incarnation of the Lord, Nrisinghadev). The Kazi told Mahaprabhu that this uncommonly sublime and yet angry personality had warned him, "Although I shall not take your life on this occasion, if you again try to obstruct the congregational chanting of My name, I shall not be tolerant. I shall kill you, your entire family, and all meat-eaters."

Upon hearing this, Mahaprabhu merely touched the body of the Kazi to surcharge Him with purification and spiritual energy. The Kazi then shed tears of ecstasy and at last realized Lord Chaitanya to be not only the Supreme Godhead of the Hindus, but the Lord of all. Some call Him Allah; some, Jehovah; and some, Krishna. But from then on, the Kazi called Him Mahaprabhu.

Then, on the order of the Lord, the Kazi boldly issued this decree: "To as many descendants as take birth in my dynasty in the future, I give this grave admonition—no one should interfere with the *sankirtan* movement of Lord Chaitanya Mahaprabhu." The Lord then began to chant and dance ecstatically, and the Kazi, having been purified by the Lord's spiritual touch, eagerly joined the *kirtan* party with the Lord's devotees. The tomb of the Kazi is today found in the village of Bamanpukur, where both Hindus and Muslims show respect and devotion to his memory.

Mahabhava Prakash

During this general period, Chaitanya Mahaprabhu often went to the house of Shrivas Thakur and sat on a special seat prepared just for Him. It was called the throne of Vishnu. Once, while seated upon this throne, the Lord addressed a problem that had arisen between His mother and Adwaita Acharya. It seems that Sachidevi had offended the sage and, in great humility, she desired to atone for her misconduct. She in fact resolved all differences between them by humbly touching the feet of Shri Adwaita. Mahaprabhu was pleased with this loving interaction.

Soon after, the Lord displayed His Universal Form to Adwaita Acharya. This inconceivable form encompasses the entire cosmic creation and can only be seen by those to whom the Lord shows special favor. (It is the same manifestation that Krishna had shown to Arjuna some 4,500 years earlier.)

It was around this time, too, that Shrivas Thakur worshiped the Lord in the traditional Vedic way—just as if Mahaprabhu were a temple Deity of Lord Krishna. After this function at the Thakur's house, Nityananda Prabhu arrived and Lord Chaitanya bestowed special mercy upon Him (revealing His divine six-armed form known as *shad-bhuj-murti*, which displays the two arms of Krishna, the two arms of Ramachandra, and Lord Chaitanya's own two arms; and finally He showed Nityananda Prabhu His original form as Lord Krishna). Nityananda Prabhu then arranged to offer Vyas-puja, or worship of the spiritual master, to Lord Chaitanya.

Navadvip Pastimes

While being worshiped in this way, Chaitanya Mahaprabhu sat on the throne of Vishnu at the home of Shrivas Thakur for twenty-one hours. As the devotees came to engage in the festivities, Mahaprabhu revealed His transcendental nature to all who were present. Vaishnava commentators call this revelation the *sata-prahariya bhava*, or "the ecstasy of twenty-one hours." Others call it the *mahabhava prakash*. A similar incident is described by Shrila Bhaktivinode Thakur in his song "Gaura-arati," and this can be found in his larger work known as *Gitavali*.

CHAPTER SEVEN

renunciation

Being the Supreme Lord, renunciation (*sannyasa*) is not necessary for Chaitanya Mahaprabhu, for He does not suffer from attachment to His creation. Renunciation is essential, however, for an ordinary being because attachment is an integral part of his conditioning and ultimately causes him great pain. Since everything belongs to the Lord, the living entity is naturally frustrated when he tries to enjoy that which is not his. Therefore, renunciation is necessary for him to overcome the misconception of proprietorship.

In India, the *sannyasi* is highly respected and even revered as one who has realized the Absolute Truth, one who is fully aware of the futility of material existence. The *sannyasi* is one who renounces the world and acts as the spiritual master of society, guiding others in a very high standard of devotion. He remains celibate, avoiding the opposite sex, and he travels and preaches incessantly. He is also reverentially called *"swami,"* because he is said to have mastered his senses by using them in the service of the Lord. When one uses one's senses in this way, it is called *bhakti-yoga*.

It was Mahaprabhu's desire, in fact, to bring all living beings to this genuine path of devotional service (*bhakti-yoga*). This path teaches that the typical, austere concept of renunciation, in which one gives up the amenities of this world, is incomplete. The perfection of renunciation, rather, is to use everything in God's service. To teach this fundamental truth and to win the respect of others, thereby enabling them to hear His message, Lord Chaitanya decided to take *sannyasa*.

Mahaprabhu's mother, Sachidevi, and His wife, Shrimati Vishnupriya, were both heartbroken when they heard of the Lord's decision. His renunciation meant that Mother Sachi would see Him only infrequently and that Vishnupriya would never see Him again. While it was certainly difficult for them, they nonetheless quickly adapted, thus showing that they truly understood the Lord's teachings. These two extraordinary devotees indeed became shining examples of womanhood throughout the annals of Vaishnava history. Later important devotional writers, such as Nityanandadas and Narahari Chakravarti, give graphic descriptions of their asceticism and contribution to the further development of the movement in Bengal.[67]

Enthusiastic in His decision to take *sannyasa*, the Lord and several of His associates went across the Ganges to Katwa (now a subdivisional town in the Burdwan district of Bengal), which is some twenty-four miles from Navadvip. There He took *sannyasa* initiation from Keshava Bharati, an ascetic of the Shankarite impersonal school. It has often been asked why the twenty-four year-old Mahaprabhu decided to take an impersonalist as His *sannyasa guru*. After all, the Lord's teaching was in direct opposition to that of the impersonalists.

Why Keshava Bharati?

During the time of Lord Chaitanya, the influence of Shankaracharya was still pervasive, even though the *acharya's* teaching was effectively refuted by great devotional leaders, such as Ramanujacharya and Madhvacharya. Since Shankara's system emphasized renunciation of the material world, many equated the *sannyasa* order of life with his particular *sampradaya* (lineage). Since the Lord's renunciation was largely to gain a following and attract public attention, He decided not to disturb the local conventions and took *sannyasa* according to time, place and circumstance. In fact, if He had done otherwise He would not have been able to deliver the Mayavadi (impersonalistic) *sannyasis*, who later agreed to hear from Him only because He had been initiated in their line of disciplic succession. It was for this reason that the Lord took initiation from Keshava Bharati.

It is also sometimes said that prior to being initiated by Keshava Bharati,

Lord Chaitanya had actually initiated him. By first whispering the *mantras* of initiation into Bharati's ear, Mahaprabhu had in reality initiated the one who would soon be known as His *sannyasa guru*. Only after this had transpired did Keshava Bharati externally initiate Lord Chaitanya.

Some scholars say that Keshava Bharati had already converted to Vaishnavism by the time of Mahaprabhu's initiation.[68] As evidence, they cite statements from *Chaitanya Bhagavat*, where Mahaprabhu asked Keshava Bharati whether the path of knowledge (*gyan*) is superior to the path of devotion (*bhakti*). Bharati answered that *bhakti* is supreme. A true impersonalist would have answered that the path of knowledge is superior. Also, it is stated that Keshava Bharati engaged in chanting and dancing with the Lord, which was abhorrent to members of the Shankarite school.

Another reason posited for Bharati's possible conversion is the fact that he gave the Lord a name which was not used in the impersonalist tradition: "Shri Krishna Chaitanya."[69] While these reasons are logical and convincing, they are not specifically stated by the authoritative biographers, such as Vrindavandas Thakur and Krishnadas Kaviraj Goswami, and must therefore remain mere conjecture.

Sannyasa

Joining Mahaprabhu at His *sannyasa* initiation ceremony were Nityananda Prabhu, Mukunda Dutt (the Lord's favorite *kirtan* singer), Chandrashekhar, and Paramananda Puri. Some biographers say that Gadadhar and a devotee named Brahmananda were there as well. Thus, in February 1510, just before His twenty-fifth birthday, the Lord took *sannyasa* in the presence of His intimate associates.

Shri Nimai was now Shri Krishna Chaitanya. At the ceremony, His head was shaved, and His associates started to weep with uncontrolled remorse. As the Lord's beautiful raven black hair began to fall to the ground, the devotees were besieged by both ecstasy and anxiety. This apparent paradox actually represents two sides of the same coin, and the Vedic scriptures teach that these two sides inconceivably coalesce in the absolute region.

Mahaprabhu was given a simple loincloth and a traditional *sannyasa* garment called a *bahirvas* (an outer cloth wrapped around the waist). He carried a *sannyasa danda* (the staff of renunciation) and a *kamandalu* (a simple vessel for carrying water).

After staying in Katwa for one night following His initiation, the Lord spent three days traveling the whole of Radhadesh by foot, and from there He went on to Fulia.

Tricked by Nityananda

Visiting many villages and inspiring literally thousands to chant the holy name of Krishna, Lord Chaitanya was led by Nityananda Prabhu to the western side of Shantipur, although after His *sannyasa* initiation the Lord had originally wanted to go to Vrindavan.

Nityananda was elected by the Navadvip devotees to deceive Mahaprabhu into coming to Shantipur so they could see Him at least one last time before He traveled all over India as an ascetic. In order to do this, Nityananda had to convince the Lord that the Ganges was actually the Yamuna (a holy river in which Lord Krishna had engaged in intimate transcendental pastimes), so Mahaprabhu would think that He was going to Vrindavan when in reality He was going to Adwaita Acharya's house at Shantipur (where His Navadvip followers were waiting to surprise Him). To put the Lord in such a delusion, Nityananda knew, would not be difficult, for every body of water reminded Mahaprabhu of the sacred Yamuna.

As they marched along the Ganges, Adwaita Acharya soon appeared with a boat to take Nityananda, Mahaprabhu and party to Shantipur. Thus the conspiracy to reunite Lord Chaitanya and His Navadvip followers at the home of Adwaita Acharya was a grand success. All of Mahaprabhu's early followers, including Mother Sachi, came to see the Lord at that time. Sometimes it is said that during this pastime, especially, Adwaita Acharya and His wife, Sita, acted as the perfect householder couple. While Adwaita's wife labored incessantly to cook for all of the devotees, her husband offered the food to Krishna before they ate the remnants.

After an ecstatic *kirtan*, everyone was drenched in the holy name of the Lord, and Mother Sachi finally (if also reluctantly) gave Lord Chaitanya permission to leave and lead the life of a *sannyasi*. But she requested that He make His headquarters Jagannath Puri instead of Vrindavan, for it was closer to Navadvip and there was thus greater likelihood that she would hear news of His activities. Mahaprabhu agreed.

Leaving Shantipur, the Lord and His followers passed through Varahanagar, Calcutta, Atisara, Chattrabhoga, and many other cities and villages along the path. The Lord specifically went to Remuna (in the district of Balasore), for there He visited the divine Gopinath Deity and showed special mercy to Madhavendra Puri, His grand-spiritual master. From there He proceeded to Jajpur, and then to Cuttak, where He saw the Sakshi Gopal Deity and heard the amazing stories connected with this divine manifestation of Krishna.[70]

Breaking the Lord's Staff

When Lord Chaitanya arrived in Kamalapur, He went to the temple known as Kapoteshvar. It was at this place that Nityananda Prabhu, who was keeping the Lord's *sannyasa* staff in custody, broke the staff in three parts and threw it into the River Bharginadi. Later, this river became known as Danda-bhanga-nadi, or "the river where the staff was broken."

According to the Lord's biographers, there is great symbolic meaning in Nityananda Prabhu's breaking of the staff. In the *sannyasa* order there are four divisions, and these are delineated according to progressive levels of spiritual advancement. Only when a *sannyasi* remains on the two primary levels does he need to carry a staff of renunciation. After that, he may renounce even the staff itself. In fact, when one reaches either of the two higher levels of *sannyasa*—known as *hamsa* and *paramahamsa* respectively—he *must* give up the *sannyasa* staff.

Nityananda Prabhu realized that although Mahaprabhu was still only a young *sannyasi*, He was nonetheless the Supreme Lord as well, and, as such, He was already far beyond the *paramahamsa* stage of life. In this way, Nityananda Prabhu decided that the Lord did not need to carry the staff of renunciation, and He thus broke the *danda* into three pieces. Parenthetically, renunciants of the Vaishnava school carry a "tridanda," which is composed of three staffs.

Gaudiya Vaishnava commentators assert that since Lord Chaitanya was initiated by a Mayavadi, He carried an "ekadanda" (single staff), which represents the "oneness" philosophy that Lord Chaitanya so vehemently opposed. But the "tridanda" (three staffs) indicates that its carrier has surrendered his body, mind, and words unto the service of the Lord. It is this tridanda philosophy that was actually endorsed by Mahaprabhu, and some say that Nityananda Prabhu broke the staff into three pieces for this reason.

Due to Nityananda Prabhu's historic act of *danda-bhanga*, or "breaking the *danda*," Mahaprabhu feigned anger so He could leave His traveling companions behind and proceed to Jagannath Puri alone. For when He arrived, He wanted to meditate on the Deity of Lord Jagannath without disturbance, to enjoy the loving exchange that He shared with the Lord (from whom He was nondifferent). Finally, by way of Bhubaneshwar, Chaitanya Mahaprabhu reached Orissa and immediately went to Jagannath Puri.

CHAPTER EIGHT

Jagannath Puri

The sacred city of Puri is one of India's most popular attractions for pilgrims and tourists. Situated on the shore of the Bay of Bengal, this city of 80,000 is most famous for its colossal temple of Jagannath (Krishna), the "Lord of the Universe." Overlooking Puri from atop Nila Hill, the temple's 215-foot solid-stone tower is visible for miles around. It was this beautiful structure that Mahaprabhu, now a *sannyasi*, gazed upon as He entered Puri. The temple's original structure disappeared long ago through a series of reconstructions, the present design dating from the first century of the Common Era.[71] The location of the temple, however, has always stayed the same. (The most recent reconstruction took place in the thirteenth century under King Chodaganga and his successor Anangabhima.) Foreigners are not allowed inside the massive temple; this age-old custom was turned into statute form by the Temple Act of 1803.[72]

Sarvabhauma Bhattacharya

An important event in the life of Lord Chaitanya soon occurred within the jurisdiction of this exclusive temple. Arriving in Puri, He was immediately drawn to the Jagannath temple, and there He met Vasudev Sarvabhauma Bhattacharya, an impersonalist scholar who excelled in logic (*nyaya*) and

Vedanta. The Bhattacharya had founded the dialectical school of Navya Nyaya at Navadvip, to which scholars were drawn from all over India and which had eclipsed the Mithila school, the most important center of learning in Northern India at that time.

The Bhattacharya was driven from Navadvip by the persecution of Hussain Shah, the Islamic ruler of Bengal, and was now living in Puri under the patronage of King Prataparudra, the king of Orissa, who held him in high esteem. The Bhattacharya was about eighty years old when Lord Chaitanya arrived in Puri.

When Lord Chaitanya first entered the temple of Jagannath, He was immediately filled with ecstasy upon seeing the transcendental form of the Deity. Mahaprabhu thought, "Oh Krishna! For so long I have wanted to see You, and now I can." He saw the Deity as nondifferent from Krishna as He exists in the Kingdom of God. Mahaprabhu's eyes were indeed smeared with the salve of love, and He relished the absolute nature of Krishna's form, which was fully revealed to Him in the Deity of Jagannath.

Lord Chaitanya was so overcome with bliss, that He could not even say the name of Lord Jagannath. Rather, He called out, "Jaga . . . Jaga . . . Jaga . . ." and in a preponderance of ecstasy He fell unconscious on the temple floor.

The Lord Tested

The temple custodians were bewildered by the actions of Lord Chaitanya. But the Bhattacharya, who was immediately brought to the temple, suspected that the Lord's loss of consciousness was not an ordinary event. Rather, it was a rare symptom of divine love, exhibited only by the most elevated souls. He therefore asked the custodians not to disturb the Lord but instead to carefully carry Him to his home. As a scholar of the *Vedas* and a scientific-minded academician, the Bhattacharya wanted to study the entranced condition of the Lord in a systematic and methodical way. By this sort of careful analysis, he sought to substantiate the symptoms exhibited by Lord Chaitanya.

The Bhattacharya was not the kind of man who could be influenced or swayed by external, physical appearances. He knew well that there were many unscrupulous people who would feign such ecstatic symptoms in order to gain personal notoriety.

Sarvabhauma Bhattacharya thus tested the condition of the Lord in the light of scientific evidence and authentic scriptures. He checked His pulse, heartbeat, stomach movements, and other vital signs, and he found that the Lord's bodily functions were all in complete suspension. But when a small cotton swab was placed in front of Mahaprabhu's nostrils, the Bhattacharya could see the tiny fibers slightly moving by His exhalation. He could thus understand that Lord Chaitanya's trance was clearly genuine. His experiments completed, he tried to revive the Lord in a standard manner. Mahaprabhu, however, did not respond to ordinary treatment. The only way that He could be revived was by chanting the holy name of the Lord, but this fact was not known to the Bhattacharya.

Soon, the companions that Lord Chaitanya had left behind during the "breaking of the staff" episode arrived on the scene, and, seeing what had transpired, they began to loudly chant the Hare Krishna *maha-mantra*. To the Bhattacharya's great surprise, the Lord was quickly revived from His trance. Impressed, the Bhattacharya invited the Lord and His followers to become his guests of honor.

Gopinath Acharya (Sarvabhauma Bhattacharya's brother-in-law) fully believed in the Lord's divinity and tried to convince the Bhattacharya that Mahaprabhu was the predicted incarnation of the Supreme Personality of Godhead. While the Bhattacharya admitted that Mahaprabhu must indeed be a greatly empowered devotee, he did not believe that He was God incarnate.

The two men, however, did not debate this point on the basis of sentiment. Each cited evidence from the Vedic scriptures to support his claim. There are many self-serving imposters who claim to be God or who are proclaimed God by their followers on the basis of emotional fervor, but no man can become God by popular vote or by the haranguing of scholars. The genuine incarnations of God are described in the *Vedas*, and it was with reference to these scriptures that their discussion took place.

The Vedanta Sutra

Although still unconvinced of Mahaprabhu's divinity, the Bhattacharya felt great paternal affection for the Lord, who was young enough to be his grandson. Out of this affection he was anxious to recite and explain the *Vedanta-sutra* for the Lord, for these texts summarized the philosophical knowledge of the *Vedas* and would help the new *sannyasi* on His path to perfection. Lord Chaitanya agreed to hear from Sarvabhauma

Bhattacharya.

The Bhattacharya instructed Mahaprabhu for seven consecutive days. The Lord listened attentively, not saying a word. But on the eighth day, the Bhattacharya exclaimed, "Krishna Chaitanya! Do You understand what I've been saying? I've been instructing You for the past week, but You haven't asked any questions or said anything about my explanations."

To this, Lord Chaitanya replied, "Yes. I am a great fool. But since you have asked Me to hear you, I've been trying to listen as a matter of duty, although I cannot follow what you have been saying."

When the Bhattacharya finally asked why the Lord had not questioned anything, Mahaprabhu replied, "Actually, I can understand the *Vedanta-sutra* very clearly; it is your explanations that confuse Me."

Sarvabhauma Bhattacharya had been explaining the *sutras* according to the impersonalistic school of Shankaracharya, especially in terms of logic, grammatical word play, and mental speculation. But Lord Chaitanya indicated that He did not accept this method. Skeptical that the *Vedanta-sutra* could be understood without relying on such devices, the Bhattacharya insisted upon hearing the Lord's explanation of the *sutras*.

"As It Is"

Lord Chaitanya responded that no interpretation was needed in order to understand Vedanta philosophy. "The *Vedanta-sutra* is as bright and clear as the sun," He said, "but if someone tries to interpret it by mental speculation and give his own meaning, he covers this sun with the cloud of his imagination." The Lord further said that because the *sutras* were already perfect, there was no need to adjust their meaning. In this way, the Lord was advocating the standard way in which adherents accept the Vedic literature. Being given by God, the texts are considered already perfect. And in India they are used, even today, as the last word in any philosophical or practical argument.

For example, it is stated in the *Vedas* that if one touches the stool of any animal, one becomes contaminated and has to take a bath. But elsewhere in the Vedic literature, it is stated that cow dung is purifying. This appears to be contradictory, but the followers of the *Vedas* accept both of these statements as indisputable facts. The apparent contradiction, incidentally, has been resolved by modern science: cow dung has all antiseptic properties. In fact, cow dung is today used in India as an effective disinfectant and is

Jagannath Puri

used both as a poultice and a cleansing agent.

Lord Chaitanya thus taught that Vedic wisdom was meant to be accepted *as it is*. Rather than read some obscure, esoteric, or abstract meaning into each text, one should accept the direct meaning as given in disciplic succession. Lord Chaitanya then explained all the *sutras* in a clear and direct way, and with extensive quotations from the Vedic literature He conclusively proved that the Supreme Truth is held to be Krishna, the Supreme Personality of Godhead. Rather than pointing to the impersonal Absolute, as the Bhattacharya had thought, Vedic literature ultimately directs one to the personal Absolute, the cause of all causes. And Mahaprabhu made this point obvious and apparent.

Atmarama Verse

Overwhelmed by Lord Chaitanya's simple and yet profound explanation, the Bhattacharya was awestruck and could not utter a word. To encourage him, Lord Chaitanya said, "My dear Bhattacharya, there is nothing wonderful in My explanations. Please take it from Me that devotional service unto the Personality of Godhead is the highest goal of human life." He then quoted a famous verse from the *Shrimad Bhagavatam*, called the "*atmarama*" verse, to prove His point that the ultimate path is to worship the Supreme Person. The *atmarama* verse appears as follows:

> *atmaramas ca munayo*
> *nirgrantha api arukrame*
> *kurvanti ahoitukim bhaktim*
> *ittham-bhuta-guno hari*

"All different varieties of genuine self-realized souls, although freed from all kinds of material bondage, desire to render unalloyed devotional service unto the Personality of Godhead. This means that the Lord possesses transcendental qualities and therefore can attract everyone, including liberated souls." (S.B. 1.7.10)

Sarvabhauma Bhattacharya was eager to hear Lord Chaitanya's explanation of the *atmarama* verse, but the Lord said, "First you explain it, and then I will." The Bhattacharya then explained the verse in nine different ways, using his method of logic and grammar. Mahaprabhu thanked him for his scholarly presentation, and then He explained the same verse in sixty-four distinctly different ways, never touching on the first nine given by the Bhattacharya. The Lord's explanations of the *atmarama* verse were superior to anything the Bhattacharya had ever heard.

The Conversion

Stunned, the Bhattacharya realized that no earthly creature could possibly articulate such explanations. Although he had previously debated with his brother-in-law about the divinity of Lord Chaitanya, he could now not avoid the inescapable conclusion that Mahaprabhu was indeed God incarnate. The Bhattacharya had agreed that all scriptural evidence pointed to this, but now the practical evidence of the Lord's inconceivable intellect pierced his reservations.

Feeling offensive for not previously recognizing the true position of the Lord, the Bhattacharya threw himself at the Lord's feet in a mood of total surrender. Mahaprabhu, being greatly pleased that such a distinguished scholar had humbly surrendered himself, revealed His identity as the Supreme Personality of Godhead. First, He revealed His four-armed form as Vishnu, the opulent ruler of the spiritual world. He then displayed a very confidential six-armed form (*shad-bhuj-murti*), revealing Krishna's two arms playing on His flute, Ramachandra's two arms with bow and arrow, and His own two arms, carrying the *danda* and the *kamandalu*. Finally, He bestowed upon the Bhattacharya a vision of His original two-armed form as Krishna.

According to the Lord's earliest biographers, Sarvabhauma Bhattacharya then spontaneously composed one hundred verses in praise of Lord Chaitanya. Of these verses, two are considered most important, for they reveal the essence of Mahaprabhu's mission in this world:

> (1) Let me surrender unto the Personality of Godhead who has now appeared as Lord Chaitanya Mahaprabhu. He is the ocean of all mercy and has come down to teach us material detachment, learning, and devotional service to Himself.
>
> (2) Since pure devotional service unto the Personality of Godhead has been lost in the oblivion of time, the Lord has appeared to renovate the principles, and therefore I offer my obeisances unto His lotus feet.

Mahaprabhu appreciated these verses so much that He embraced the Bhattacharya, who at once became filled with even greater ecstasy. In this way, Sarvabhauma Bhattacharya, the great logician and grammarian, became a great devotee of the Lord.

Enlivened by this profound spiritual conquest, Mahaprabhu decided to tour South India, to spread the holy name throughout the countryside. The Bhattacharya asked the Lord to look for a great devotee named Ramananda Roy while in the south, for this soul would be of great assistance to Mahaprabhu's mission.

The year 1510 was thus full of important events in the history of Gaudiya Vaishnavism. The Lord accepted *sannyasa* in the very beginning of that year. After a month of extensive travels, He reached Jagannath Puri and soon encountered Sarvabhauma Bhattacharya. And as spring approached, the Lord began His historic 4,000-mile walking pilgrimage throughout the South.

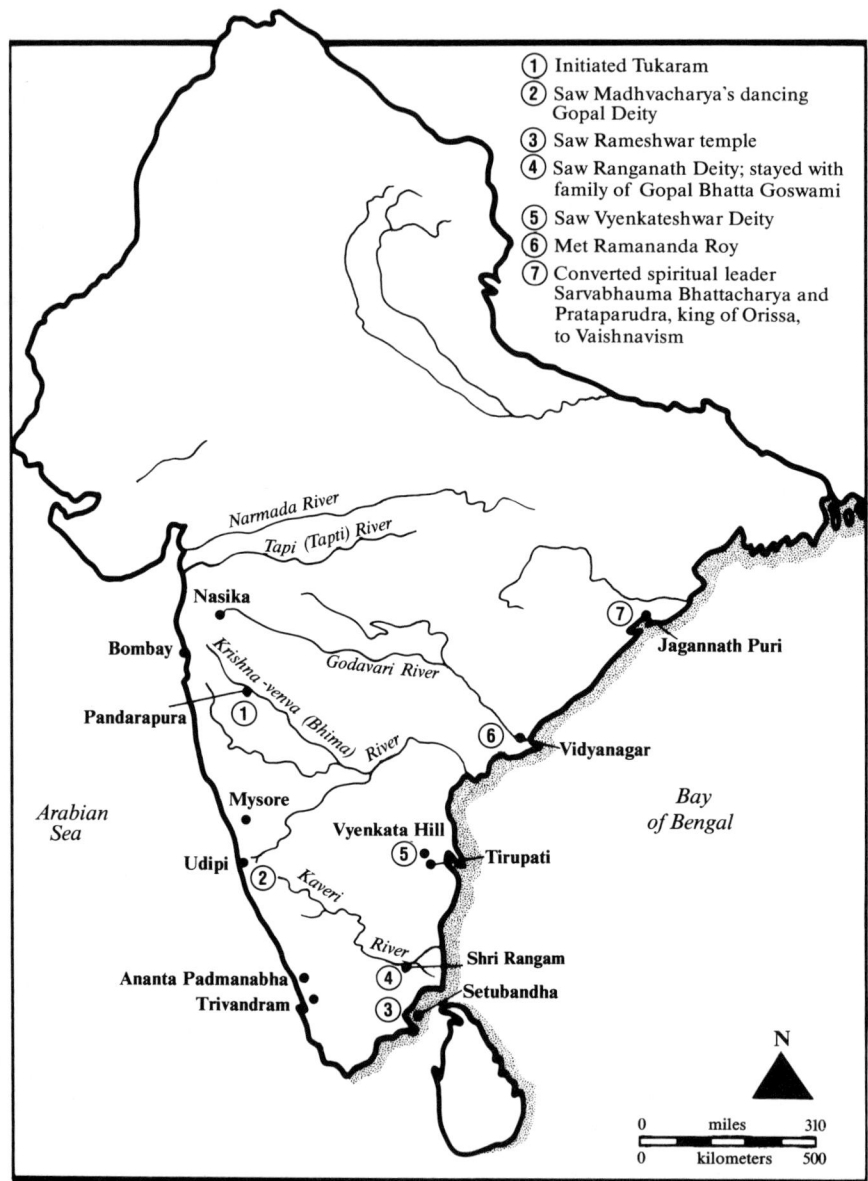

SOUTH INDIA/IMPORTANT PILGRIMAGE SITES OF THE LORD
The Lord traveled throughout the Indian subcontinent for two years, when He was twenty-five and twenty-six years old.

CHAPTER NINE

Ramananda Roy

Although Mahaprabhu wanted to travel alone in order to enjoy His intimate and confidential relationship with Krishna, Nityananda Prabhu succeeded in convincing the Lord to take at least one attendant. Otherwise, who would protect Him in those moments of transcendental abandon, when He was totally given to ecstatic symptoms? Thus a *brahmana* named Krishnadas accompanied the Lord, carrying His waterpot and four sets of fresh clothes supplied by Sarvabhauma Bhattacharya.

Nityananda, Gopinath Acharya, and several other devotees followed the Lord to a village called Alalanath, where people came from long distances to see Mahaprabhu, the incarnation of Radha and Krishna. Throughout the day enthusiastic pilgrims received the blessings of the Lord, which He would give them along with the holy name. "Always chant the Hare Krishna *maha-mantra*," He would say, "and in this way you can be in Krishna's presence."

The next morning, the Lord started out with only Krishnadas. In whatever village He spent the night, if a person came to see Him, the Lord implored that person to take up the chanting of the holy name. After teaching the people of one village, the Lord proceeded to other villages in order to increase the number of devotees. In this way, Mahaprabhu broke open the storehouse of love for Krishna and freely distributed the bounty.

Miracles

The Lord and His attendant reached Kurma-sthan (Kurma-kshetra), which is about 150 miles from Alalanath.[73] Here, Mahaprabhu visited the famous temple of Kurmadev, the tortoise incarnation. While at Kurma-sthan, the Lord bestowed His mercy upon a *brahmana* named Vasudev, who was suffering from leprosy. After Lord Chaitanya miraculously cured him, the leper became His staunch follower, and the Lord was thus soon glorified as *Vasudevamrita-prod*, meaning "One who has delivered nectar to the leper Vasudev." Such miracles were not uncommon in the pastimes of Lord Chaitanya Mahaprabhu. Once, Sarvabhauma Bhattacharya's son-in-law, Amogha, was stricken with cholera for offending the Lord. He was on his deathbed and his disease seemed irreversible. Forgiving him for his offense, Mahaprabhu touched his body and asked him to get up and chant the holy name of the Lord. This he did, with great ecstasy, as the Lord's associates watched in astonishment.[74] Another miracle was displayed when Shrivas Thakur's son passed away. Mahaprabhu succeeded in bringing the boy back to life.[75]

Miracle after miracle occurred in the courtyard of Shrivas Thakur. Once, when Mahaprabhu's followers were hungry, He asked them what they would like to eat. When they replied that they would like mangoes, even though the fruit was out of season, Mahaprabhu immediately sowed a mango seed in the ground. Within seconds a large tree miraculously appeared with more ripened fruits than the devotees could eat.

Other miracles include appearing in seven different chanting parties at once; embracing two *tal* trees, thus revealing and freeing the demigods who were trapped inside; and in His final pastimes, He escaped from the Gambhira (a small room where, in His last years, He enjoyed complete meditative trance and its concomitant ecstatic symptoms). According to the Lord's order, Gopinath Acharya and Ramananda Roy would bolt the doors and guard it so the Lord could not wander in His state of spiritual absorption and perhaps disappear altogether by walking into the sea. Nonetheless, Mahaprabhu was often found wandering the beach at Puri, His servants confused about how He could possibly have gotten out of the Gambhira.

In what is considered one of the Lord's most inconceivable miracles, the giant cart of Lord Jagannath once stopped in its tracks during the yearly Ratha-yatra Festival. Although the masses—and there were thousands—

all endeavored together, the cart could not be moved. Even elephants were brought in, but nothing could get the cart to resume its journey. Mahaprabhu, however, by leaning His divine head into the cart, accomplished what the others could not. And as the cart began to move, thousands of devotees watched and relished this inconceivable pastime of the Lord.

On another occasion, Mahaprabhu filled a large concavity in the ground with tears of love as He remembered the transcendental pastimes of Radha and Krishna. Freely distributing this sense of divine love to all who came within His path—and inducing them to accept it—was perhaps the greatest miracle ever performed. In the modern age, this miracle was repeated by His Divine Grace A. C. Bhaktivedanta Swami Prabhupada, who influenced religionists, agnostics, and even atheists, and transformed them into devotees of the Lord, giving them a chance to live as strict Vaishnavas with a very high standard of purity.

In commenting on such miracles as those performed by Lord Chaitanya, Dr. J. Stillson Judah, Professor Emeritus of the Graduate Theological Union and Pacific School of Religion, has insightfully written:

> If to the outsider the "pastimes of Krishna" [or those of Lord Chaitanya] appear miraculous and illogical, the following question must be asked. Does not the awareness of a higher reality, which all religions declare to be a divine mystery, come most often through participation in the irrational, the paradox—and for the disbeliever, the absurd? For many Buddhists it may emerge through meditating on the paradoxes of the *pragya-paramita* or the nonsensical *ko-ans*; for the Pentecostals it speaks through the incoherent babble of glossolalia; for the Roman Catholics, it involves the mystery of the transubstantiation of the bread and wine into the body and blood of Christ during the Mass; for the Moslem, it may occur during the pilgrimage to Mecca when he trots between the hills of Safa and Marwah imitating Hagar's search for water.[76]

If miracles are commonplace within other religious traditions, why would the Gaudiya Vaishnava tradition be devoid of such occurrences? If we readily accept miracles that were performed by religious figures with which we are more familiar, would it be reasonable to assume that Mahaprabhu was incapable of performing similar feats of supernatural wonder? Naturally, the miracles performed by Lord Chaitanya will confound those who are given to religious skepticism. But these very miracles stand as irrefutable evidence of the Lord's sublime effect on His immediate followers and those who appeared in subsequent generations. All of these exalted devotees fully support the wondrous and supernatural events that occurred in the career of Lord Chaitanya. Although these suprahuman activities are not accepted by disbelievers, their very existence and inclusion in canonical Vaishnava literature attest to Lord Chaitanya's greatness, for He inspired the faith of exalted, stalwart devotees. In other words, whether or not the miracles of a Moses, a Jesus, or Mahaprabhu Himself are accepted as factual, the testimony of such occurrences speaks highly of the persons who inspired them. Thus, the miracles associated with any religious tradition serve to establish the love and faith that adherents have toward their masters. Clearly, an ordinary person could not evoke such praise, and, accordingly, there are only a handful of personalities who are remembered for miraculous deeds. In a sense, the love that such praise gives rise to is more important than whether the miracles themselves had actually occurred.

Governor of Rajahmundry

After curing the leper Vasudev at Kurma-sthan, Lord Chaitanya continued His South Indian pilgrimage by proceeding to Jaiyada Nrisingha, now known as Shri Nrisingha-chalam, where a beautiful Deity of the Lord's half-man/ half-lion manifestation is still worshiped. The temple is located five miles to the northwest of Vishakapatnam, in Andhra Pradesh. Here, Lord Chaitanya taught the eternal truths of Vaishnavism to many sincere souls.

Moving further south, Mahaprabhu then followed the old route from Sabaran (near Nrisingha-chalam), and soon entered the Rajahmundry district, where He went to bathe in the Godavari River. Seated on the western bank, He noticed the governor of Rajahmundry, Ramananda Roy, who had also come to the river for the same purpose. The governor was easily recognizable because he had some one hundred servants with him, and there was great fanfare and music. But still he humbly walked over to the beautifully effulgent *sannyasi* and introduced himself: "I am the unworthy Ramananda Roy. While acting in some important capacity, I am simply a *shudra*,[77] a low-born individual." With this, Mahaprabhu embraced him, and they both relished utterances of Krishna's name.

Actually, Ramananda Roy was not an ordinary personality.[78] According to Vaishnava tradition, he was actually an incarnation of the *gopi* named Lalitadevi, who was one of Lord Krishna's most intimate devotees.

Others say that Ramananda Roy was both Vishaka (Radharani's chief attendant in Her service to Krishna) and Arjuna (Krishna's dear friend to whom He revealed the philosophical instructions of *Bhagavad-gita*). As we shall see, Mahaprabhu Himself values the instructions He receives from Ramananda Roy as the highest spiritual knowledge.[79]

Some biographers point out that while the Lord received initiation into the holy name from Ishvara Puri and *sannyasa* initiation from Keshava Bharati, for entrance into the highest realm of spirituality, He took *raga-marg* initiation from Ramananda Roy. Of course, none of these three ever considered themselves Mahaprabhu's *guru* in any real sense. But such pastimes were enacted for the sake of setting an example for the world to follow.

Conversations

On the day that they first encountered one another, Mahaprabhu and Shri Ramananda agreed to again meet before nightfall. After taking their evening baths at the Godavari, they sat on its cooling banks to discuss the philosophy of Krishna consciousness. Before Shri Ramananda and the Lord could even exchange simple pleasantries, the Lord had asked him to quote some scriptural verses about the ultimate goal of life.

Ramananda Roy replied at once: "A person who is sincere in his occupational duty will gradually develop a sense of God consciousness." He also quoted a verse from the *Vishnu Purana* (3:8:9) which states that the Supreme Lord is worshiped by one's occupational duty and that there is no alternative for satisfying Him. The idea is that if one uses one's God-given propensity in the Lord's service, then one is properly using one's ability and will gradually reach perfection as a result. For this purpose, the *Vedas* divide society into four natural sections: the intellectuals and priests (*brahmanas*); the administrators and warriors (*kshatriyas*); the merchants and farmers (*vaishyas*); and the laborers and artisans (*shudras*).

Varnashram Dharma

For each class there are prescribed rules and regulations as well as occupational functions. The main emphasis, however, is on one's natural quality and work. Unlike the Hindu caste system, as later witnessed by the British, the original "caste system" had little to do with birthright. Rather, one naturally fit into a particular social status according to one's inclinations and behavior. In this sense, the *Vedas* simply gave formal definition to that which normally occurs in nature.

In addition to the four social orders, the *Vedas* recognize four spiritual orders as well: celibate student life (*brahmacharya*), marriage (*grihastha*), retirement (*vanaprastha*) and renunciation (*sannyasa*). These four progressive stages were recommended for the gradual upliftment of humanity to ultimately attain the spiritual platform. Each level was characterized by new and deeper modes of realization and commitment. Gradually, by following this system, one would become ready for renunciation, which was necessary both to face death gracefully and to enter into the Kingdom of God.

Ramananda Roy stated that those who rigidly follow this system could please the Supreme Lord and reach perfection in this very lifetime.

After hearing Shri Ramananda expound on this Varnashram system (as it is properly called), Mahaprabhu readily acknowledged its validity. Still, the Lord cautioned, it is merely external. The highest perfection transcends even the Varnashram system. The Lord then asked Shri Ramananda to dive deeper into the truths of transcendence.

In response, Shri Ramananda quoted a verse from *Bhagavad-gita* (9:27) in which Lord Krishna recommends that absolutely everything one does—all one's daily activities—be done as an offering unto Him.

Although this verse deals with total surrender in that it says one should give the results of one's work to the Lord as an offering, Mahaprabhu was still dissatisfied, saying there is a principle that is even higher. Previously Shri Ramananda recommended the *Varnashram* system. He now stressed, however, that in order for the system to work, all of one's occupational duties had to be centered on loving service to the Lord (*daivi*, or "divine" Varnashram). Otherwise, the whole system is a waste of time. This was certainly true, Mahaprabhu agreed, but was still only superficial. "If you know something more," Lord Chaitanya encouraged him, "then go further."

Higher Truth

After having his suggestions rejected twice, Shri Ramananda next proposed that one should abandon occupational duties altogether and simply develop detachment from the material world, which would in turn allow one to rise to the transcendental plane. In other words, he was now saying that all activity within society should be rejected and total surrender to

God should permeate one's existence. As evidence, he cited Lord Krishna's final instruction in *Bhagavad-gita*: "Abandon all varieties of religion and simply surrender unto Me. I will protect you from all sinful reaction. Do not fear, worry or hesitate." (Bg. 18.66)

Lord Chaitanya, however, also rejected this third proposal, for He wanted to demonstrate that such renunciation, in and of itself, was not sufficient. Then Shri Ramananda went further. Having said that one should render devotional service with renunciation of fruitive activities, he was now saying that devotional service with appropriate knowledge and spiritual realization is superior.

When Mahaprabhu heard this, He asked Shri Ramananda to go a little further, for although this is correct, there is a slightly higher platform. Ramananda Roy now gave scriptural references for the highest accomplishment in spiritual realization: to render pure devotional service without any attachment to even the subtle attainments of knowledge and liberation.

The Ultimate End

This answer catapulted Lord Chaitanya into ecstatic bliss, for His mission was to teach such unmixed devotional service—service without any tinge of material conditioning. At once, Mahaprabhu said, "Yes! This is it!" Now, having agreed upon the topmost spiritual path, He wanted Ramananda Roy to expound on *advanced* devotional service.

If *bhakti-yoga* is elevated to the personal platform, Shri Ramananda taught, it is called *prema-bhakti*. In the early stages of self-realization, a particular relationship between the Supreme Lord and the devotee is not yet established. But when *prema-bhakti* develops, a relationship with the Supreme Personality of Godhead unfolds, manifesting one of five basic interactions (*rasa*), including passive adoration, servitorship, friendship, parenthood, and conjugal love.

Since the neutral position of passive adoration is fundamental, Ramananda Roy began by discussing the level of servitude, wherein the devotee is eternally found as the servant of his divine master. Worship in this mode is often full of opulence and regalia, motivated by a sense of awe and reverence, without the full sweetness that manifests in the remaining three relationships. Mahaprabhu was enjoying this explanation and encouraged Shri Ramananda to discuss the other transcendental *rasas*.

Highest Rasa

Ramananda Roy proceeded to tell the Lord about the fraternal relationship one may have with Krishna, which is considered to be on a higher platform than the master/servant mode. In fraternity, one's reverence matures into affection, and awareness of the Lord's superiority begins to dwindle. As a result, one can relish a disinct relationship with God in the mood of friendship.

Lord Chaitanya's appreciation for these subjects was beyond words. He simply kept telling Shri Ramananda, "Go further!"

Understanding the Lord's mind, Shri Ramananda immediately discussed the conjugal relationship, in which one has an intimate pastime of confidential love with the Supreme Person. Then he backtracked, discussing more elaborately relationships in neutrality, fraternity, and paternity. Finally, he elaborated upon the conjugal relationship as the perfect state of love for God. In one sense, he cautioned, all of these relationships are absolute and thus equal. In the realm of spiritual variegatedness, however, there are definite distinctions and the conjugal relationship is considered the highest. This relationship, moreover, is perfectly expressed in the activities of the *gopis*, the simple cowherd girlfriends of Krishna, who, out of love for Him, knew of nothing beyond His service.

The "love" under discussion is not the sort to which we are accustomed in the material world. It is not beleaguered by the unsavory characteristics of the mundane sphere: superficiality, carnality, and temporality. In contrast, the spiritual love of the *gopis* is profound, wholesome, and eternal. In comparison to *this* love, the mundane counterpart may be considered nothing more than lust. Ramananda Roy described the difference between the two, and how material lust can be transformed into spiritual love by the process of Krishna consciousness.

Mahaprabhu could not control Himself. Upon hearing these words, His bliss knew no bounds and both He and Shri Ramananda were saturated in love of God. Although He agreed that this was the last word in Krishna consciousness, Mahaprabhu asked Ramananda Roy to go even further. Surprised, for it is difficult to imagine that there is anything superior to the conjugal relationship, Shri Ramananda expounded on the details of the foremost of all the *gopis*, Shrimati Radharani, who is none other than the Lord's eternal consort.

Confidential Knowledge

Shrimati Radharani's position is extremely confidential and is only understood by the most advanced devotees. She is the female counterpart of the Personality of Godhead. Her love for Krishna is perfectly complete, and Her beauty attracts the heart of that Supreme Attractor. Her attributes are so overpowering, in fact, that She makes Krishna self-conscious, and He becomes bewildered by Her beauty and the love that She feels for Him. So intense is Her love, the scriptures inform us, that it makes the standard color of love (Krishna's color) change from dark to a glowing light (Her own hue: *Ujjvala*). In this totally spiritual experience, as Krishnadas Kaviraj Goswami says, "lover, beloved and love itself dance in one body,"[80] and this is personified in Lord Chaitanya Mahaprabhu.

There are two reasons for Mahaprabhu's appearance in this world, one external and the other internal. The external reason for His appearance was simply to inaugurate the *sankirtan* movement. The internal reason is highly esoteric, based on God's desire to fully taste the love that His devotees feel for Him. This love is felt most intensely by Shrimati Radharani. Thus, the Lord descends as Mahaprabhu in order to realize the depth and bliss of Her love for Him. Furthermore, by adopting Her devotional attitude, He comes to appreciate His own sweetness and charm through the eyes of His own devotee.

It may be argued that God is already omniscient, and He does not need to make some extraneous endeavor to realize these internal truths about Himself. The Vaishnava response to this argument, however, is that the manifestation of Lord Chaitanya is not at all extraneous to God's self-existent nature. Vaishnava philosophy, in other words, accepts the premise of the above argument, but it goes even further by asserting exactly *how* the Lord happens to know Himself—He knows Himself and His internal potency, Shrimati Radharani, by manifesting in the form of Chaitanya Mahaprabhu.

Shrimati Radharani

Shrimati Radharani is worshiped *before* Krishna, according to Shri Ramananda. For instance, They are traditionally referred to as "Radha-Krishna"—the energy first (Radha) and then the energetic source (Krishna). Even the *maha-mantra* is a prayer *first* to Radha and *then* to

Krishna. The first word of the *mantra* is "hare," which is the vocative form of "hara." In other words, the Hare Krishna chant is an address to Mother Hara that pleads with Her to engage one in the service of the Lord.

It is interesting that even the Vedic literature is reserved in disclosing the truth of Shrimati Radharani. The Vedic sages knew that people would misconstrue the confidential reality of Radha-Krishna (possibly mistaking it for some mundane love affair), and they therefore described it in very few places.

The *Shrimad Bhagavatam*, for instance, which is considered the most important Vedic work, only mentions Radharani in one obscure text (10.30.28) of its eighteen thousand verses. And even then, She is only alluded to with the oblique word *aradhita*, implying that She is that one special personality who has won Krishna's heart. Nonetheless, even this verse is indirect, with neither Her name or divinity fully described. This is because Shukadev Goswami, the narrator of the *Bhagavatam*, would go into fits of ecstasy upon the recitation of Her name.

Nonetheless, She *is* clearly mentioned in other Vedic texts, such as the *Harivamsa*, and the *Naradiya, Padma, Brahmanda*, and *Brahma-vaivarta Puranas*, where Her name and theology are elaborately described. Her exact identity, too, has been revealed by the great teachers in disciplic succession and in later Vedic works, such as the *Gita Govinda* and the *Shri Chaitanya Charitamrita*. In these works, especially, Shrimati Radharani is fully described in regard to her morphology and ontology, and thus the female aspect of God is dealt with as a detailed science. Shri Ramananda expounded upon these esoteric truths while Mahaprabhu listened in a state of blissful absorption.

The Delusions of Love

Finally gathering His wits about Him, Lord Chaitanya begged Shri Ramananda, "Please, go further, further, further . . ."

Ramananda Roy then informed Lord Chaitanya Mahaprabhu that there was another, highly evolved spiritual topic, known as *prema-vilas-vivarta*. In an attempt to convey this esoterica to Lord Chaitanya, Shri Ramananda began to recite a poem that embodied these higher truths. The Lord immediately covered Ramananda Roy's mouth, however, symbolically indicating that materialists, philosophers, and even spiritualists and devotees of a lower order cannot enter into such confidential understandings. Mahaprabhu finally relented, and Ramananda Roy began to sing two verses that reflect the sum and substance of spiritual life. After these verses were sung, Mahaprabhu said, "This is the limit of the goal of human life, and only by your mercy have I come to understand it conclusively."

The essence of the spiritual transaction reflected in *prema-vilas-vivarta* is as follows: unlike their material counterpart, transcendental loving affairs are as relishable during separation as during enjoyment. But such affairs manifest a special sweetness when experienced in separation, culminating in a sort of spiritual longing, a sublime desperation that otherwise remains unknown. Shrimati Radharani, for instance, once mistook a black *tamal* tree for Krishna and embraced it out of love in separation. Such a mistake is a manifestation of the level called *prema-vilas-vivarta*. This advanced stage of spiritual life is rarely achieved in this world.

In this way, the Lord and Ramananda Roy discussed the highest spiritual philosophy for some time. Shri Ramananda went deeper and deeper into the completely spiritual loving exchanges of Radha and Krishna, and Mahaprabhu kept insisting that he go further still. Soon, Lord Chaitanya admitted, "I came to you to understand the transcendental loving affairs of the Divine Couple, and now I am very satisfied that you have described them so nicely. I can understand from your pure lips that this is the highest loving state of Krishna consciousness."

Shri Ramananda Roy replied: "I do not know how it is that I am saying these things, but I do know that You have mystically made me speak. I am simply repeating Your message." In this way, Ramananda Roy acknowledged that all truth emanates from the Supreme Lord, Shri Chaitanya Mahaprabhu.

Satisfied with Shri Ramananda, Lord Chaitanya revealed His essential ontological form as a combination of Radha and Krishna. Blessed with this vision, Ramananda Roy became an important follower in Mahaprabhu's line and eventually settled in Puri, where he served as one of the Lord's most intimate associates.

Incidentally, as governor of an entire district (known today as Madras), all of Shri Ramananda's subjects also became devotees of Lord Chaitanya. The place where the esoteric conversation between Mahaprabhu and Ramananda Roy had occurred has become exalted as a holy site for pilgrims. Shrila Bhaktisiddhanta Saraswati identified the exact meeting place of the two transcendentalists as the Gospada Ghat on the Godavari at Kovvur.[81] Here he established a monastery called the Ramananda

Gaudiya Math, and he installed the footprints of Chaitanya Mahaprabhu that are honored in memorial to this day.[82]

After leaving Shri Ramananda's district of Vidyanagara (Rajahmundry), Mahaprabhu visited such important places of pilgrimage as Gautami-ganga, Mallikarjuna, Ahovala-nrisingha, Siddhavata, Skanda-kshetra, Trimatha, Vriddhakashi, Bauddha-sthan, Tripati, Trimalla, Pana-nrisingha, Shiva-kanchi, Vishnu-kanchi, Trikala-hasti, Vriddha-kola, Papanasanam, and many others. To each and every one of these districts He brought love of God, as an aromatic flower brings a delightful fragrance on a spring day.

CHAPTER TEN

Shri Rangam

From Papanasanam, Lord Chaitanya followed the western route along the bank of the Kaveri. Finally, on a hot summer day toward the end of July, He arrived in Shri Rangam, one of the holiest cities in all of South India. There, He would spend the next four months (*chaturmasya*) to perform austerities during the rainy season and enliven the devotees.

As He saw its seven surrounding concentric walls and its towering *gopurams* (gateways), the magnificent temple of Ranganath Swami (Krishna) brought joy to Mahaprabhu's heart. And when He entered the temple compound, He began dancing in ecstatic love of God as He chanted the holy names. The news of Mahaprabhu's arrival spread throughout the city, and many people began to assemble just to see Him.

Conversations with Vyenkata Bhatta

Vyenkata Bhatta was the head priest, so he and his two brothers, Tirumalla and Prabodhananda Sarasvati, invited Lord Chaitanya to be their guest. Since they lived quite close to the temple, Mahaprabhu would have easy access to the Lord of His heart, Ranganath Swami, the presiding Deity of Shri Rangam. Parenthetically, this temple is the largest and one of the richest in all of India. Established by Ramanujacharya, it still serves as a central headquarters for devotees of the Shri Sampradaya.

Lord Chaitanya spent many days at Vyenkata's house, and they often discussed the comparative value of God's majesty (*aishvarya*) and love (*madhurya*). Mahaprabhu strongly conveyed the superiority of God's loving feature, whereas Vyenkata was trained, as a member of the Shri Sampradaya, to appreciate the Lord's majestic opulence (in the form of Narayana). Eventually, Mahaprabhu convinced Vyenkata that while both features of God are certainly praiseworthy, the loving side of the Supreme is sweeter and more intimate. Prabhodananda Saraswati and Vyenkata's son, Gopal Bhatta, heard these discussions and were also convinced of Mahaprabhu's conclusions.

Lord Chaitanya's Jagannath

In the early morning hours, Lord Chaitanya Mahaprabhu would regularly go to the temple to see the Deity (Ranganath Swami). Sometimes, however, Mahaprabhu felt separation from the particular forms of God at the temple in Puri—Lord Jagannath, Baladev, and Subhadra—who had thrown Him into an ecstatic trance while He was there. Tradition relates that He carved similar Deities with His own hands. Those sacred Deities, created by the Lord Himself, are still worshiped at the Shri Jagannath Mutt, a temple that today stands where Vyenkata Bhatta's house used to be.

Sometimes Mahaprabhu would go out into the road and perform *sankirtan*. Upon seeing the beautiful form of Lord Chaitanya, and the ecstatic way in which He chanted and danced, the people were astonished. Many thousands would come and see the Lord in this way, and when they did, they could not help but join in the chanting and dancing, as if mystically possessed. Indeed, after chanting and dancing with the Lord, they gave their lives to His service and became devotees of Krishna.

The Illiterate Brahmana

On one occasion Lord Chaitanya came upon a devotee who was trying to read *Bhagavad-gita*. The Lord noticed that this great soul exhibited ecstatic symptoms—hair standing on end, tears welling in the eyes, trembling, and perspiration. Mahaprabhu was pleased to meet such a pure devotee.

Some of the townspeople standing nearby, however, did not share Lord Chaitanya's fondness for the humble sage with the *Gita*. They were laughing and joking about the way he was turning the book rightside up and upside down. Actually the poor sage was illiterate. And that's why the cruel townspeople were laughing at him.

Lord Chaitanya asked the devotee, "My dear sir, why are you in such ecstatic love? Which portion of the *Bhagavad-gita* gives you these transcendental symptoms?"

"I am illiterate," the devotee replied, "and therefore I do not know the meaning of the words. Sometimes I read it correctly and sometimes, well, You saw them laughing . . .

"In any case," the devotee continued with renewed enthusiasm, "I am trying to study *Bhagavad-gita* because my spiritual master told me to do so. Although I cannot read, I am greatly moved by this picture of Lord Krishna acting as Arjuna's charioteer. Taking the reigns in His hands, He appears very beautiful and merciful. As the Supreme Lord, He does not have to serve anyone. Still, because Arjuna is His dear friend and devotee, He agrees to act as his servant. I am simply appreciating the love He feels for His devotees."

Then, much to everyone's surprise, Lord Chaitanya embraced the illiterate devotee and proclaimed that he was actually the real knower of *Bhagavad-gita* because he had realized its most profound purport: love for Krishna and Krishna's love for His devotees.

Being embraced by Mahaprabhu, the illiterate devotee went into a fit of ecstasy, chanting the holy name and dancing in blissful remembrance of Krishna's pastimes. He then realized that Lord Chaitanya was Krishna Himself.

After four months, Lord Chaitanya prepared to leave Shri Rangam and continue His pilgrimage of South India. Vyenkata Bhatta, who became very close to the Lord during His short visit, was overwhelmed with lamentation and fainted. Mahaprabhu also left a deep impression on Vyenkata's son, Gopal Bhatta, who would one day become one of the Lord's six most important disciples, the Goswamis of Vrindavan.

All the residents of Shri Rangam felt their hearts ache and developed the mood of love in separation when Mahaprabhu continued His travels. Even though five full centuries have elapsed since the Lord's visit, the residents of Shri Rangam have not forgotten the great fortune Lord Chaitanya brought to their city. A shrine at Shri Rangam's main entrance displays the Lord's footprints and commemorates His arrival.

The family descendants of Vyenkata Bhatta still live at Shri Rangam.

The head of the temple, Rangaraj Bhatta, continues to carry on the tradition and heritage of his forefathers by serving on the Ranganath temple advisory committee. And Shri Rangam has become one of India's most famous temples.

The glories of Ranganath Swami are being spread all over the world, too, for when visited by a devotee of the International Society for Krishna Consciousness, Rangaraj Bhatta said, "The members of ISKCON, headed by His Divine Grace A. C. Bhaktivedanta Swami Prabhupada, are fulfilling the mission of Ranganath Swami by preaching Lord Chaitanya's *sankirtan* movement all over the world. This is very wonderful, and it has been predicted by the Lord Himself."[83]

After leaving Shri Rangam, Mahaprabhu went further south to Risava Parvata. There, He met Paramananda Puri, who was later to become His intimate associate when He returned to Orissa. Next, the Lord visited Madurai, and there He met a great devotee of Lord Ramachandra. This devotee was grief-stricken because Sitadevi, the divine consort of Lord Rama, was once abducted by the demon Ravana. Out of pain for Sitadevi, the devotee was observing a fast until death.

Lord Chaitanya consoled the faithful devotee, however, explaining that the real Sita disappeared in a mystical fire as soon as Ravana approached Her. She thus remained in an unmanifest state while an illusory Sitadevi was abducted by the demon in Her place. After the death of Ravana, when Sita was put through the ordeal of a fire sacrifice, the false Sita vanished and Her real counterpart appeared for Lord Rama.

Having heard the Lord's explanation, the devotee broke his fast and began to cry in ecstatic love. He then became a follower of Lord Chaitanya.

Converting the Buddhists

Once, during His travels in South India, the Lord encountered a group of Buddhist philosophers. After a rigorous debate, Mahaprabhu pierced their impersonalistic reasoning and heterodox views with the strong arguments of Krishna consciousness. Unfortunately, a large gathering that had witnessed the debate began to laugh at the defeated Buddhists. Thus these Buddhists went away unhappy and proceeded to plot against the Lord.

According to their plan, they brought the Lord a beautiful plate of food, claiming it was offered to a temple Deity of Lord Krishna. However, the food was untouchable by Vaishnava standards (as it was not offered to

God with love and devotion, but rather was offered by non-Vaishnavas). Thus, the Buddhists sought to defame the Lord by broadcasting the fact that He had eaten unoffered food. Nonetheless, when the contaminated food was about to be given to Lord Chaitanya, a large bird immediately swooped down, picked up the plate in its beak, and flew away. While the bird was soaring through the sky, the food actually fell off the plate and dropped on the head of the chief Buddhist teacher. The plate itself fell as well, gashing the teacher's head. Seeing this, the small group of Buddhist philosophers realized the Lord's mystic opulence and ran to Him for mercy and shelter. The Lord then formally initiated them and taught them to chant the holy name of the Lord.

Thereafter, the Lord went to Durvasana, Rameshvaram, Udipi, and literally all over South India. Krishnadas Kaviraj Goswami says the tour lasted two years.[84] And in that time the Lord changed the lives of thousands upon thousands, turning sinners into devotees, and devotees into pure devotees. According to Kavi Karnapur, Lord Chaitanya succeeded in establishing Vaishnavism as the state religion of Karnata country.[85] This influenced a large part of the South to also turn toward Vaishnavism. Mahaprabhu then paid a short visit to Kurukshetra and some other places that are not specifically noted in His authorized biographies.[86] Having completed His tour, Mahaprabhu soon returned to Puri.

During His journeys throughout South India, the Lord's associates and followers, such as Nityananda Prabhu and Sarvabhauma Bhattacharya, spread His message throughout Orissa. The conversion of the Bhattacharya and the Lord's reputation in general soon reached the ears of King Prataparudra, who had great respect for the Bhattacharya (employed as the court counselor) and so he was easily convinced of Mahaprabhu's divinity. Soon, the king knew, the Lord would return to Orissa from His pilgrimage. And when He did, the king would be happy to entertain Him and see if all that He had heard was true.

CHAPTER ELEVEN

King Prataparudra

Although His first stay in Orissa was relatively short, Mahaprabhu would now stay for almost two years. Puri, as His mother had requested, was becoming His headquarters, and many of His followers from Navadvip would either move there or make regular pilgrimage.

King Prataparudra was a sincere devotee of Krishna, the Supreme Personality of Godhead, and he worshiped Him in the form of the Jagannath Deity at the great Jagannath temple in Puri. In 1512, when Mahaprabhu returned from South India to live in Puri, King Prataparudra was naturally eager to talk with Him, having heard His glories from the Bhattacharya.

Aversion to Opulence

Nonetheless, Lord Chaitanya had adopted the role of a monk (*sannyasi*) to teach pure devotional service, and He strictly followed the injunctions forbidding a *sannyasi* to meet people absorbed in material affairs. Therefore, although the king was also a great devotee, Mahaprabhu desired to use the king as an example and was therefore reluctant to meet him.

On behalf of the pious king, however, Sarvabhauma Bhattacharya boldly approached Mahaprabhu, "King Prataparudra is very anxious to meet You. He wanted me to ask You if You would see him."

As soon as He heard this proposal, Lord Chaitanya covered His ears with His hands and said, "My dear Bhattacharya, why are you making such an undesirable request? I am in the renounced order of life, and for Me to meet a king is just as dangerous as meeting a woman. To meet either would be just like drinking poison." Considering His words carefully, the Lord said, "For a man seriously desiring to cross the ocean of material miseries and obtain the Lord's mercy, seeing either a materialist or a lusty woman is more abominable than drinking poison."

Sarvabhauma Bhattacharya replied, "My dear Lord, what you have said is correct. But this king is not ordinary. He is a great devotee and servant of Lord Jagannath."

"Although the king is certainly a great devotee," said Lord Chaitanya, "as a *sannyasi* I must still consider him a venomous snake. Bhattacharya, if you continue to speak like this you will never see Me here again." Afraid of further angering the Lord, the Bhattacharya returned home and began to meditate on the matter.

Petitioning the Lord

Meanwhile, King Prataparudra, who had gone to his capital city of Cuttak, sent a letter to the Bhattacharya begging him to get the Lord's consent for a meeting. The Bhattacharya wrote the king that Lord Chaitanya had not given His permission. The king immediately wrote another letter: "Please appeal to all the devotees associated with Lord Chaitanya Mahaprabhu to submit my petition at the lotus feet of the Lord. By the mercy of the devotees, one can attain the shelter of the Lord's lotus feet. If Lord Chaitanya does not show mercy to me, I shall give up my kingdom, become a mendicant, and beg from door to door."

This letter disturbed Sarvabhauma Bhattacharya. He met with all the devotees and described the king's wishes, showing the letter to each one. Everyone was astonished that King Prataparudra had so much devotion for Lord Chaitanya Mahaprabhu. One devotee said, "The Lord will never consent to meet the king, and if we ask Him to do so, He will feel very unhappy."

"We shall go once again to the Lord," the Bhattacharya suggested, "but we shall not request Him to meet the king. Rather, we shall simply describe the king's good behavior." Having reached this decision, they all went to the place where Lord Chaitanya was staying. When the Lord saw them, He said, "Why have you all come here?" Although they had intended to speak, they could not utter a word. "I see that you want to say something," said Chaitanya Mahaprabhu, "but you do not speak. What is the reason?"

The Lord's Garment

Nityananda Prabhu, the Lord's closest associate, answered, "We want to tell You something, but we are afraid to speak on such a delicate matter. Nevertheless, we must inform You that unless he sees You, the king of Orissa will become a beggar. It is the nature of an attached man to give up his life if he does not attain his desired object." Knowing the king's seriousness, the devotees were trying to save him from committing suicide. Nityananda Prabhu then suggested, "There is a way by which You need not meet the king, but which would enable him to continue living. If You would mercifully send one of Your garments to him, he would remain alive, hoping to see You sometime in the future."

Lord Chaitanya agreed to this proposal, and Nityananda Prabhu then obtained a garment used by Him and delivered it to Sarvabhauma Bhattacharya who, in turn, sent it to the king. When the king received the sacred cloth, he began to worship it exactly as he would have worshiped the Lord directly.

Ramananda Roy

Soon, King Prataparudra came to Jagannath Puri from Cuttak, along with his entourage of secretaries, ministers, and military officers. Also with him was one of his governors, Ramananda Roy, who had met Lord Chaitanya on His tour of South India and had at that time established a close friendship with the Lord. In fact, Mahaprabhu had asked Ramananda Roy to resign from his governmental post and join Him at Jagannath Puri so that they could talk together every day about the activities of Lord Krishna and share their understanding.

Thus, when Ramananda Roy arrived in Jagannath Puri, he hurried with great anticipation to see Lord Chaitanya. After they greeted each other, he said to the Lord, "I informed King Prataparudra of Your order. I said, 'Your majesty, I cannot continue my political activities. I desire only to stay at the lotus feet of Chaitanya Mahaprabhu. Kindly give me permission.' Upon hearing Your name, he immediately rose from his throne and embraced me. My dear Lord, as soon as the king heard Your holy name, he was overwhelmed by great ecstatic love. He granted me full salary as a pension and requested me to engage in Your service without anxiety. Then he humbly said, 'Because I am most fallen and abominable, I am unfit to receive an interview with the Lord. Lord Chaitanya Mahaprabhu is Krishna Himself, and service to Him makes life successful. He is very merciful, and I hope that He will allow me an interview in one of my future lives.' My Lord," said Ramananda Roy, "I don't think I have even a fraction of King Prataparudra's ecstatic love for You."

"My dear Ramananda," the Lord replied, "you are the foremost of Krishna's devotees, and whoever serves you is blessed by Krishna. The king has shown so much devotion for you that Krishna will certainly accept him."

The King's Determination

In the days that followed, the Lord enjoyed the company of Ramananda Roy, talking with him about Lord Krishna and His pastimes. While they were absorbed in these conversations, King Prataparudra called for Sarvabhauma Bhattacharya. The king made him sit on an elegant chair and offered him respectful greetings. Then he began lamenting, "Lord Chaitanya Mahaprabhu has descended just to deliver all kinds of sinful, lowborn persons. But has Lord Chaitanya incarnated to deliver all kinds of sinners except a king named Prataparudra? If He is determined to avoid me," cried the king, "then I am determined to give up my life."

The Bhattacharya was astonished at the king's strength of purpose. He thought that such determination would be impossible for a worldly man. King Prataparudra continued, "If I do not receive Lord Chaitanya Mahaprabhu's mercy, both my body and my kingdom are useless."

At last, Sarvabhauma Bhattacharya said, "My dear king, don't worry. Your firm determination will surely inspire Lord Chaitanya to bestow His mercy upon you. Only pure love can attract the Supreme Lord, and since your love for Mahaprabhu is very deep, He will undoubtedly be merciful to you."

The Bhattacharya felt great compassion for the king and wanted to help him as much as he could. By making the following suggestion, he blessed the king that he might receive the mercy of the Lord: "There is one way to see Lord Chaitanya directly. On the day of the Ratha-yatra festival, He will dance before the Deity in great ecstatic love. Afterward He will enter the Gundicha garden. At that time you should go there alone, in plain dress, and read the five chapters from the *Shrimad Bhagavatam* about Krishna's dancing with the *gopis* (cowherd girls). Mahaprabhu will be in a mood of ecstatic love, and He will embrace you, knowing you to be a pure devotee. Do not worry: the Lord has already changed His mind about you due to Ramananda Roy's description of your pure love for Him."

After thus encouraging the king, Sarvabhauma Bhattacharya returned home. In the days that followed, Ramananda Roy would remind the Lord of the king's desire to see Him. Using expert diplomacy, Ramananda Roy gradually softened the Lord's heart.

"My Lord," Shri Ramananda said, "You are the Supreme Personality of Godhead. You have nothing to fear from anyone."

Lord Chaitanya objected, "I am not the Supreme Personality of Godhead. I am just an ordinary human being, and I fear public opinion. As soon as the general public finds a little fault in a *sannyasi*, they advertise it like wildfire. A black spot of ink on a white cloth cannot be hidden; it is always very prominent." (Actually, the traditional commentators explain that Mahaprabhu, as the perfect devotee, was always adverse to being identified as God. He, of course, was aware of His divinity and had even proven it several times in the past, to Shri Ramananda and to many others. Yet He also felt that if people found any discrepancy in His behavior—such as associating with a worldly minded king—their criticism would minimize the importance of the *sannyasa* order and hamper His mission of preaching Krishna consciousness.)

The King's Son

"My dear Lord," Ramananda Roy continued, "You have delivered so many sinful people. But King Prataparudra is not at all sinful. He is actually the Lord's servant and devotee."

"There may be much milk in a big pot," Lord Chaitanya Mahaprabhu replied, "but if it is contaminated by one drop of liquor, it is untouchable. The king certainly possesses many good qualities, but simply by taking the title 'King,' he has infected everything. However, if you are still very eager for Me to meet the king, please bring his son to Me first. The *Vedas* say that the son is a representative of the father. So meeting King Prataparudra's son would be just as good as meeting the king himself."

Ramananda Roy then went to tell the king about his talk with Lord Chaitanya Mahaprabhu, and following the Lord's order, he brought back the king's son to see Him. The young prince's blackish complexion, large lotus eyes, yellow garments, and jeweled ornaments reminded everyone of Lord Krishna.

"Here is a great devotee," Lord Chaitanya Mahaprabhu said, "for anyone who sees him remembers the Supreme Personality of Godhead, Krishna. Just by sending Me this boy, the king has put Me very much in his debt." Seeing all this, the devotees praised the boy for his great spiritual fortune. Shri Ramananda took him back to the king's palace. The king was very glad to hear of his son's experience, and when he embraced him, he also felt ecstatic love—just as if he had touched Lord Chaitanya Mahaprabhu directly.

The King Sweeps the Road

At last the day came for Lord Jagannath's annual Ratha-yatra festival. After bathing early in the morning, Lord Chaitanya Mahaprabhu saw the Deity of Lord Jagannath transferred from His throne to the cart, while musicians played various melodies and thousands looked on.

Although King Prataparudra was the exalted owner of the royal throne, he wanted to do some menial service for Lord Jagannath. Therefore, he personally swept the road with a gold-handled broom and sprinkled the road with sandalwood-scented water. Seeing the king sweeping the street and sprinkling it with water, Lord Chaitanya became very happy.

As the huge carts moved along the road toward the Gundicha temple, the devotees danced and chanted Hare Krishna with great enthusiasm. Lord Chaitanya Mahaprabhu divided the devotees into seven parties, with two drums in each group. King Prataparudra was astonished by the tumultuous and enchanting sound of the *sankirtan* party.

All the devotees chanted the holy names in great ecstasy, with tears falling from their eyes, and Lord Chaitanya wandered through all seven groups chanting, "Hari! Hari!" Raising His arms, He shouted, "All glories to Lord Jagannath!"

The King Sees the Lord

King Prataparudra could hardly believe his eyes. Suddenly, he saw Lord Chaitanya simultaneously appear in seven different *sankirtan* parties! Appreciating the Lord's mystic opulence, the king became stunned with ecstatic love. Although Mahaprabhu had previously rebuffed the king, He now showered His favor upon him by revealing His transcendental power.

Although the other devotees could not see the Lord appearing in seven places, they were also overwhelmed with spiritual ecstasy just to see His dancing. Everyone was dancing and chanting, and as the sound echoed everywhere, Lord Chaitanya gracefully danced through the crowd.

When the servants of Lord Jagannath had pulled the carts of the Lord as far as the Gundicha garden, they stopped, and all the devotees offered the Deities some simple food they had prepared. The king with his queens, the ministers, and all other residents of Jagannath Puri offered preparations to the Lord, and a large crowd gathered to watch.

At that time Lord Chaitanya stopped His dancing and went into the garden to rest. The Lord was covered with perspiration, and He enjoyed the cool, fragrant breezes in the garden. All the devotees who were chanting and dancing with Him also went there and rested under many different trees.

Service to the Lord

While Lord Chaitanya Mahaprabhu was resting peacefully, King Prataparudra entered the garden. Following Sarvabhauma Bhattacharya's instructions, the king had replaced his royal garments with the simple clothes of a devotee. He was so humble that he first offered respects with folded hands to all the devotees in the garden. Then, taking courage, he fell down and touched the lotus feet of the Lord. Finally, the king started to recite verses about Krishna's dancing with the *gopis*. When Lord Chaitanya heard these verses, He was pleased beyond limit and said again and again, "Go on reciting! Go on reciting!"

Then King Prataparudra recited a very special verse:

My Lord, the nectar of Your words and the descriptions of Your activities are the life and soul of those who are always aggrieved in this material world. These narrations are transmitted by exalted personalities who can eradicate all sinful reactions. Whoever hears these narrations attains all good fortune. These narrations are broadcast all over the world and they are filled with spiritual power. Those who spread the message of Godhead are certainly the most munificent welfare workers. (S.B. 10.31.9)

As soon as the king recited this verse, Lord Chaitanya embraced him and cried, "*You* are the most munificent!

"You have given me invaluable gems," the Lord further exclaimed, "but I have nothing to give you in return!" Saying this, the Lord began to recite the same verse again and again. Both the king and Lord Chaitanya were trembling, and tears were flowing from their eyes. Finally the Lord asked, "Who are you? You have done so much for Me. All of a sudden you have come here and made Me drink the nectar of Lord Krishna's pastimes."

The king replied, "My Lord, I am most obedient to You. It is my ambition that You accept me as the servant of Your servants." Then Lord Chaitanya displayed some of His divine opulences to the king, revealing His identity as God, but forbade him to disclose these secrets to anyone. Although Mahaprabhu knew who the king was, He pretended not to know.

Seeing that the king had received the Lord's special mercy, the devotees became blissful and praised his good fortune. After submissively offering prayers to the devotees and obeisances to Lord Chaitanya Mahaprabhu, the king left the garden.

In this way, King Prataparudra received the mercy of Lord Chaitanya. Ordinarily, the king would not have had a chance to meet the Lord, but when the Lord saw that he was serving Lord Jagannath as a menial sweeper, He bestowed His full mercy upon him. In the years that followed, King Prataparudra had many more opportunities to render service to Lord Jagannath, and he maintained his humble attitude in spite of his wealth and power. Even to this day, King Prataparudra's descendants remember his example. At the Ratha-yatra festival each year, the present king of Orissa takes a gold-handled broom and sweeps the road in front of Lord Jagannath's cart.

Late in the year 1513, after almost two years of memorable pastimes with His increasing number of followers, the Lord was ready to travel once again, primarily to see Vrindavan, the place of Krishna's pastimes. However, this was not to be.

Dabir Khas and Sakara Mallik

While stopping at Ramakeli en route to Vrindavan, Mahaprabhu met Dabir Khas and Sakara Mallik, two high officials in the court of Hussain Shah. These two brothers were scholars of a very high caliber, and in their official position, they commanded great respect and high social prestige.

Their meeting with Mahaprabhu, however, was to become a great turning point in their careers. Lord Chaitanya's intensely spiritual personality made such a deep impression on them that they completely abandoned their worldly pursuits and became two of the Lord's staunchest followers. The elder brother Sakara Mallik was given the name "Sanatan," and Dabir Khas was called "Rupa." Together, they would soon be the leaders of the Vaishnava community in Vrindavan and compose theological literature, under the Lord's direction, that clearly systematized and expounded upon Mahaprabhu's teachings.

After meeting the two brothers, Mahaprabhu decided to return to Puri. Biographers suggest that the political tension between Muslims and Hindus was severe at this juncture, and both Rupa and Sanatan, who were previously employed by Hussain Shah, knew of many possible dangers the Lord might face at his hands. They thus pleaded with Mahaprabhu to continue His journey at another time. In addition, the two brothers felt that it was not proper for a *sannyasi* to go on pilgrimage with a large group of followers. Since the Lord did indeed amass a large following in His travels, this advice appealed to Him, and, complying with His two new disciples' wishes, He returned to Puri. Mahaprabhu only remained there for a few months, however, before again setting out for Vrindavan.

THE LIFE AND TIMES OF LORD CHAITANYA

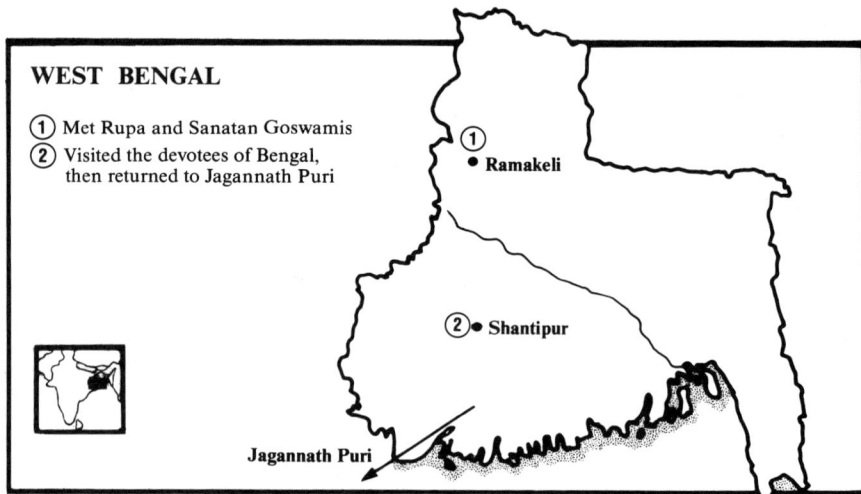

After staying in Jagannath Puri for one year, the Lord attempted to visit Vrindavan when He was twenty-eight years old. But He was detained by Rupa and Sanatan Goswamis in Bengal. Thus, He returned to Jagannath Puri for a short time before once again proceeding to Vrindavan.

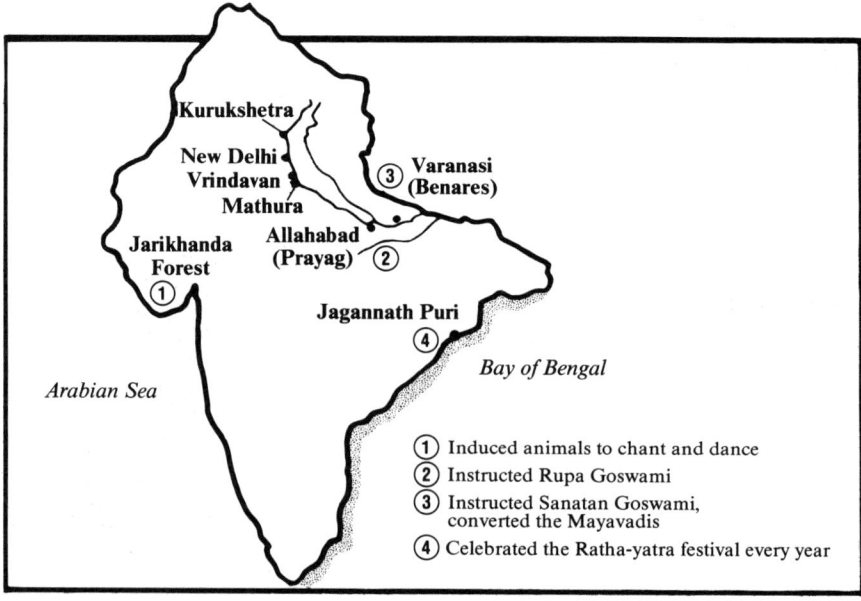

From His twenty-ninth through thirtieth year, He visited Vrindavan and then returned to Jagannath Puri, where He remained for the rest of His life.

CHAPTER TWELVE

Vrindavan

Vrindavan, according to the *Vedas*, is the highest paradise. It is a manifestation of the Kingdom of God on earth. And it is Krishna's most holy abode, from which He never steps foot. Since Mahaprabhu is nondifferent from Krishna, He is also inextricably related to Vrindavan. Consequently, one cannot properly think of the divine abode without acknowledging that it is Mahaprabhu's original transcendental dwelling place, a spiritual counterpart of Navadvip.

Thus, the Lord's journey to Vrindavan was more a homecoming than a first visit. But even this perspective can only be considered partially accurate. If it is true that the Lord *never* leaves Vrindavan, then Mahaprabhu's journey to that holiest of places is merely an external occurrence. Since it is definitely accepted that the Lord eternally remains in that transcendental region, the authentic biographers say that His journey there was primarily to show ordinary living beings the importance of such a pilgrimage. Thus, to relish the nectar that a pure devotee feels upon entering Vrindavan, and to set an example for the world, the Lord passed through Benares and Prayag, finally reaching His own transcendental dwelling place, some ninety miles southeast of present-day Delhi.

The Animals Chant and Dance

Traveling to Vrindavan with His attendant, now a *brahmana* named Balabhadra, Chaitanya Mahaprabhu walked through the dense jungle of Jharikhanda toward the Ganges at Benares. If he were not an eyewitness, Balabhadra would scarcely have believed what happened as he accompanied the Lord through the forest. Chanting the holy name in complete ecstasy, Mahaprabhu induced the lions, tigers, and elephants to sing along in their respective tongues. Indeed, it is said that His sweet, melodious voice touched the soul of every creature in His path, and it inspired them to quickly reach the level of perfect God consciousness.

After some time, He reached Benares (also called Varanasi or Kashi) and bathed at the Ganges tributary called Manikarnika Ghat. There, He met Tapan Mishra, who had received instruction from the Lord when they were in East Bengal. Mishra was now living in Benares according to Mahaprabhu's earlier advice, and he was acting as the Lord's host during His visit.

Eager to reach Vrindavan, however, Mahaprabhu only stayed in Benares for ten days. En route, He stopped at Prayag (now Allahabad) and took His bath in the Triveni Sangam, which is where the Ganges meets the Sarasvati and the River Yamuna. Swooning and singing in uncontrollable bliss, the Lord happily splashed about with Balabhadra in Lord Krishna's favorite river.

Mathura

Mahaprabhu soon reached the city of Mathura, where, almost 5,000 years ago, Lord Krishna was born. Here, Lord Chaitanya prostrated Himself in the holy dust with total reverence for the Lord of His life. He then bathed at the famous Vishram Ghat, which is now bordered by Dori Bazaar Road. According to the Vaishnava tradition, Lord Krishna rested at this *ghat* after killing the demon Kamsa. The *Skanda Purana* says that by once bathing there, one can wash away more sins than one is able to commit.

From Vishram Ghat, Mahaprabhu went to Janma Bhumi, Lord Krishna's birthplace, and there He offered prayers to the Deity of Keshavadev. This Deity is still worshiped in the same place, but it is now overshadowed by a mosque that was built in the vicinity by the dictator Aurangzeb.

While at the Keshavadev temple, the Lord met a humble *brahmana* who showed Him all of the places of pilgrimage that relate to Shri Krishna's pastimes. They went to the sacred temples of Swayambhu, Dirgha Vishnu, Bhuteshwar, Mahavidyadevi and Gokarna. They also traveled throughout the forests of Vrindavan, which are associated with Krishna's most confidential pastimes.

Recognizing Mahaprabhu

Naturally, Mahaprabhu was in a state of transcendental fixation during the entire pilgrimage. Blissfully passing through the Vrindavan forests, the deer and cows would snuggle up and lick the Lord's body, putting Him into even deeper ecstasy. The animals of Vrindavan recognized their darkish Lord Krishna, although He now had a golden hue, and they followed Him for a brief part of His pilgrimage. Even the trees and plants felt spiritual bliss upon having the good fortune to acquire the Lord's embrace.

Holiest Places in the Universe

Mahaprabhu then came to Aritagram (now called Aring) and rediscovered the nearby Radha kunda and Shyama kunda; it is sometimes said that these are the holiest places in the entire universe. The two lakes were at that time called Gauri and Kali, their sanctity forgotten over the course of time. When Mahaprabhu arrived, however, He felt loving emotions and, recognizing the lakes as places that Radha and Krishna had frequented, began to apply the mud of these ponds as *"tilok"* (the Vaishnava daily marks his body as a temple of God by applying sacred clay) on the traditional twelve places of the body.

Govardhan Hill

From here the Lord went to Sumanah Lake (now called Kusham Sarovara) and bathed within her holy waters. Next, Lord Chaitanya visited Govardhan Hill, sometimes called *Giriraj*, or "the king of hills." Although a revered place of pilgrimage because of its connection with Krishna's pastimes, the hill was cursed centuries ago by a sage: it was to shrink the size of one sesame seed each day. In fact, historical records do show that Giriraj was much higher several hundred years ago, even when Mahaprabhu was there. Although in length Mt. Govardhan is still almost seven miles, in height it is in some places hardly the size of one's fist.

Gopalaji

From Govardhan, the Lord went to Brahma kunda, and from there He journeyed to the Manasa Ganga and took His bath. Then He went to Gantholli Gram to see the beautiful Deity of Gopalaji. This Deity, which was previously worshiped by Mahaprabhu's grand spiritual master (Madhavendra Puri), was originally installed atop Govardhan Hill. If the Deity had still been there, Lord Chaitanya would never have gone to visit Him, for the Lord felt that the hill was too holy to be walked upon.

By Lord Krishna's divine arrangement, however, a battalion of Turkish soldiers invaded the area and, to protect the Deity, local devotees brought Gopalaji to Gantholli Gram. Thus, Mahaprabhu was able to see the Deity. Now worshiped as the famous Lord of Nathwara, this Deity is presently known as Nathji.

Childhood Pastimes

Soon Mahaprabhu went to Nandagram, where Lord Krishna had 4,500 years earlier enacted His childhood pastimes under the care of Nanda Maharaj and Mother Yashoda. Here the Lord bathed in all the holy rivers, beginning with Pavana Sarovara, where Krishna used to tend His cows and give them water to drink. In Nandagram, too, Mahaprabhu heard from local farmers that within a nearby cave there were three beautiful Deities that had been hidden from the Moghul invaders. Entering this cave, the Lord found these Deities: Nanda Maharaj, Mother Yashoda, and Baby Krishna.

After this, Lord Chaitanya went to Khadiravana and then to Sheshashai. It was at Khadiravana that Lord Krishna bifurcated the Bakashura demon after the monster tried to kill the Lord by swallowing Him. Sheshashai is where Krishna manifested Himself in His majestic feature as Vishnu, and Radharani manifested as Vishnu's consort, Lakshmidevi. At the temple of Sheshashai, Mahaprabhu prayed before the Deity of Lakshmidevi by offering devotional outpourings from *Shrimad Bhagavatam*.

Next, the Lord went to Khelanavana, where Krishna and Balarama used to play and sport together. Visiting Gokula, where Krishna enacted His early childhood pastimes, Lord Chaitanya swooned in ecstasy when He beheld the twin Yamalarjuna trees that were broken by Baby Krishna. In this way, Mahaprabhu saw all of the holy places in Vrindavan and appreciated them with great relish.[87]

Once, while crossing the Yamuna River in a boat, Chaitanya Mahaprabhu gazed upon the glossy black water and was immediately bewildered with ecstatic love. Indeed, as soon as Lord Chaitanya saw the holy river, He made a wailing sound and jumped straight into the water. This put the devotees into a fearful state, and they all hastily went to grab the Lord, pulling Him out of the river. On another occasion, a similar incident occurred when the Lord got up in the boat and proceeded to dance in ecstatic abandon. As the boat started to tilt, it began to fill with water. But the devotees eventually managed to calm the Lord and save the situation from getting out of hand. In this way, the Lord would sometimes frighten the devotees with His symptoms of transcendental ecstasy. This would also increase their love for Him.

The Highest Paradise

According to Shrila Krishnadas Kaviraj Goswami, "Lord Chaitanya's mind was absorbed in ecstatic love at Jagannath Puri, but when He passed along the road on the way to Vrindavan, that love increased a hundred times.

"The Lord's ecstatic love increased a thousand times," the Goswami continues, "when He visited Mathura, Lord Krishna's birthplace. And it increased a hundred thousand times further when He actually wandered in the forests of Vrindavan."[88]

Only in Vrindavan can one attain exclusive loving service to the Lord. Elsewhere, service is always mixed. Consequently, Vrindavan, also called Vraja (although it is actually only a part of Vraja-mandala), brings the supreme level of spiritual pleasure, and this was demonstrated by Lord Chaitanya.

This topmost category of exclusive service and resultant spiritual pleasure is hinted at in the final instruction of *Bhagavad-gita* (18.66):

> *sarva dharman parityajya*
> *mam ekam sharanam vraja*

aham tvam sarva papebhyo
mokshayishyami ma suchaha

"Abandon all varieties of religion and simply surrender unto Me," says Lord Krishna, "I shall protect you from sinful reactions. Do not fear, worry or hesitate."

According to the *Gita*, the ultimate perfection of the religious pursuit ironically culminates in abandoning the formalities of religion. In other words, after many frustrating lifetimes of trying to pursue material happiness, one gradually learns to fully embrace the religious path in earnest. When one reaches an even higher level of spiritual evolution, however, one follows the rules and regulations of religiosity only to set an example for those who are less advanced. Meanwhile, in one's heart, one surrenders wholly unto the Lord with spontaneous love and devotion. This level transcends ordinary religious observance. Nonetheless, this is a very advanced stage, the scriptures warn, and it should not be imitated by those who are spiritually immature. Rather, one should study under a bona fide spiritual master who will direct a sincere disciple to gradually attain the spontaneous platform of love of God.

This spontaneous love is found in Vrindavan, or Vraja-mandala, for it is ultimately here that one finds Krishna. The word *vraja*, as mentioned in the above verse from the *Gita*, refers to the directive "go," indicating that one should go only to Krishna and place one's surrender at His lotus feet. According to Vaishnava commentators, such as Vishvanath Chakravarti Thakur, *vraja* can also refer to Vrindavan, and in this way the word again points to exclusive devotion to Krishna. More importantly, it points to exactly *where* the mood of this single-minded devotion is found: in Vraja, the land of Vrindavan.

CHAPTER THIRTEEN

Rupa Goswami

Although Vrindavan held an incomparable spiritual attraction for the Lord, He did not remain there for long. Late in January, in the year 1516, Mahaprabhu and His servant Balabhadra (along with Balabhadra's assistant; a Rajput chief named Krishnadas; and the humble *brahmana* who took the Lord on His tour of Vrindavan) left Akrura *ghat* to start their return journey to Puri via Prayag (Allahabad). There, the Lord would meet Rupa Goswami (1489–1564),[89] whom He had previously initiated at Ramakeli, and to whom He would now deliver invaluable instruction.

On the way to Prayag, the Lord passed a herd of cows who were grazing to the music of their cowherd flutist. This, of course, reminded Mahaprabhu of Krishna and sent Him into uncontrollable ecstasy. The Lord then fell unconscious due to His divine absorption.

Muslim Soldiers

At that moment, ten Muslim horsemen, known as *pathans*, a distinct military class, arrived on the scene. Seeing Mahaprabhu unconscious, they mistakenly thought that His four attendants were responsible for His condition and that they had robbed Him of His valuables. After binding the party in chains, the *pathans* threatened to kill them. Balabhadra and his assistant were paralyzed with fear. The brave Rajput Krishnadas, however, was undaunted, as was the humble *brahmana*, who calmly described himself as a local priest. He further explained that the man who lay unconscious on the ground was his *guru*, who occasionally was given to epileptic seizures.

With this, Lord Chaitanya regained consciousness and began crying aloud: "Hari! Hari!" The *pathans* were startled, but they nonetheless proceeded to tell the Lord that the four men were about to rob Him and kill Him with *dhatura*, a poisonous flower. Mahaprabhu laughingly denied even the remote possibility of such a scenario; these were His faithful companions, He told the *pathans*, and besides, He was a *sannyasi* with no money for anyone to steal.

One of the *pathans* was dressed as an ascetic, perhaps of the Sufi order, for he initiated a religious discussion with Mahaprabhu that centered around the pantheistic doctrine of the Sufis. Although the *pathan* was a great scholar and a master of logic, Lord Chaitanya refuted his arguments using references from the *pathan's* own scripture, the Koran. Establishing the monotheistic truth of all religion—that there is one supreme and personal God—Mahaprabhu defeated the impersonalism of the Sufi *pathan*.

Lord Chaitanya's spiritual insight and knowledge of the Koran impressed the *pathan*, and as a result the sincere soldier asked to become one of the Lord's followers. Mahaprabhu accepted him with open arms and gave him the name Ramadas.

The leader of the *pathans*, whose name was Vijuli Khan, had listened to the entire conversation between Lord Chaitanya and the Sufi scholar, and now he too wanted to become the Lord's disciple. Likewise, all ten soldiers decided to devote their lives to Chaitanya Mahaprabhu, and later these humble converts became famous as the "*pathan* Vaishnavas."

When Mahaprabhu finally arrived in Prayag, He approached the famous Bindhu Madhava temple, and the crowds roared with glorification and feelings of love. Shrila Krishnadas Kaviraj Goswami says that although the united streams of the Yamuna and the Ganges could not submerge Prayag, Chaitanya Mahaprabhu overflooded the area with love of God.[90]

The Prayers of Rupa Goswami

Later, while the Lord was staying at the house of a *brahmana* that He had

Rupa Goswami

met in South India, Rupa Goswami and his younger brother Vallabha (who was given the name "Anupama" by Lord Chaitanya) came to meet Him.

With all humility at their command, the two brothers stood before Mahaprabhu and offered prayers: "O most munificent incarnation of the Lord! You are Krishna Himself appearing as Chaitanya Mahaprabhu. You have assumed the golden color of Radharani, however, and You are widely distributing pure love of Krishna. We offer our respectful obeisances unto You.

"We offer You our obeisances," Shrila Rupa and Anupama continued, "because You are that merciful Supreme Personality of Godhead who has converted the entire cosmic creation, which was full of living entities who were maddened by ignorance. Further, You have saved them from their diseased condition by making them mad with the nectar from the treasure house of love of God. We pray, then, to take full shelter of that Personality of Godhead, Shri Krishna Chaitanya, whose activities are wonderful."

Lord Chaitanya was pleased by their prayers. Then, for ten consecutive days, at a place called Dashashvamedha Ghat, the Lord instructed Rupa Goswami in the entire science of Krishna consciousness.

Mahaprabhu began: "The ocean of the transcendental juice (*rasa*) of devotional service is so pervasive that it is impossible to describe it completely. No one can estimate its length and breadth. Just to help you taste it, I will describe one drop." He then proceeded to fully describe the nature of the spirit soul, supporting His statements with references from the Vedic scriptures.

Journey of the Soul

With exacting detail, the Lord explained that the dimensions of the soul are inconceivably small: one ten-thousandth the size of the tip of a hair. These infinitesimal living entities, the Lord continued, are unlimited in number and, according to what they deserve,[91] they incarnate in one of the 8,400,000 species. If they are pious, they receive a good human body, both in terms of outward prosperity and the ability to pursue spiritual life (or sometimes only one of these qualities).

Impious beings, however, devolve into the lower species and gradually work their way up to the human form once again.

All souls are in this way wandering throughout the various species of life—birth after birth—in a never-ending quest for peace, happiness, and fulfillment. Sometimes they enjoy heavenly pleasures, and sometimes they suffer hellish miseries. The goal, however, is to receive a human form, and in that form to somehow or other receive the grace of a pure devotee of the Lord.

Devotional Service

The human form serves as a gateway into spirituality, or transcendence, for only a human being can inquire into the Absolute Truth, receive answers, and conduct his life accordingly by engaging in devotional service to the Lord. Those who reach perfection in this process attain the kingdom of God.

Lord Chaitanya warned Rupa Goswami that living beings who are given the opportunity to engage in devotional service must be careful not to offend others on this path, for sincere devotees are particularly dear to the Lord. One's "creeper" of devotion, according to Mahaprabhu, can be totally trampled by this "mad elephant" offense. The devotee "gardener" must be extremely careful to avoid this pitfall in devotional service and to treat other devotees with respect and even reverence.

Mahaprabhu pointed out another danger: The weeds of material desires may grow alongside the devotional creeper. The variegated subtleties of these desires are unlimited and difficult to overcome, and the gardener must be careful not to nourish them while watering his devotional creeper.

Avoiding these and other offenses outlined by Lord Chaitanya, the determined, patient gardener ultimately reaps the fruits of love of God. These fruits are so relishable, says Lord Chaitanya, that the four kinds of material aspirations—economic development, sense gratification, religiosity and liberation—seem pale and even worthless by comparison.

Devotional Sweetness

The Lord next compared the various stages of love of God to sugar. First is the seed of the sugarcane, then the sugarcane itself, and then the juice extracted from the cane. When the juice is boiled, it forms a liquid molasses, then a solid molasses, then sugar, candy, rock candy, and finally a refined rock candy.

Analogically, all these stages combined are called *sthayibhava*, or continuous love of Godhead in devotional service. Gradually, by performing any or all of the nine processes of devotional service (which include hearing, chanting, remembering, serving, worshipping the Deity, praying, carrying out orders, serving Krishna as a friend, and sacrificing everything for Him) one invariably evolves to more concentrated levels of love for God, which correspond to the various configurations of sugar. Mahaprabhu concludes, however, that the sweetness found in the development of one's love for God has no exact counterpart in this world.

On the platform of pure love, there are still further stages, and Lord Chaitanya described these in detail to Rupa Goswami. Basically, these stages reflect one's eternal relationship with Krishna and are five in number: *shanta-rasa*, neutral appreciation of the Lord; *dasya-rasa*, servitude; *sakhya-rasa*, friendship; *vatsalya-rasa*, parental affection; and *madhurya-rasa*, conjugal love. The Lord described these in detail and also explained how one can gradually uncover one's eternal relationship with Krishna.

Mahaprabhu thus concluded His instructions to Rupa Goswami, saying: "I have simply given a general survey of the truths of devotional service. You can consider how to adjust and expand upon this. When one thinks of Krishna constantly, love for Him naturally manifests within the heart. Even though one may be ignorant, one can reach the shore of the ocean of transcendental love by Lord Krishna's mercy."

"Rupanuga"

Shrila Rupa Goswami did indeed understand Mahaprabhu's instructions and was later to become one of His most important followers. Even today, devotees in the line of Chaitanya Mahaprabhu are sometimes called *Rupanugas*, or followers of Shrila Rupa Goswami.

Shrila Rupa Goswami was instructed by Mahaprabhu to go to Vrindavan and uncover the places of Lord Krishna's pastimes, which, due to neglect and the passage of centuries, had been obscured. Also, he was instructed to systematize and codify Gaudiya Vaishnava philosophy as he had heard it from the Lord Himself.

Many of the books attributed to Srila Rupa Goswami are extant. The most important are the *Bhakti-rasamrita-sindhu* (an extensive lawbook with elaborate rules and regulations for developing pure love of God); the *Vidagdha-madhava* (a drama about Lord Krishna's pastimes in Vrindavan); the *Ujjvala-nilamani* (a spiritual account of loving affairs using metaphor, analogy, and culminating in higher *bhakti* sentiments); and the *Lalita-madhava* (a drama about Lord Krishna's pastimes in Dvaraka).

Some of Shrila Rupa Goswami's other important books include the *Upadeshamrita, Hamsadutta, Laghu-bhagavatamrita, Dana-keli-kaumudi, Stavavali, Lilacchanda, Padyavali, Govinda-virudavali, Mathura-mahatmya,* and the *Nataka-varnana*. Rupa Goswami's pen never tired; Shrila Krishnadas Kaviraj notes that Mahaprabhu actually invested the Goswami with full spiritual power.[92] Thus, the entire world is indebted to Rupa Goswami for his outpouring of genuine spiritual knowledge in the form of literature, and he can be repaid, say his followers, only by becoming a Rupanuga.

CHAPTER FOURTEEN

Sanatan Goswami

After revealing the confidential secrets of love of God to Shrila Rupa Goswami and then sending him to Vrindavan, Mahaprabhu proceeded toward Puri via Benares. Here, the Lord would meet with Shrila Sanatan Goswami (1488-1558) and instruct him in the *bhakti* religion much as He had instructed Rupa, Sanatan's younger brother.

Upon entering the holy city of Benares, the Lord was overcome with appreciation, for this was one of India's most important centers of learning and devotion. Benares was in fact an extremely significant place for the Lord to introduce His *sankirtan* movement. Although much of Southern and Eastern India had long embraced His teachings, and some of the provinces in Northern and Central India had felt His influence, Benares had remained untouched and was still largely a center of the Shankarite impersonal teaching. By the time Mahaprabhu left Benares, however, it had been turned into a second Navadvip.[93]

Benares

Before the dawn of Western civilization, Benares occupied its high bank overlooking the sacred Ganges. Also known as Varanasi (and sometimes Kashi), the ancient city was already a popular place of pilgrimage some

2,500 years ago, attracting such luminaries as Buddha, Mahavira, and Shankara. In fact, according to Rev. M. A. Sherring, a nineteenth-century missionary in Benares, "Twenty-five centuries ago, at least, it was famous. When Babylon was struggling with Nineveh for supremacy, when Tyre was planting her colonies, when Athens was growing in strength, before Rome had become known, or Greece had contended with Persia, or Cyrus had added lustre to the Persian monarchy, or Nebuchadnezzar had captured Jerusalem, and the inhabitants of Judaea had been carried into captivity, she had already risen to greatness, if not glory."[94] Mark Twain added his realization: "Benares is older than history."[95]

The antiquity of Benares is more than equaled by her sanctity. This was eloquently conveyed by Count Hermann Keyserling, who visited Benares just after World War I: "Benares is holy. Europe, grown superficial, hardly understands such truths anymore. . . . I feel nearer here than I have ever done to the heart of the world; here I feel every day as if soon, perhaps even today, I would receive the grace of supreme revelation. . . . The atmosphere of devotion which hangs above the river is improbable in its strength: stronger than in any church that I have ever visited. Every would-be Christian priest would do well to sacrifice a year of his theological studies in order to spend this time on the Ganges. Here he would discover what piety means."[96]

Shiva or Vishnu?

Although Benares is popularly known as a center of Shiva[97] worship, it is the Personality of Godhead, Vishnu (or Krishna), who is actually at the heart of Benares. Thousands of years ago, in fact, the ancient Vedic scripture known as the *Narada Purana* refers to "the Vaishnava city of Kashi." To make it even more clear that "Kashi" is indeed Benares, the *Purana* gives details of Kashi's location and the exact way in which Vishnu was worshiped there.

Why, then, is Benares associated with the worship of the demigod Shiva? Diana Eck, associate professor of Hindu religion at Harvard, cites a tradition explaining that Lord Vishnu gave Benares to Shiva as his "dwelling place."[98] Shiva, who is celebrated in the Vedic texts as the greatest devotee of Vishnu, was thus given a gift by his Lord and has consequently been revered in Benares for many centuries. Especially noteworthy, however, is the fact that two of the most important temples in Benares are still Vishnu temples—Adi Keshava and Bindhu Madhava—and both are exceedingly ancient.

Mahaprabhu In Benares

According to the Gaudiya Vaishnava tradition, the most significant event ever to grace the holy city of Benares took place in the winter of 1516, when Lord Chaitanya Mahaprabhu, the incarnation of the Supreme Personality of Godhead, went there to expand His *sankirtan* movement. At that time, the Lord stayed in the house of His devotees Tapan Mishra and Chandrashekhar Vaidya, which was located in a part of Benares now known as Chaitan-ghar. Benares was soon to take part in Mahaprabhu's spiritual renaissance.

Shrila Sanatan Goswami was to take part in this renaissance as well, for he arrived in Benares soon after Mahaprabhu so that he might receive the Lord's holy association. Having experienced great hardships in his travels, Sanatan appeared like a poor, disheveled mendicant, unshaven and unrecognizable, even by the devotees of the Lord. Mahaprabhu, however, recognized him immediately and sent him to the Ganges for a bath, to don clean clothes, and to shave.[99]

Instructions to Sanatan Goswami

Lord Chaitanya then instructed Shrila Sanatan Goswami for two months, explaining the intimate details of the science of devotional service. A summary of the Lord's teaching to His eager student is given by Shrila Bhaktivinode Thakur: "First they discussed the constitutional position of the living entities, and Lord Chaitanya Mahaprabhu explained to Sanatan Goswami how the living entity is one of Lord Krishna's energies. After this, the Lord explained the way of devotional service. While discussing the Absolute Truth, Shri Krishna, the Lord analyzed *Brahman*, *Paramatma*, and *Bhagavan* [the three progressive manifestations of the Absolute: His impersonal feature, His all-pervading feature and His personal feature respectively]."[100]

Brahman

These three distinct levels of realization were thoroughly addressed by Mahaprabhu. The *brahman* level is fundamental, He taught. When a living being who is conditioned by material nature begins the cultivation of spiritual knowledge, he can elevate himself, by study and speculation, to a facsimile of *brahman* realization, perhaps achieving a vague concept of God as an all-pervading force. If he is determined, he can bring himself to genuine *brahman* realization by the process of *gyan-yoga* and can attain an awareness of eternity.

But the *brahman* level is not without its pitfalls. What goes up must come down. This is particularly true for the *gyan-yogi*, as the vast impersonalism of eternity prompts him to hanker after natural, interpersonal relationships. His realization is hallowed, but somehow hollow as well. His avowed search for impersonalistic truth soon gives rise to an earnest desire for personalism.

The neophyte seeker's quest for truth only brings him to the Lord's impersonal effulgence, known as the *brahmajyoti*, and it is into this that the *gyanis* merge after death. Empiricists with a spiritual bent are inclined to this realization. Precious few ever reach the level of genuine *brahman* realization, however, and instead they are generally left with a vague conception of the Absolute Truth. According to Mahaprabhu, the authentic concept of *brahman* is the first step in God realization. When one achieves perfection on this path, one can develop a tangible understanding of immortality and begin to approach a state of supramundane happiness. Today, however, it is rare to find someone who can genuinely reach this stage, much less go beyond it.

Paramatma

If a *gyani* is fortunate, Lord Chaitanya taught, he may raise himself to the level of a *yogi* and realize the localized form of the Lord in the heart and within every atom. This manifestation of the Lord is called Paramatma, and upon realizing Him, one achieves awareness of more than immortality: one realizes the essence of spiritual cognition as well.

As one sun may appear reflected in countless jewels, Mahaprabhu told Sanatan Goswami, so the Lord within every atom may appear like many, though He is one. In other words, the sun exists in one specific location in the same way that Krishna appears (in His original form) in His transcendental kingdom. And just as the sun may be reflected in innumerable jewels, so the same one Lord pervades all of existence as Paramatma, or "Supersoul," His reflected expansion.

One inherent danger in pursuing the path of Paramatma realization is that one could mistake one's self for the Superself (Paramatma). This would constitute dismal failure and is not uncommon on this path. One should thus always be aware of the distinction between Supersoul (God) and the ordinary living entity.

In the Vedic literature, the Supersoul and the individual soul are compared to two birds sitting in the same tree. The ordinary living being is enjoying the fruits of the tree, while the Supersoul stands by and watches, waiting for His companion to give up his foolish pursuit of temporary pleasures. This, of course, may take many lifetimes. But the Supersoul patiently waits. And when the living being finally turns to Him in love and devotion, He agrees to direct and purify him, giving him the association of a pure devotee of the Lord, one who is accomplished in *bhagavan* realization. If a *yogi* actually reaches perfection, he will become a *bhakta* and devote his entire life to Krishna, the Supreme Personality of Godhead.

Bhagavan

Bhagavan is the Sanskrit equivalent of "God." It literally means "He who is full in all opulences." The sages of the East have narrowed all opulences down to a basic six: strength, beauty, wealth, fame, knowledge, and renunciation. No one but the Supreme Personality of Godhead has all these qualities in full. One who becomes adept at worshipping Him becomes aware of eternity and knowledge, and develops a profound sense of transcendental bliss as well. According to Mahaprabhu, the *bhakta* (devotee) of *Bhagavan* (God) is on the highest path and receives the greatest result. Lord Chaitanya taught Sanatan Goswami that *Bhagavan* realization is the perfection of *gyan*, *yoga*, and indeed all spiritual pursuits.

An Analogy

In order to make these three levels of realization more clear, later Vaishnava commentators have supplied the apt analogy of three backward villagers and their guide at a railway station.

Having never seen a train, the three villagers were grateful that their guide was finally bringing them to see one. Observing the headlight on the front of the train (pulling in at a distance), one villager asked just what the light in the distance represented. The guide curtly responded: "That is the train." Confident that he had thus seen the train, the first villager left feeling satisfied with what he saw.

When the train approached the platform, one of the remaining two villagers exclaimed, "Oh! *This* is the train!" He was also confident that he had seen all there is to see, and he left feeling content that he had indeed experienced the train.

But the third man patiently remained. And when the train came into the station, he had the opportunity to meet the conductor and see the various individual passengers on board.

The three villagers went back to their small village and began to tell everyone what they saw. But their descriptions of the same train were diverse; their realizations were different. Though it was an undeniable truth that they each saw the same train, they had each visualized different objects.

The third villager, however, obviously had a more complete experience than the other two. Furthermore, he was able to convince the others of this, for he perfectly described what they had seen, and more. He had seen the big light and the train from a distance, but he had met the conductor as well. And this is something the other two villagers had not experienced.

Analogically, the big light represents the effulgent, impersonal aspect of the Lord (*Brahman*); the big light with something more concrete behind it conveys the idea of divine substance, a vague concept of personality that pervades all of existence (*Paramatma*); and the third villager's vision represents the most complete aspect of God realization (*Bhagavan*), wherein one meets the Supreme Personality of Godhead Lord Shri Krishna, and develops a loving, devotional relationship with Him.

All of the above are different aspects of the same Absolute Truth, Mahaprabhu taught, and all are valid. But one views these different aspects of God according to one's level of spiritual advancement, and one's level of advancement can be determined by which aspect of the Supreme one focuses on. Mahaprabhu, of course, recommended that Sanatan Goswami focus on the highest truth: *Bhagavan* realization.

Expansion of God

After extensively explaining these three levels of attainment to Sanatan Goswami, Mahaprabhu further explained the various expansions of *Bhagavan* Shri Krishna, which are called *svayam-rupa*, *tad-ekatma*, and

Sanatan Goswami

EXPANSIONS OF KRISHNA

(A simplified rendering of the information given to Sanatan Goswami)

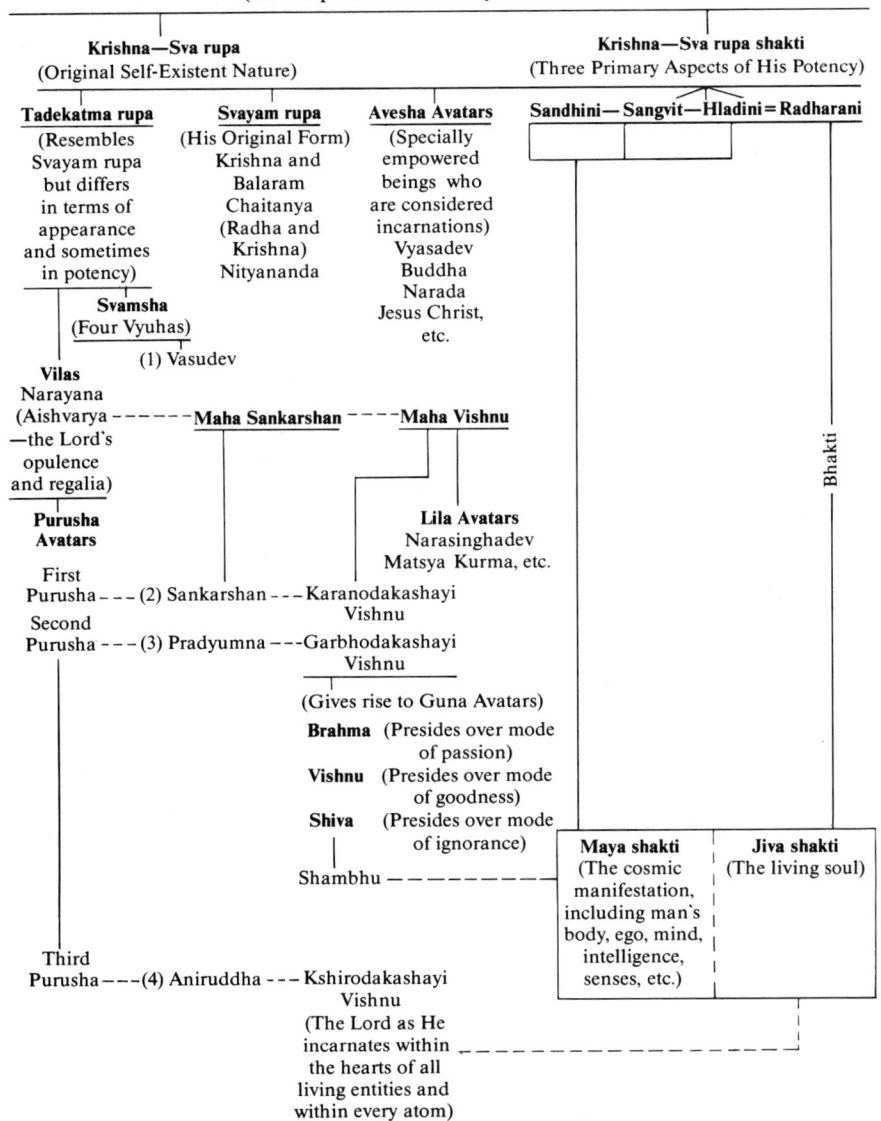

avesha. His personal form (*svayam-rupa*) manifests His original, self-existent nature; His hypostatic manifestation (*tad-ekatma*) is identical in essence to His original form but may differ in appearance and, sometimes, in potency; finally, His manifestation in which He inspires or empowers a living entity (*avesha*) is substantially different from His essential nature and yet inconceivably it is similar at the same time.

These three aspects of the Supreme are further divided into branches known as *vilas* and *svamsha*, which in turn have various features and can be divided into *vaibhava* and *prabhava* expansions. In other words, Mahaprabhu revealed to Shrila Sanatan Goswami extremely technical information about the Lord's original form and His various expansions and manifestations.

In essence, Chaitanya Mahaprabhu described the contents of the *Shrimad Bhagavatam*: *sambandha*, *abhidheya*, and *prayojana*. Sambandha refers to knowledge of our relationship with the Supreme Lord; *abhidheya* refers to the process of developing that relationship; and *prayojana* is the perfection of that relationship, realized in tangible and direct service to God through love and devotion. Thus, Mahaprabhu explained to Sanatan Goswami that the ultimate goal and purpose of the Vedic literature is to give its readers an understanding of their relationship with God; a practical methodology by which one can function according to that relationship; and, ultimately, the ability to go back home, back to Godhead.

After revealing these secrets of devotional service to Shrila Sanatan Goswami, the Lord requested that he join his brother, Rupa, in Vrindavan. While still in Benares, however, the Lord and His associates, including Sanatan Goswami, danced up and down the city streets, blissfully chanting the holy name of the Lord: Hare Krishna, Hare Krishna, Krishna Krishna, Hare Hare/ Hare Rama, Hare Rama, Rama Rama, Hare Hare. And in this way the *sankirtan* movement flourished, influencing everyone who came in contact with its potent singing and dancing.

Prakashananda Saraswati

There were, however, nondevotee philosophers in Benares at the same time, and many of them were opposed to the glorification of God's name. Some were followers of Shankara, known as *Mayavadis*, and while superficially they seemed very much like the Vaishnavas, they ultimately taught that God is formless and that the living entity, when freed from illusion, realizes his oneness with the Supreme. Mayavadis, or impersonalists, are fond of preaching this absolute oneness. But they neglect the essential difference between God and the living being. Vaishnavas, on the other hand, while acknowledging the oneness, stress the difference as well. Thus, although Mayavadi philosophy espouses a partial truth, it is Vaishnava philosophy that engenders the all-inclusive truth of the Vedic literature.

Although Vaishnavas (and especially Gaudiya Vaishnavas) consider chanting and dancing in glorification of God to be the highest form of spiritual expression, there are a class of Mayavadis that shun such chanting and dancing as obnoxious sentimentality.

When Chaitanya Mahaprabhu was teaching Shrila Sanatan in Benares, He heard about the leader of the Mayavadis, Prakashananda Saraswati, a *sannyasi* of the Shankarite school. At every opportunity, Prakashananda criticized Lord Chaitanya and the entire *sankirtan* movement. "Lord Chaitanya is also a *sannyasi*," Prakashananda would say, "and so should engage in serious Vedanta study. Instead," the Mayavadi leader continued with distaste, "He simply engages in chanting and dancing." In this way, Prakashananda denounced Lord Chaitanya as a mere sentimentalist.

Although this sort of criticism was typical when a Mayavadi *sannyasi* spoke about Vaishnava practices, the Lord's devotees became very unhappy when the news reached them that Lord Chaitanya Himself was being ridiculed in this way. Unable to tolerate the blasphemy, the devotees approached Lord Chaitanya and, after giving Him all of the details concerning Prakashananda's statements, they waited anxiously to see what the Lord would do.

Just then, a *brahmana* entered and invited Mahaprabhu to have lunch at his house on the very next day. The *brahmana* explained that he had invited all the Mayavadi *sannyasis*—headed by Prakashananda Saraswati—and the festivities would not be complete unless the Lord appeared as well. Smilingly, Lord Chaitanya accepted the invitation.

The next day, Lord Chaitanya went to the *brahmana's* house, where he saw all the Mayavadi *sannyasis* and even Prakashananda, who was seated on a raised platform. Lord Chaitanya entered the house, His biographers tell us, as the rising sun enters the world to drive away the darkness of ignorance. Out of great humility, Mahaprabhu sat in a dirty place meant for washing the feet of weary travelers. His form exhibited a shining effulgence that attracted the other *sannyasis* to come over and offer Him their own sitting places. This was to their advantage, for unless they had rendered some service to the Lord, even unconsciously, they could not understand the instructions He would soon give them. After humbly accepting His seat, Lord Chaitanya began to discuss philosophy with Prakashananda Saraswati.

The Conversion

The central theme of the discussion was Vedanta, the ultimate philosophical thesis presented by Shrila Vyasadev, the divinely inspired author of the Vedic literature. *Vedanta* literally means "the end of knowledge." And Lord Chaitanya explained that the real end of knowledge was Krishna and devotional service to Krishna. Mahaprabhu then went on to scientifically describe the chanting process, by which one can attain self realization in this age. He quoted the Vedic literature: "Chant the holy name! Chant the holy name! Chant the holy name! In this age there is no alternative for spiritual progress."[101] Using scripture and logic, Mahaprabhu forcefully and yet politely convinced the Mayavadis of Vaishnavism on an intellectual basis. There was little debate.

Upon hearing the wonderfully disarming explanations of Lord Chaitanya, the hearts of the Mayavadis began to change. So moved were all who listened that only Prakashananda himself had the power to speak: "My dear Lord, Your direct explanation of Vedanta is certainly enlivening and wonderful. You are the Supreme Personality of Godhead and thus are all-knowing and have inconceivable energies."

Sankirtan In Benares

At this point, Prakashananda and all of his followers—numbering in the tens of thousands—joined Lord Chaitanya in a fabulous *kirtan*, enthusiastically chanting and dancing throughout the streets of Benares. The name of Krishna resounded with unabashed glory as Lord Chaitanya led the procession all over the holy city, now made even more holy by the *sankirtan* movement.

"When Shri Chaitanya Mahaprabhu passed by the people," wrote Krishnadas Kaviraj, "He would raise His arms and say, 'Please chant Krishna! Please chant Hari!' All the people received Him by chanting Hare Krishna, and they offered Him their sincerest respects by this chanting."[102] Thus, all Benares' citizens became full-fledged devotees of the Lord.

Historical Controversy

The conversion of Prakashananda brought great fame to Mahaprabhu.[103] The majority of his earliest contemporary biographers, however, do not mention the account. Only Krishnadas Kaviraj Goswami describes it. The remarkable silence of Murari, Jayananda, Lochandas, and Kavi Karnapur has caused a controversy among several modern scholars of Gaudiya Vaishnavism. S. K. De and B. B. Majumdar are not quite convinced that the conversion actually occurred.[104] A. K. Majumdar, however, accepts it implicitly.[105]

More importantly, the Prakashananda episode is accepted by His Divine Grace A. C. Bhaktivedanta Swami Prabhupada, who represents a pure, unbroken chain of masters in the Gaudiya Vaishnava tradition and is thus considered the foremost authority on Lord Chaitanya in the modern age. It should be noted, furthermore, that the silence of biographers other than Shrila Krishnadas Kaviraj Goswami does not minimize the historicity of the event. The Goswami is considered Lord Chaitanya's most authoritative biographer and is accepted in the Gaudiya Vaishnava tradition as a pure soul, with access to information that others may not have had. In this connection, it is noteworthy that Krishnadas Kaviraj received his account from two important eyewitnesses: Shrila Sanatan Goswami and Raghunath Bhatta Goswami, who were both in Benares at the time.

Further, since Vrindavandas Thakur disclosed the Lord's early pastimes with such exacting detail, Krishnadas Kaviraj Goswami saw no need to do so. Similarly, since the Lord's later pastimes were not elaborately described by the Thakur, Krishnadas Kaviraj took it upon himself to detail those events. The Prakashananda conversion was part of those later pastimes.

CHAPTER FIFTEEN

return to Puri

Lord Chaitanya Mahaprabhu returned to Orissa in April 1516 and lived in Puri for the remaining eighteen years of His life. For the first six years He preached tirelessly to all the residents of Puri, who reciprocated by enthusiastically taking His *sankirtan* mission to heart. In 1522, when He was thirty-six years old, Mahaprabhu was convinced that His elder followers could carry on His movement, and thus the Lord went into a state of constant spiritual absorption (*samadhi*).

Still, during the years of His active preaching in Puri, the Lord enacted many instructive and relishable pastimes, and these could fill several large volumes. What follows is a summary of the pastimes that stand out as particularly significant, for space does not allow a detailed chronicle.

Ballabhacharya

Shortly after Mahaprabhu's return to Puri, the famous Ballabhacharya came to visit Him. Earlier, when the Lord was in Prayag, Ballabha had invited Him to his native village of Adeli-gram, which was nearby. At that time, they enjoyed lunch together, and they relished topics about Krishna for many hours. Now, while at Puri, Ballabha would have Mahaprabhu's association for an even greater length of time, and it would be to his eternal benefit.

Ballabha, it seems, was in the middle of writing a commentary on *Shrimad Bhagavatam*, and he wanted Mahaprabhu to read it. Unfortunately, Ballabha's scholarly explanation, which he had hoped would impress Lord Chaitanya, ran counter to the authoritative Vaishnava commentary of Shridhar Swami.[106] Consequently, Ballabha's version was completely dismissed by Mahaprabhu. It is significant, moreover, that Ballabha never completed his commentary, for it is believed that he became convinced of Lord Chaitanya's perspective.[107] It is further stated that Ballabha eventually received initiation from one of Mahaprabhu's most intimate followers, Gadadhar Pandit.[108]

Guru Nanak

A sixteenth-century Oriyan manuscript called the *Chaitanya Bhagavat* says that Mahaprabhu met with the founder of Sikhism, Guru Nanak.[109] The author, Ishvar Das, one of Mahaprabhu's followers in Puri, was the only biographer to mention the event, perhaps because the meeting was brief and only the eyewitness devotees of Puri would know about it.

According to Ishvar Das, "Shri Chaitanya, the Lord, joined in the *kirtan* with Nanak, who was accompanied by his disciple Sarang. Rupa and Sanatan were also there, as were Jagai and Madhai. They all engaged in *kirtan*, dancing in ecstasy." (Ishvara Das' *Chaitanya Bhagavat, Adhyaya* 61)

Ishvara Das continues: "In the congregational singing led by Shri Chaitanya and Guru Nanak, Nagar Purushottama followed suit. Two disciples, Jangli and Nandni, also joined in. Gopal Guru, for whom Guru Nanak felt deep affection, was there as well, along with Nityananda Prabhu, who was considered an incarnation of Balarama. They all relished the *kirtan* at Jagannath Puri." (Ishvara Das' Ch. B., *Adhyaya* 64) Thus there are scholars in the Gaudiya tradition who are confident that Mahaprabhu and Guru Nanak resolved all religious differences in the holy name of Krishna.

There are scholars in the Sikh tradition, too, who have documented the meeting of Lord Chaitanya and Guru Nanak. Ganda Singh, for instance, says that the meeting actually occurred in 1510, during one of Mahaprabhu's earlier trips to Puri.[110] And Trilochan Singh fixes the date at 1512.[111] Still others place the meeting at a much later date, perhaps in 1518.[112] Regardless of the disagreement over when the meeting took place, all these references acknowledge the historicity of the event.

Devotees come to Puri

Great devotees came to Puri from all over India. Raghunath Das (1495-1571), who originally met the Lord at Shantipur, and Raghunath Bhatta (1505-1579), the son of Tapan Mishra (the Lord's host in Benares), were instructed at Puri and soon were sent to meet up with Rupa and Sanatan in Vrindavan. These four were later joined by Gopal Bhatta (1503-1578), Vyenkata's son from South India, and Jiva (1513-1598), who was widely known as the scholarly nephew of Rupa and Sanatan. Together, they would become the famous six Goswamis of Vrindavan. All would regularly travel to Puri for the Lord's association.

Mahaprabhu's movement in Puri was tremendous. In addition to the six Goswamis, the Lord's most intimate associates would gather there to engage in loving pastimes with Him. Along with Swarup Damodar, Ramananda Roy, Sikhi Mahiti, and his sister, Madhavidevi (the four most confidential devotees of the Lord's later pastimes), Nityananda Prabhu, Adwaita Acharya, Gadadhar Pandit, Shrivas, Haridas Thakur, Jagadananda Pandit, Bhavananda Roy (Shri Ramananda's father), Kasi Mishra, Bhagavan Acharya, Vakreshvara Pandit, Sarvabhauma Bhattacharya, Shivananda Sen, Kalidas, Raghava Pandit, and other pure devotees too numerous to mention, helped Mahaprabhu turn Puri into the kingdom of God.

The Perfect Example

During His many years at Puri, Lord Chaitanya lived as an ideal *sannyasi*, showing an overt abhorrence for luxury of any kind. He even rebuked His dear disciple Jagadananda for trying to arrange comfortable bedding for Him. He happily slept on the bare ground and had a minimum of personal requirements. In addition, His eating habits were simple: only *prasadam*, strict lacto-vegetarian food that had been offered as a sacrament to God. Even then, the Lord ate in small portions, only what was required to keep body and soul together. The exceptions, of course, were when His loving devotees brought Him varieties of eatables as token of their devotion (which happened frequently) and on Vaishnava holidays. On such occasions, the Lord would outdo everyone else, eating as if it were a central religious principle. In this way, Mahaprabhu showed how a perfect *sannyasi* and religious leader should set a dual example of austerity and celebration.

As the ideal ascetic, Lord Chaitanya never allowed Himself to get involved in matters concerning finance. Once, Gopinath, Ramananda Roy's brother, had embezzled two hundred thousand rupees that was supposed to have been paid as tax to King Prataparudra. When detected, Gopinath had to stand trial in a court of law. And although Mahaprabhu's disciples pleaded with Him to speak on Gopinath's behalf, the Lord flatly refused and threatened to leave Puri if they asked Him again. The burden of finance was relegated to the householders (*grihastas*); *sannyasis*, Mahaprabhu taught, should try to avoid such dealings.

He was equally strict in avoiding the association of women. While His philosophy espoused that they were equal to men spiritually, He also recognized that there was obviously a material difference. A *sannyasi*, according to Vedic tradition, must be strict in his vow of celibacy,[113] and should be careful when in proximity to the opposite sex.

Consequently, Mahaprabhu was often scrupulous in this regard. For example, He completely banished His follower Chota ("junior") Haridas[114] for conversing with an elderly female devotee. As the story goes, Mahaprabhu's intimate devotee, Bhagavan Acharya, sent Chota Haridas to collect alms from Sikhi Mahiti's sister, Madhavidevi, who was considered one of the most important devotees of the time. As a *sannyasi*, however, Chota Haridas should have completed his transaction and left immediately. Instead, he talked intimately with her for a long period. Mahaprabhu chose to use this incident as an example by denying Chota Haridas His association for all time, and, despite the fervent requests of the Lord's elder disciples, He never rescinded His judgment.

Some modern scholars thus say that Mahaprabhu was downright stubborn in regard to women. Mrinal K. Ghosh, Bipin Bihari Das Gupta, B. B. Majumdar, and others hold this perspective, saying that the Lord rarely if ever associated with women after His *sannyasa*.

In fact, it is generally accepted that Mahaprabhu strongly discouraged any unnecessary association with the opposite sex for one who is serious about celibacy and spiritual life. Once, when the Lord heard someone beautifully singing the *Gita Govinda*, He ran directly toward the sound of the chant. His intention was to embrace the singer for such an enchanting expression of devotion. But His servant stopped Him in His tracks, informing Him that it was a woman who was the singer of the devotional song. Lord Chaitanya thanked His servant profusely, saying that the boy had in fact saved His life by stopping Him when he did.[115]

Further, Mahaprabhu taught that a *sannyasi* should be disinclined to hear the name of a woman.[116] Indeed, the Lord also said that a piece of wood carved in the form of a woman was capable of putting one into illusion.[117]

While strictness in regard to association with the opposite sex was definitely a part of the Lord's teachings, there were some notable exceptions as well. That Mahaprabhu had at times met with His mother, Sachidevi, is accepted by all. Strictly speaking, this is also forbidden to a *sannyasi*. There is evidence, however, that Mahaprabhu also was cordial and had a friendly relationship with Sarvabhauma Bhattacharya's wife and with Sitadevi Thakurani (Adwaita Acharya's wife).[118] But these two were many years His senior and were exceptional devotees.

In addition, as a regular visitor to the Jagannath temple in Puri, the Lord one day met an Oriyan woman, who had also gone there to see the Deity of the Lord. Finding it difficult to see the altar as a result of the large crowds that would go there daily, she climbed atop the Garuda pillar to get a better view. While one foot rested on the pillar, she inadvertantly rested the other on Mahaprabhu's shoulder. When Govinda, the Lord's servant, saw what was happening, he started to rebuke the pious woman.

"Oh uncivilized man," Mahaprabhu objected, "do not forbid this women to climb the Garuda pillar. Let her see Lord Jagannath to her satisfaction." When the woman heard the Lord defend her, however, she quickly came to her senses. Climbing back to the ground, she begged the Lord for forgiveness. Eager to see the Lord of the Universe, she said, she had forgotten all about social etiquette.

In Mahaprabhu's eyes, of course, her spontaneous eagerness to see Lord Jagannath superseded her offense. Looking at the woman with transcendental love, Mahaprabhu humbly said, "Lord Jagannath has not bestowed so much eagerness upon Me. She has fully absorbed her body, mind, and life in Lord Jagannath. Therefore she was unaware that she was putting her foot on My shoulder.

"How fortunate this woman is!" the Lord concluded, "I pray at her feet that she favor Me with her great eagerness to see Lord Jagannath."[119] In addition to this incident, there are scholars who even say that Mahaprabhu at times enjoyed watching dramas performed by women (*devidasis*), which is also considered taboo for *sannyasis*.[120] While there is scanty evidence in support of this latter incident, Lord Chaitanya did teach that practicality in such matters should always be the rule.

Both strictness and leniency, then, can be found within Lord Chaitanya's *sannyasa* pastimes. While His association with women was indeed minimal, it was not out of the question. And although He set the highest example of renunciation, He was always practical, and He always acted in a way that would be most beneficial for His *sankirtan* movement.

Beyond the exemplary teaching established by His *sannyasa* vows, scholars say that there are five events in Mahaprabhu's later life that are particularly significant[121]: His appreciation of Kalidas; His meeting with Kavi Karnapur; the death of Haridas Thakur; His ecstatic love (*mahabhava*) as exhibited in the Gambhira-lila; and the composition of His *Shikshashtakam*, eight concise prayers that were written by the Lord Himself.

Kalidas

Kalidas was the uncle of Raghunath Das Goswami, and he was best known for his appreciation of *prasadam*. It is said that throughout his entire life he only ate the remnants of such food when other devotees had eaten their fill. After the devotees threw out their plates, Kalidas would sneak up and steal the leftovers. This is in keeping with the scriptural tradition, which says that holy food becomes even more sacred after it is touched by the lotus-like lips of a Vaishnava.

Mahaprabhu appreciated Kalidas' realization of this concept. And it is said that He bestowed His supreme mercy, unattainable by anyone else,[122] upon this faithful devotee. Further, the Lord openly praised Kalidas and suggested that others learn from his example.

Kavi Karnapur

Kavi Karnapur's original name was Paramananda Sen (although he was sometimes called Puridas), and he was the youngest son of Shivananda Sen, the Lord's intimate devotee. Mahaprabhu met young Paramananda for the first time in 1531, when the boy was only seven years old.

One day, Lord Chaitanya asked him to utter the name of Krishna, but the boy remained silent. Shivananda asked the boy as well. Still, young Paramananda would not speak. Then, one day, Mahaprabhu again tried: "Recite, My dear Puridas."

Just then, the young boy spontaneously composed a beautiful Sanskrit verse, much to the astonishment of all who were present: "Lord Shri Krishna is just like a bluish lotus flower for the ears; He is ointment for the eyes, a necklace of *Indraneela* gems for the chest, and universal ornaments for the *gopi* damsels of Vrindavan. Let that Lord Shri Hari, Krishna, be glorified."[123]

Mahaprabhu was greatly pleased. Although the boy was only seven and had no formal training, he had composed a verse that would be the envy of experienced Sanskritists. This was, for the Lord, an enlivening example of Krishna's mystic opulence.

Seeing the talent of the young boy, and knowing the quality and importance of his future literary works, Mahaprabhu gave him the name Kavi Karnapur, which means "the ear ornament of poets."

Haridas Thakur

The passing of Haridas Thakur occurred around the same time as the Kavi Karnapur incident, just two years or so before Lord Chaitanya departed from this world. The Thakur was one of Mahaprabhu's most cherished disciples. In fact, the Lord once asked Haridas for advice in regard to saving the fallen souls who are bereft of Vedic culture. To this, Haridas assured Him that only the loud chanting of the Hare Krishna *mantra* could help them.

After describing this incident in some detail, Krishnadas Kaviraj Goswami proceeds to explain how the Thakur's faith and chastity were tested at Benapola, a village near Shantipur.

A person named Ramachandra Khan, who was envious of Haridas Thakur, hired a professional prostitute named Lakshahira to defame him. By the mercy of the Thakur, however, the prostitute eventually became a great devotee of the Lord. Because Ramachandra Khan had attempted to offend the pure Haridas, he was later cursed by Nityananda Prabhu and ruined.

From Benapola, Haridas went to Chandapur, where he lived at the house of Balarama Acharya. Soon after, the Thakur was received by two brothers, Hiranya and Govardhan Majumdar. While at their home, Haridas was unfortunately offended in the course of a discussion with an unqualified *brahmana* named Gopal Chakravarti. Because of his offense, Chakravarti was miraculously stricken with leprosy.

Haridas Thakur soon left Chandapur and went to the house of Adwaita

Acharya, where his devotion was tested by Mayadevi herself (illusion personified). The Thakur, of course, fully passed the test, as he had with the prostitute sent by Ramachandra Khan, and he even initiated Mayadevi into the chanting of Krishna's holy name.[124] Haridas Thakur was thus one of the primary exponents of Lord Chaitanya's spiritual renaissance.

Fearful of this renaissance, Muslim political leaders began to throw "Hindus," and especially low-caste Hindus, into prison. Haridas Thakur, as a Muslim convert to "Hinduism," was a prime target for this hostility and prejudice. Thus, when the Muslim governor of Bengal heard of Haridas' activities, he dispatched a band of soldiers to immediately arrest the Thakur.

Being transcendentally situated, however, Haridas Thakur simply viewed his arrest as an opportunity to preach to the other prisoners, especially Hindu leaders, who were also in the same prison. Reflective due to a life behind bars, the prisoners were particularly religious, and they were anxious to associate with Haridas Thakur, the great saint. Although, as they had hoped, the Thakur gave his blessings to them, these blessings were quite different from that which they expected: "May you all remain in your present condition."

Confusion covered their faces. Haridas explained, "My veiled benediction is rightly meant, for, due to your incarceration, you are now thinking of Krishna. Your minds should always be fixed on His lotus feet. If you are released from prison, your minds may become distracted from Krishna, and you may become worldly-minded once again. I do not necessarily wish for you to remain in your present state of captivity, but just chant the name of Krishna always and never forget Him, no matter what may happen to you."

After blessing the prisoners in this way, Haridas presented himself before the Muslim governor, to whom he explained that there is essentially no difference between "the Koran and the Puran[a]." Thus, according to Haridas, Islam and the Vedic religion (and all other genuine religious paths as well) are ultimately one, for they unanimously acknowledge the final goal as love of Godhead.

The Islamic leaders of Bengal could not tolerate (or understand) Haridas Thakur's catholic view of religious truth and his "conversion" to Hinduism. Consequently, a harsh verdict was soon bestowed upon the Thakur: "Let him be whipped at the twenty-two marketplaces of the city." Strong deputies seized Haridas and carried him into the streets. As they dragged his body and beat him for all to see, Haridas continued to sweetly chant the holy name of the Lord, apparently unaffected by the beating. By the time they reached the twenty-second marketplace, the deputies were tired of whipping the Thakur, and, in dismay, they said, "Haridas, you will be the death of us. We beat you until our arms are exhausted, and still you do not die. But what's worse, from time to time you even smile."

Upon hearing the frustrated statements of the perpetrators, Haridas replied, "If my presence on earth troubles you, then I will gladly depart." The Thakur then fell into spiritual trance, immersed in love for Krishna. Thinking he was dead, the deputies threw his body into the Ganges River. Soon his body washed up on shore, and he awoke, chanting the holy name in ecstasy. Some days later, the Thakur met with Chaitanya Mahaprabhu, who exhibited many cuts and bruises upon His own body. Haridas became confused, so Mahaprabhu explained to him, "Because you are My pure devotee, I have accepted all the pains of your whipping." This was the loving relationship that Haridas Thakur enjoyed with Lord Chaitanya.

The Passing of Haridas Thakur

Naturally, then, the passing away of such an exalted personality had special meaning for Mahaprabhu, who felt that all His happiness was simply due to Haridas' association.

As the story goes, the Thakur knew that the Lord would soon end His manifest pastimes in this world. And he could not bear to be a witness. He begged the Lord that he instead be allowed to depart first. Mahaprabhu reluctantly consented. At this point, the Thakur begged Mahaprabhu to sit in front of him, and with this opportunity he blissfully stared directly into the Lord's eyes. It is said that he then took the Lord's holy feet on his chest and proceeded to chant the holy name of Shri Krishna Chaitanya again and again. As he simultaneously chanted and appreciated the sweetness of the All-Attractive Lord who sat before him, tears of divine love glided down from his eyes. While in this state, he allowed his own life force to divorce the body.

Out of love for Haridas Thakur, the Lord conducted the funeral ceremony Himself, personally carrying the Thakur's body out to sea. With the accompaniment of a massive *kirtan*, the Lord personally entombed the body, covered it with sand and erected a special platform on the site. After bathing in the sea, Mahaprabhu went to all the people of Puri, begging for Jagannath *prasadam*, as He wanted to distribute the sacred food to all of the devotees in honor of the great Haridas.

Shrila Bhaktivinode Thakur has written a beautiful poem containing the Vaishnava perspective on the death of a great devotee. Today, this poem is posted in Jagannath Puri above the tomb of Haridas Thakur: "He reasons ill who says that Vaishnavas die. For thou art living still in sound. The Vaishnava dies to live. And in living tries to spread the holy life around."

Gambhira Lila

During His final two or three years of manifest pastimes, the Lord stayed, almost exclusively, in the garden house ("Gambhira") of Kasi Mishra. It was at this Gambhira that Vakreshvara Pandit, one of the Lord's favorite Bengali *kirtan* dancers, eventually established the daily worship of a quilt and waterpot used by the Lord. To this day, in fact, these items are worshiped at that place, which has since been turned into a Vaishnava monastery called Radha Kanta Math.

Toward the end of His manifest pastimes, the Lord would have His intimate servants lock Him in the Gambhira, especially at night, when He was given to mystical trance and convulsive fits of ecstasy. Once, when the Lord was chanting the holy name of Krishna late into the night, He suddenly heard the rapturous melody of Krishna's flute. Although the three doors of the Gambhira were bolted from the outside, and the little house was even guarded by His servant Govinda, Swarup Damodar, and Ramananda Roy, the Lord somehow managed to disappear. Noticing that they could no longer hear the Lord's chanting from within the Gambhira, Govinda and Swarup Damodar opened the door and saw that Mahaprabhu had gone.

Greatly alarmed, they went to search for Him and eventually found Him lying unconscious amidst a small group of cows at the Lion's Gate of the Jagannath Temple. His form was unusual, with arms and legs receding into His body like a tortoise. He was foaming at the mouth, while His hair stood on end and tears flowed relentlessly from His eyes. Although He externally resembled a large pumpkin gourd, the Lord was thoroughly enraptured with love of God.

Not able to revive Him, His followers brought Him back to the Gambhira. And by loudly chanting the holy name of Krishna, they were able to bring Him back to external consciousness. His arms and legs came out of the trunk of His body, and He started to explain what had happened. As His devotees listened to the story of His beatific vision of Krishna's pastimes, they all shared transcendental emotions. This incident is fully described by Raghunath Das Goswami in his book entitled *Gauranga-stava-kalpavriksha*.

While at the Gambhira, the Lord exhibited the highest transcendental emotion, known as *prema-vilasa-vivarta*, wherein one mistakes ordinary phenomena for spiritual reality. This occurs due to an intense mood of love in separation. For example, Mahaprabhu once saw a large sand dune and mistook it for Govardhan Hill. Fully convinced that it was the holy mountain of Lord Krishna's pastimes, He ran in its direction while exhibiting symptoms of ecstatic love. His devotees ran after Him, but they could not keep up. They finally reached Him when He soon fainted out of sheer ecstasy.

On another occasion, while the Lord was walking along the seashore near the Aitota temple in Puri, He mistook the sea for the Yamuna River. In a state of uncontrollable bliss, He jumped into it, attempting to immerse Himself in her holy waters. As the turbulent waves forcefully carried His body, He felt certain that Radha and Krishna would be splashing about nearby. In due course, however, He was washed several miles away to the Konarka temple. There, a fisherman, thinking that the Lord's body was a big fish, caught Him in his net and brought Him ashore.

The fisherman could immediately see that this was no ordinary being, and as soon as he touched the Lord's body, he became mad with ecstatic love for Krishna. His own madness frightened him, however, and, thinking that he was possessed, he went in search of someone who could perform an exorcism. While wandering the beach in this way, he came upon Swarup Damodar and the other devotees, who had been frantically looking for Lord Chaitanya. After deciphering the jibberish of the fisherman, Swarup Damodar could understand that it was actually the Lord who the fisherman had captured in his net. Loudly chanting the holy name of Krishna near the unconscious body of Lord Chaitanya, Swarup Damodar succeeded in reviving the Lord and convincing the fisherman that he was not possessed.

Many similar pastimes occurred while the Lord stayed at the Gambhira of Kasi Mishra. And in each incident He could only be pacified by the loud recitation of the holy name. Sometimes, His devotees would recite the works of Chandidas, Vidyapati, Jayadev Goswami, or Ramananda Roy's

Jagannath Ballabha (a drama about the pastimes of Radha and Krishna), and these would soothe Him as well.

The Shikshashtakam Prayers

While at the Gambhira, the Lord fell into constant spiritual absorption, recalling Krishna's most intimate transcendental pastimes with the damsels of Vraja. Overcome by such intense feelings of spiritual longing, it is said, Lord Chaitanya recited His Shikshashtakam prayers, with commentary, in the presence of His intimate devotees, Swarup Damodar and Ramananda Roy.

According to Krishnadas Kaviraj Goswami, this is the last known event in Mahaprabhu's manifest career. The Shikshashtakam, in fact, are the only composed prayers that can be attributed to the Lord Himself.

The first of the eight prayers espouses the sevenfold efficacy of chanting the holy name of Krishna[125]: "Let there be all victory for the chanting of the holy name of Krishna, which (1) can cleanse the mirror of the heart and (2) stop the miseries of the blazing fire of material existence. That chanting is (3) the waxing moon that spreads the lotus of good fortune for all living entities. (4) It is the life and soul of all education. The chanting of the holy name of Krishna (5) expands the blissful ocean of transcendental life. (6) It gives a cooling effect to everyone and (7) enables one to taste full nectar at every step."

The second verse expounds upon the misfortune of not having the desire to chant: "My Lord, O Supreme Personality of Godhead, in Your holy name there is all good fortune for the living entity, and therefore You have many names, such as Krishna and Govinda, by which You expand Yourself. You have invested all Your potencies in these names, and there are no hard and fast rules for remembering them. My dear Lord, although You bestow such mercy upon the fallen, conditioned souls by liberally teaching Your holy names, I am so unfortunate that I commit offenses while chanting the holy name, and therefore I do not achieve attachment for chanting." Shrila Bhaktivinode Thakur has commented that four impediments in particular are responsible for diminishing one's natural taste for the holy name: (1) ignorance of eternal principles, (2) frailties of heart, (3) evil propensities, and (4) offenses.[126]

The third verse describes the humble person who is eligible to chant the name purely: "One who thinks himself lower than the grass, who is more tolerant than a tree, and who does not expect personal honor but is always prepared to give all respect to others, can very easily always chant the holy name of the Lord."

The fourth verse establishes the exclusivity of purpose necessary for pure chanting: "O Lord of the Universe, I do not desire material wealth, materialistic followers, a beautiful wife, or fruitive activities described in flowery language. All I want, life after life, is unmotivated devotional service unto You."

In Lord Chaitanya's fifth verse one can find the reason for one's conditioning and the required humility needed to become free: "O My Lord, O Krishna, Son of Maharaj Nanda, I am Your eternal servant, but because of My own fruitive acts, I have fallen into this horrible ocean of nescience. Now please be causelessly merciful to Me. Consider Me a particle of dust at Your lotus feet."

Here, in the sixth verse, a hint is given of the three external symptoms that accompany the dawn of true love: "My dear Lord, when will (1) My eyes be beautified by filling with tears that constantly glide down as I chant Your holy name? When will (2) My voice falter and (3) all the hairs of My body stand erect in transcendental happiness as I chant Your holy name?"[127]

The next verse describes the soul who is nearing perfection. In a mood of inconceivably blissful separation, the pure devotee becomes mad after Krishna: "My Lord Govinda, because of separation from You, I consider even a moment to be a great millennium. Tears flow from My eyes like torrents of rain, and I see the entire world as void in Your absence."

The eighth and final verse of the Shikshashtakam delineates the highest end in chanting the holy name: "Let Krishna tightly embrace this maidservant, who has fallen at His lotus feet. Let Him trample Me or break My heart by never being visible to Me. He is a debauchee, after all, and can do whatever He likes, but He is still no one other than the worshipable Lord of My heart."

During His last months in this world, Mahaprabhu remained in a state of complete spiritual absorption, day and night, and with His two intimate devotees fully tasted the meaning of the verses He had composed.

CHAPTER SIXTEEN

the Lord's disappearance

In all of the earliest authentic biographies of Lord Chaitanya Mahaprabhu, His death is described by the words *antardhana* or *sangopana*. These words literally mean "disappearance," and are generally used in the Vedic literature to describe the passing away of the Lord, which is of a miraculous nature and unlike ordinary death as we know it.

Since the Lord's form is perfectly spiritual, when He departs for His own abode He leaves nothing behind, no outer shell to serve as food for worms. When we, on the other hand, shed our mortal frame, we leave it to be buried or burned as our soul earnestly seeks its next body. But the Lord's body is transcendental, and He thus "disappears" from the world. In this way, His pastimes are existing eternally, but they are either in a manifest or unmanifest state, according to His sweet will.

In general, the most authoritative biographers are silent about the Lord's disappearance. Krishnadas Kaviraj, Vrindavandas Thakur, Kavi Karnapur, and Murari Gupta mention the year of the Lord's passing (1534), and nothing more. This is chiefly because these biographers were all lovingly devoted to Mahaprabhu and could not bear to discuss His departure.

Drowning at Sea

Following the narration in the *Chaitanya Charitamrita*, some scholars believe that the Lord, in a fit of ecstasy, threw Himself into the sea, mistaking it for the River Yamuna. Since the book does not describe Mahaprabhu's disappearance, the speculation has arisen that Krishnadas Kaviraj, in mentioning this episode at the sea, alludes to the Lord's final manifest pastime.[128] And there is a very strong oral tradition that says He left the world in that way.

But this hypothesis cannot be relied upon. Krishnadas Kaviraj Goswami himself concludes his narration of Mahaprabhu's drowning by saying that the Lord was actually rescued by a fisherman. Although His followers felt that He was going to depart at this time, the Lord clearly regained consciousness and continued to instruct His devotees for several months.[129] Further, Shrila Bhaktisiddhanta Sarasvati Thakur has firmly stated that this drowning hypothesis carries no validity.[130]

A Natural Death

There are a class of scholars[131] who believe that Mahaprabhu died of septic fever after injuring his left foot (while dancing at the *Ratha-yatra* festival). This version is obviously taken from Jayananda's *Chaitanya Mangal*, which is an early biographical account.

After hurting His foot, the story goes, the Lord entered the Gopinath Temple and died "a natural death." There, the priests closed the doors and would not allow any of His followers to come in. Just outside, Kasi Mishra, Sanatan Goswami, Haridas Thakur, and Shrivas were weeping in separation.

Conservative members of the scholarly community tend to defend this account, chiefly because it is divorced from any supernatural detail. However, it is equally divorced from reality. Jayananda's version can be readily dismissed because Haridas had already passed away several years earlier (being buried by Mahaprabhu Himself) and could not have possibly been at the alleged disappearance. To be mistaken about such a major event in the history of Gaudiya Vaishnavism (the passing of Haridas Thakur) indicates that Jayananda was an ill-informed devotee, or, giving him the benefit of the doubt, his book was later interpolated by nondevotional academicians. In either case, this theory collapses.

Tota Gopinath

According to Shrila Bhaktivinode Thakur, Mahaprabhu disappeared into the Deity of Tota Gopinath in Puri.[132] To this day, a golden streak can be seen on the Deity's thigh, and the *brahmana* priests of the temple assure visiting devotees that this is where Lord Chaitanya merged with the Lord of His heart.

This theory is supported by stalwart devotees and scholars of Gaudiya Vaishnavism. In Chapter Eight of Narahari Chakravarti's book, *Bhakti-ratnakar* (circa, eighteenth century), the Lord is described as entering the temple of Tota Gopinath and never coming out. This version is echoed in Chapter Thirty-six of Sadananda Kavisurya Brahma's important work, *Prema Tarangini*. Merging into the Tota Gopinath Deity, in fact, is the second most widely accepted tradition in regard to the disappearance of Mahaprabhu. Shrila Bhaktisiddhanta Sarasvati supports the Tota Gopinath theory as follows: "His disappearance is traced to His amalgamation with Gopinath at Tota in Puri. . . . Some are of the opinion that He merged into the Jagannath Deity at the Gundicha temple in Sundarachal."[133] Shrila Bhaktisiddhanta Sarasvati appears to have found virtue in both the Tota Gopinath and Jagannath explanations.

The Jagannath Deity

The most prominent tradition concerning the Lord's disappearance states that He merged into the Deity of Lord Jagannath. This perspective was accepted by His Divine Grace A. C. Bhaktivedanta Swami Prabhupada,[134] and it is also supported by very early biographers, one of whom was an eyewitness.

Achyutananda, for instance, was an Oriyan disciple who was actually at the Jagannath temple at the time of the Lord's departure. In the first chapter of his authoritative work, *Shunya Samhita*, he clearly says, "Lord Chaitanya, the great dancer, chanted the name of Radharani and like a flash of lightening immersed Himself within the sacred body of Jagannath." This, then, is considered the most authoritative account of the Lord's final manifest pastime, since it was described by an eyewitness.

Further, Divakara Das, another early devotee from Orissa, mentions the Lord's disappearance in his book, *Jagannath Charitamrita*, as follows: "Thinking thus [that He should return to His own abode] He absorbed Himself within the image of Jagannath. Thus He vanished into Jagannath's body (which is identical with His own) in strict confidentiality."[135] This version is supported, too, by Ishvara Das' *Chaitanya Bhagavat*.

Thus, it is concluded by orthodox Vaishnavas that either the Tota Gopinath story or the similar Lord Jagannath version is the authentic rendition of Mahaprabhu's disappearance. It is often accepted that both are true, for just as the Lord appeared in seven *kirtan* parties, He can certainly disappear into two different Deities without any difficulty. If it is accepted that God is unlimited, the Vaishnavas say, then He need not be restricted by only one disappearance story.

Mahaprabhu as God

According to the Gaudiya Vaishnava canon, Lord Chaitanya is a combined manifestation of Radha and Krishna, and He is thus considered the most complete and perfect aspect of the Personality of Godhead. To be more accurate, in fact, He is not a "manifestation" or an "aspect" of God at all, but rather He is the original *Manifestor,* the totally complete Absolute Truth. Consequently, any question of death in the usual sense is *a priori* absurd. It is for this reason, too, that Gaudiya Vaishnavas in general are usually silent in regard to Mahaprabhu's last days.

Nonetheless, due to the ontologically absolute similarity between Mahaprabhu and Shri Krishna, some light may be shed upon the mystery of the Lord's disappearance. For example, in the *Shrimad Bhagavatam*, Krishna's departure is philosophically analyzed in the following way: "My dear king, you should understand that the Supreme Lord's appearance and disappearance, which resemble those of embodied conditioned souls, are actually a show enacted by His illusory energy, just like the performance of an actor. After creating this universe He enters into it, plays within it for some time, and at last winds it up. Then the Lord remains situated in His own transcendental glory, having ceased from the functions of cosmic manifestation." (S.B. 11.31.11) These same truths naturally exist for Lord Chaitanya Mahaprabhu.

The *Bhagavatam* further states that as soon as Krishna left the earth, truth, religion, faithfulness, glory, and beauty immediately followed Him (S.B. 11.31.7). In other words, with the passing of the Lord, many auspicious qualities pass from the world as well, and the people in general tend to suffer. It is this suffering that constitutes yet another reason why Mahaprabhu's followers have been reticent in regard to the Lord's disappearance; out of a profound sense of empathy, the devotees feel the pain of other living entities.

The Lord's Disappearance

Still, there is a positive side as well. When the Lord departs for His eternal abode, one has the opportunity to serve Him in separation. Such service brings with it a special bliss, culminating in the kind of spiritual lovesickness exemplified by Chaitanya Mahaprabhu. Finally, of course, one may be reunited with his Lord in loving service and find that spiritual relationship is even sweeter than previously imagined. The anticipation intensifies the union.

It should also be pointed out that endeavoring to understand the Lord's disappearance is itself a gateway to perfection. In *Bhagavad-gita*, Lord Krishna says, "One who knows the transcendental nature of My appearance and activities does not, upon leaving the body, take his birth again in this material world, but attains My eternal abode." (Bg. 4.9)

The Lord's disappearance—whether we are speaking of Mahaprabhu or Krishna Himself—is one of His activities. And as the *Gita* points out, it is these very activities that should be our object of meditation; our ultimate goal being to enter into these confidential pastimes as a humble servant. With a devotional mind, then, one can contemplate the disappearance of Lord Chaitanya, trying to penetrate its mystery, and in this way attain the kingdom of God.[136]

AFTERWORD

After Mahaprabhu's disappearance, Puri gradually lost its importance as the primary center of Krishna worship. Under the able care of the six Goswamis, Vrindavan soon became the new Vaishnava metropolis, with devotees and scholars making special pilgrimages just to see the excavated holy places associated with Krishna's pastimes.

Raghunath Bhatta had settled in Vrindavan even while Mahaprabhu was still in Puri. So did Rupa and Sanatan. Still, all three regularly visited Lord Chaitanya whenever possible. Raghunath Das left for Vrindavan soon after the Master's disappearance, while Gopal Bhatta and Jiva followed close behind. According to historian F. S. Growse: "The recognized leaders of the Vrindavan community were known by the names of Rup and Sanatan, the authors of several doctrinal commentaries, and also, as is said, of the *Mathura Mahatmya*. With them were associated a nephew, named Jiva, who founded the temple of Radha Damodar; Gopal Bhatta, founder of the temple of Radha Raman; Raghunath Das, a *Kayastha*; and completing the six, Raghunath Bhatta."[137]

Among the six Goswamis, Jiva became the most systematic preacher, and as a result he was widely acclaimed as the greatest philosopher in all of India. Initiated by Rupa Goswami, it was Jiva who planned the proselytizing strategies that would later emerge as the saving grace of Bengal and Orissa. To elaborate, in the early seventeenth century Jiva Goswami personally trained Shyamananda, Shrinivas Acharya, and Narottam Das Thakur. Thoroughly imbibing the tenets of Vaishnavism, these three were deputed to return to the eastern provinces with the devotional literature of the Goswamis.[138] Further, they were successful in implementing the philosophy among the common people.

Patronage

At this juncture in history, the Goswamis' fame reached great proportions, and in the year 1570, the Muslim Emperor Akbar came to Vrindavan just to meet them.[139] As a result, the emperor had an exclusive interview with Jiva Goswami and was thus inspired to order the construction of a library in Vrindavan.[140]

King Man Singh of Amber was equally drawn to the Goswamis and became a disciple of Sanatan and Rupa. The king built the temple of Govindadev in 1590 under the direction of his two *gurus*. The original temple of Madan Mohan was built with the financial support of Krishnadas Kapoor, a merchant from Multan who, according to Narahari Chakravarti, was a disciple of Sanatan.[141]

Devotees in Vrindavan

Along with the six goswamis, large numbers of pure devotees thronged to the gates of Vraja, for the political unrest that led to the loss of Orissa's independence in 1568[142] made Puri too unsettling for peaceful religious contemplation. The leading Vrindavan Vaishnavas of the time included Lokanath Goswami, Bhugarbha, Subuddhi Roy, Kashishvar, and Paramananda. Soon after, the new generation of leaders was Krishnadas Kaviraj Goswami, Yadavacharya, Raghava Pandit, Uddhava Das, and Gopal Das.

Shyamananda and Baladev

During the latter half of the seventeenth century and the first half of the eighteenth century, two advanced souls, Shyamananda and Baladev Vidyabhushan, spread the teachings of Mahaprabhu across the Indian subcontinent. Even these two great Oriya Vaishnavas, however, lived in

Afterword

Vrindavan and not in their own state (Orissa), where they would go only to preach and visit the holy places associated with Lord Chaitanya's pastimes.

Shyamananda was a disciple of Hridai Chaitanya and Jiva Goswami, who were both dedicated to the teachings of Lord Chaitanya. Shyamananda and his own disciple, Rasikananda, are remembered as the two devotees who propagated the Gaudiya Vaishnava doctrine all over Orissa. This they did by following in the footsteps of their illustrious predecessors: Nityananda Prabhu's consort, Jahnavidevi, and His son, Bhirabhadra, who, in the generation after Mahaprabhu's disappearance, were also quite successful in preaching throughout Bengal.

Baladev Vidyabhushan was an incarnation of Gopinath Acharya, Mahaprabhu's intimate follower, and was also the disciple of Vishvanath Chakravarti, an important seventeenth-century Gaudiya Vaishnava. Both Baladev and his *guru* were prolific and exceptional in all areas of devotional service. By writing a commentary on the *Vedanta Sutra*, moreover, Baladev proved that the Gaudiya school was not of obscure origin, but rather an affiliate of the Madhva *sampradaya*. His commentary, too, served to silence the opponents of Mahaprabhu's mission, who in 1628 at Galta (near Jaipur) had claimed that every bona fide Vaishnava tradition must have such a commentary.[143] Baladev's version was so eloquent, in fact, that it was entitled "Govinda Bashya," indicating that it was dictated to him by Govinda (Krishna) Himself. Furthermore, his celebrated commentary won Baladev the title *Vidyabhushan* ("the ornament of knowledge") by the Gaudiya patriarchs of Vrindavan.[144]

Every Town and Village

In the generation immediately following Baladev Vidyabhushan, a great devotee named Jagannath Das Babaji became the instructing *guru* of Shrila Bhaktivinode Thakur. And it was the Thakur who took to heart Mahaprabhu's mandate that the nonsectarian, spiritual principles of Gaudiya Vaishnavism should be spread to every town and village of the world.[145]

In Calcutta in 1896, the teachings of Lord Chaitanya began their journey to the West. In Bengali-speaking Calcutta on August 20 of that year, Shrila Bhaktivinode Thakur published a small English treatise entitled *Lord Chaitanya: His Life and Precepts*.

Seventy-one years later, in 1967, in Montreal, Canada, a graduate student came across a copy of this book while browsing through the rare-book collection of the McGill University library. The book was a wonderful find for him because he was a dedicated follower of Lord Chaitanya, having been convinced of Lord Chaitanya's teachings by His Divine Grace A. C. Bhaktivedanta Swami Prabhupada, whom he had accepted as his spiritual master. It was Shrila Prabhupada, in fact, who spread the teachings of Lord Chaitanya throughout the world.

Shrila Prabhupada was born in Calcutta on September 1, 1896, a little over a week after *Lord Chaitanya: His Life and Precepts* was published. Thus by a spiritual arrangement that can be attributed to Mahaprabhu Himself, this significant book and he who would fulfill the purpose of the book appeared in this world simultaneously. The rest is history.

APPENDIX ONE

Chaitanya Mahaprabhu and the festival of Lord Jagannath

In order to avoid breaking the continuity of the biographical narrative, the intimate facts surrounding Chaitanya Mahaprabhu's deep, personal relationship with Lord Jagannath and the Ratha-yatra festival is related here. Lord Jagannath is a confidential manifestation of Krishna, the Supreme Lord. And Ratha-yatra is a yearly festival that celebrates this particular manifestation in a most blissful and colorful way.

The inner meaning of the festival, especially as it relates to Mahaprabhu, may be summarized as follows.

Although Lord Krishna became a great king in His time, He spent His childhood in the village of Vrindavan. There He sported with the cowherd boys and girls, and of all of them, Radharani was His most beloved. Radha and Krishna's spiritual love cannot be imitated by any mortal couple.

When Krishna left Vrindavan to become king of Dvaraka, however, Shrimati Radharani's lamentation was unequaled anywhere in the cosmic manifestation. Nonetheless, She never gave up hope that He would someday return to Her. And in this way She enjoys a special transcendental longing.

Once, while Krishna was king, the divine couple planned a clandestine meeting. But when Radharani saw Krishna in His princely garb, with full opulence and regalia, She longed to see Him as the simple cowherd boy She once knew. She longed to bring Him back to Vrindavan.

This mood of wanting to bring Krishna back to the intimacy of Vrindavan is the confidential theme of the Ratha-yatra festival. When devotees pull the long, sturdy ropes of the Ratha-yatra cart, they are in essence pulling Krishna back into their hearts—back to the land of Vrindavan.

Radha and Krishna were spiritually reunited as Chaitanya Mahaprabhu, who appeared in Mayapur some 500 years ago. Yet in Lord Chaitanya's last years, which He spent in Jagannath Puri, He fully assumed the mood of Radharani, relentlessly lamenting the divine tragedy of Radha and Krishna's separation.

Every year in Jagannath Puri, Lord Chaitanya celebrated the Ratha-yatra festival in Radharani's mood of pulling Krishna back to the simple, village-like atmosphere of Vrindavan. Mahaprabhu taught that this feeling of separation actually evokes the presence of Krishna. This is the internal meaning of Ratha-yatra.

Ratha-yatra and the British Imperialists

The Ratha-yatra festival—or "the Festival of the Chariots"—has baffled Westerners for over a century. Although the festival first appeared in the West some twenty years ago, in the 1800s the British brought back stories from India that were more fanciful than factual. Today, however, we can see for ourselves just what the Festival of the Chariots is really all about.

In fact, Ratha-yatra is an ancient cultural affair, full of mystic symbolism and profound meaning. It originated as an offering to God by the Vaishnavas of ancient India, and today it is still celebrated by the Vaishnavas—but now it is replicated in most major Western cities as well. The largest Ratha-yatra, however, is still invariably held in Jagannath Puri, where literally millions come to see the parade of Lord Jagannath.

It was in Puri that the British imbibed their first impressions of India's sacred culture. Of course, without any knowledge of Vedic tradition, the British were at a natural disadvantage, and they mistakenly thought of India as engendering a backward culture. Considered illiterate because they could not read English and irreligious because they did not know the Bible, the residents of Jagannath Puri appeared barbaric—uncivilized. Nevermind their highly developed Sanskrit language. Nevermind their finely detailed Vaishnava tradition.

More strange perhaps than anything else in Puri was the Deity of Lord

Jagannath, whom the British would describe as "a frightful visage painted black, with a distended mouth of bloody horror." Their superficial view of Lord Jagannath was representative of their racial, social, and religious prejudices, and the onus developed upon the Indian people: theirs was the backward, heathen culture of idol worshipers, while the British were progressive and civilized.

Never imagining that anything of value could be gained from "primitive Hindoos," the British carried away nothing more than a new word for their "highly evolved" vocabulary: from the word Jagannath they derived "juggernaut," which came to indicate an overwhelming force that crushes everything in its path. Dr. Claudius Buchanan, who landed in Bengal in 1790, was the first British missionary to witness and describe "the horrors of juggernaut." Some say that much earlier, perhaps in the fourteenth century, Friar Odoric brought similar misinformation back to Europe.

In reality, however, Jagannath was less brutal than the picture painted by the British. In fact He was lovingly worshiped by devotees throughout the Indian subcontinent as the merciful and compassionate Lord Krishna Himself.

Jagannath literally means "Lord of the Universe." And the Deity of Jagannath, along with His brother Baladev (His immediate expansion) and sister Subhadra (His internal energy), was the very life of the Indian people. They saw in Him not some vicious fiend but a very endearing and loving manifestation of God, to whom they were completely devoted. One devotee, in fact, composed the following verses in praise of Lord Jagannath, and it hardly describes "a horrible blood-thirsty idol."

> (1) Sometimes in great happiness Lord Jagannath, with His flute, makes a loud concert in the groves on the banks of the Yamuna. He is like a bumble bee who tastes the beautiful lotus-like faces of the cowherd damsels of Vraja, and His lotus feet are worshiped by great personalities such as Lakshmi, Shiva, Brahma, Indra, and Ganesh. May that Jagannath Swami be the object of my vision.
> (2) In His left hand Lord Jagannath holds a flute. On His head He wears the feathers of peacocks and on His hips He wears fine yellow silken cloth. Out of the corners of His eyes He bestows sidelong glances upon His loving devotees and He always reveals Himself through His pastimes in His divine abode of Vrindavan. May that Jagannath Swami be the object of my vision.
> (3) Lord Jagannath is an ocean of mercy and He is beautiful like a row of blackish rain clouds. He is the storehouse of bliss for Lakshmi and Saraswati and His face is like a spotless full-blown lotus. He is worshiped by the best of

demigods and sages, and His glories are sung by the *Upanishads.* May that Jagannath Swami be the object of my vision.

(4) When Lord Jagannath is on His Ratha-yatra cart and is moving along the road, at every step there is a loud presentation of prayers and songs chanted by large assemblies of *brahmanas.* Hearing their hymns, Lord Jagannath is very favorably disposed toward them. He is the ocean of mercy and the true friend of all the worlds. May that Jagannath Swami be the object of my vision.

Idol Worship

The perspective brought back by the British, then, was hardly accurate. They were obviously swayed by religious and cultural prejudice. As inheritors of the Judeo-Christian tradition, the British naturally found the worship of Lord Jagannath to be distasteful, for "idol worship" was a cosmic taboo set down in the Bible. And the form of Jagannath hearkened back to the primitive, "graven" idols with which they were familiar. Indeed, they referred to Lord Jagannath as "that Indian Moloch."

But the Vedic literature informs us that there is a vast difference between idol worship and deity worship. One is based on the imaginative, speculative efforts of an ordinary man. The other has its basis in divinely inspired writings and is scientifically conveyed in ancient Vedic texts.

According to the *Vedas,* God *can* appear in wood, marble, stone or other material elements (just as much as He can appear in His original spiritual form). To be sure, Western theologians admit that God is unlimited and omnipotent, and that nothing is beyond His ability and scope. Yet the practical application of this eludes them. If God can do anything, as the Western theologians admit, then why can He not incarnate in material elements? The Supreme Lord, by definition, need not be confined by our limitations, by our sense of the reasonable. Indeed, He is inconceivable! He is not constricted by what we, limited beings, can understand. *Therefore* He is supreme. He manifests as spirit, or wood, marble, stone—He even manifests within one's heart. He can do whatever He likes.

Moreover, the *Vedas* give explicit instructions for carving and worshiping deities such as Jagannath. And while idol worship is condemned, even in the Vedic literature, deity worship is considered a must. It's something like mailing a letter. One doesn't just drop his letter in any box. It must be a box that is authorized by the post office, by the government. Then one can be sure that one's letter will arrive at its destination. Similarly, a deity must be conceived and worshiped according to the revealed scriptures. Then the faithful Vaishnava can be sure that his worship will arrive at the proper destination. This is a central tenet of Vaishnavism, and Lord Jagannath has been worshiped as such an authorized deity by the residents of Puri for countless generations. The story of how this came to be is quite complex, but the scriptures summarize it as follows.

The Story of Lord Jagannath

Once, millennia ago, a great king named Indradyumna ruled a province called Malava. A pious king, he searched vigorously for the beautiful bluish form of the Lord he had heard so much about from the sages. Known as Nila Madhava, the Lord one day came to Indradyumna in a dream, revealing to him that he would soon arrive in the form of a *daru*, or a wooden log. The Lord told the king that his transcendental piece of wood, once found, should be carved and worshiped as was the tradition.

The next day, Indradyumna indeed found the log floating in a holy river. With great labor, he managed to procure the log and engage a host of sculptors in trying to carve the form of the Lord. But this was no ordinary log. Try as they may, their tools were inadequate. Hammer and chisel alike would break when applied to the divine log. Finally, the king engaged Vishvakarma, architect of the demigods, to fashion the Lord's form out of the *daru brahman* piece of wood.

Vishvakarma, however, would only do his work if he was allowed to meditate in perfect tranquility. He stipulated that his meditation could not be broken. And if someone were to come in and disturb him while carving the form of the Lord, he said, he would immediately leave, even if he was not finished and the deity was incomplete.

Indradyumna agreed. But as time wore on, he became impatient. Nonetheless, he remained tolerant and continued to honor the strictures laid down by his prestigious sculptor. Unfortunately, the king's wife, Gundicha, did not share her husband's maturity in patience. And so after a few short days, she burst in, hoping to see all that the sculptor had done. (Sometimes it is said that, at the behest of his wife, the king himself was the one who burst through the doors.)

To her consternation, as well as the king's, the sculptor had vanished, as he said he would. Three half-completed images were left behind:

Jagannath, Baladev, and Subhadra. But because love and devotion were imbued into these deities by a genuine devotee of the Lord, Indradyumna appreciated the work anyway, proclaiming that the divine sculptor had actually captured the Lord in essence. So while Jagannath may appear materially incomplete—no hands, no feet, etc.—He is *spiritually* complete. All of the great Vaishnava scriptures and saints attest to this. And Jagannath has been worshiped in that form, especially in Puri, for many centuries.

Jagannath Puri

The city of Puri, shaped like the silhouette of a conchshell, was fashioned around Lord Jagannath, and even today He remains the center. His temple, sometimes known as "Shri Mandir," is situated on elevated ground, known as *Nilgiri,* "the blue hill." According to the palm leaf chronicles of the *mandir,* the temple is in fact ancient. It has, however, been refurbished more than twelve times, although it still stands in exactly the same area. The current frame was constructed under the patronage of King Chadoganga Deva, sometime in the twelfth century. Since then it has been recognized as a sort of Vaishnava metropolis and pilgrims come from all over to pay homage to the Lord of the universe.

A brief description of the temple is in order. The central shrine is typical of Orissa, consisting of a miniature kingdom of four buildings. These are referred to as (1) *Bhoga Mandap,* where some fifty-four food offerings are daily prepared for the deities; (2) *Naata Mandap,* which is a large dancing hall for the Lord's pleasure; (3) the *Mukhasala,* where the Lord gives His *darshan,* or "audience" for all of His devotees to see. And last but not least is (4) the *Bada-deula,* or the area of the main temple.

This temple is some 215 feet in height—the tallest in all of Jagannath Puri. Indeed, it is the tallest in all of Orissa. Superbly built, the temple is surrounded by two compound walls. The outer wall extends to about 665 feet in length and 644 in width. The inner wall is smaller, covering only some 420 feet in length and 315 in width. There are fabulous gates surrounding all enclosures.

The eastern gate is called "the Lion Gate," while the gates on the southern, northern, and western sides are called the Horse, Elephant, and Tiger gates, respectively. Through these gates throng the multitudes for a glimpse of their mighty Lord, who stands enthroned on His *Ratna Singhasan,* which is about five feet in height. This is about the same size as Jagannath Himself. His elder brother Baladev is about six feet, whereas Lady Subhadra is at least four feet.

Despite Their limited size, however, the deities appear gigantic, and one naturally becomes reverential upon attaining the good fortune to see Them. Most of the residents at Puri see the deities every day, when they come to get the *"mahaprasad,"* food offered to the deity that invariably feeds thousands every day. But the visage of the deity is especially glorious during the great Puri festivals, when onlookers can see the deity being glorified in full regalia.

Ratha-yatra

Puri is a city of festivals. And it has been said that there are sixty-two major festivals held throughout the year. The most important festival, of course, is Ratha-yatra, wherein the Lord comes out into the streets in His own cart, which is then pulled by huge ropes by His loving devotees. Baladev and Subhadra are given Their own carts as well. Literally millions come from far and wide to enjoy the annual Ratha-yatra festival, while the Lord is served by a multitude of happy devotees in a fabulous and elaborate parade.

The Ratha-yatra carts are mammoth in size and are a sight to behold. Jagannath's own cart projects some fifty feet into the sky, and it is about thirty-six feet wide as well, making it a formidable "juggernaut." Sixteen large wheels help the giant cart of the Lord move down the road, which is then followed by two slightly smaller carts, one for Baladev and one for Subhadra. Over two thousand priests climb aboard the three carts to accompany the Lord as He is pulled through the teeming masses.

As millions follow along in the summer heat, praises of the Lord permeate Jagannath Puri: "Jai Jagannath! All glories to the Lord of the universe!" This continues for several miles until the parade arrives at the Lord's pavillion, the Gundicha Temple, and seven days later a similar festival ensues signifying the return of the Lord. The return festival is enacted with all the pomp and vigor of the initial parade.

The Ratha-yatra festival is easily the most cherished event in Jagannath Puri, and it is anticipated all year by those to whom it is familiar. As one of India's most colorful summer festivals, it has been the subject of artistic interpretation as well. One famous bas-relief, from the eighth century A.D., is now found in the Museum of Bhubaneshwar, and it is easily one of their most popular pieces. The relief beautifully illustrates the whole parade, and viewers are often moved at the unique display of devotion generated by the artist's work. Of course, the festival is itself unique, and so any artistic representation is bound to catch an attentive art observer's eye. When the subject-matter is already profound, a talented artist has a natural advantage. Be that as it may, crores of Indian sages and holymen—and foreigners as well—journey thousands of miles just to behold Ratha-yatra, an artist's dream come true.

Shri Chaitanya Mahaprabhu, the Personality of Godhead who manifested in the guise of His own devotee, also took part in this festival some five hundred years ago. In 1510, having entered the renounced order of life, He decided to leave Bengal and bring the chanting of the holy name to all parts of India. At the very beginning of His journey, however, the Lord traveled to Puri, where He developed deep attraction for Lord Jagannath. Still, due to His mercy on the fallen conditioned souls, Chaitanya Mahaprabhu continued His travels, touring South India for several years. He soon returned to Lord Jagannath, however, and was to take part in the Ratha-yatra festival, preparations for which were underway when the Lord arrived.

Desiring to make the festival a grand success, Lord Chaitanya gathered hundreds of devotees together and cleaned the Gundicha Temple in preparation for Jagannath's arrival. In great ecstasy, Lord Chaitanya swept and polished the temple complex until it was immaculate. Chanting "Hare Krishna, Hare Krishna, Krishna Krishna, Hare Hare/ Hare Rama, Hare Rama, Rama Rama, Hare Hare" as He and the others performed their service, Mahaprabhu was contributing in a practical way and teaching His followers a lesson as well: Cleaning the Lord's temple is tantamount to cleaning one's heart.

Lord Jagannath's destination prepared by Lord Chaitanya, the festival was ready to begin. Singers, dancers, and a great number of enthused participants gathered around. The chanting started, the march began, and the massive ropes were pulled. Jagannath was coming down the road in time to the music and fanfare, and no one was more ecstatic than Lord Chaitanya, who was none other than Jagannath Himself in the mood of Radharani. Krishna was finally returning to Her.

In fact, Chaitanya Mahaprabhu relished this exchange for the next twenty years of His manifest pastimes in Puri, where He took part in the Ratha-yatra festival on a yearly basis. His followers have since popularized this festival throughout all of India.

In the mid-1960s, moreover, this Ratha-yatra festival was brought West by His Divine Grace A. C. Bhaktivedanta Swami Prabhupada, founder and spiritual master of the International Society for Krishna Consciousness. Now known as "the Festival of the Chariots," Ratha-yatra is celebrated all over the globe, replicated in all major cities. Today, in fact, people become shocked when they hear the original descriptions brought back from India by the British. They see the love, warmth, gaity and devotion of the whole festival. Rather than criticize India and her culture, people are beginning to see what India has to offer. The Festival of the Chariots is Jagannath Puri's offering to the West.

APPENDIX TWO

devotion and reflection in the Gaudiya Vaishnava tradition [146]

by William H. Deadwyler, Ph. D.

One of the signs of health in a religious tradition is its ability to integrate emotion and intellect so that all thought is energized by feeling, and all feeling is disciplined and directed by thought. A. C. Bhaktivedanta Swami Prabhupada, the founder-*acharya* of the International Society for Krishna Consciousness, recognized this, and in his commentary to the *Bhagavad-gita*, he remarked that devotion and reflection "are interdependent as religion and philosophy. Religion without philosophy is sentiment, or sometimes fanaticism, while philosophy without religion is mental speculation."[147]

The ideal of integrating feeling and thinking in religion is not always or even often realized. More often than not we encounter religious traditions in which the two have been separated. They become two-tier religions, so to speak. The lower tier is made up of a fervently emotional, relentlessly enthusiastic, and obstinately convinced following which understands its tradition's scriptures and "symbols" literally and feels threatened by reason and even education. The upper tier is made up of an urbane intelligentsia, often clergy, which is embarrassed by the naively faithful, and which has worked out a sophisticated piece of intellectual machinery enabling them to indulge in the same language and rituals as the naively faithful while intending something quite different by it—allegiance to a rational ethics or metaphysics, which is what their religion *really* amounts to, mythically conveyed.

I think that this sort of two-tiered religion is religion in a disintegrated form, even though theologies have been composed to justify it, e.g., those of Shankara in the East and Tillich in the West. In such cases the anti-intellectualism of the naively faithful may have justification, given this sort of *trahison des clercs*. At any rate, it is a problem for religions to stay integrated, and all of them go through phases of relative integration and disintegration, although it must be said that there are intrinsic characteristics that may make a particular religion more prone to one or the other. I myself believe that the Vaishnavism of Shri Chaitanya inherently provides for optimal integration of emotion and intellect, but to make the case here would take us too far into theological issues. For now, I just want to show that there was a strong and important intellectual tradition in Chaitanya's movement in India and that this tradition has come with the movement to the West. This intellectual side of Chaitanyite Vaishnavism is not as evident or as well-known as its devotional side, and the tradition has been criticized both here and in India as being deficient in rationality and reflection. For Chaitanyite Vaishnavism does exhibit, on the face of it, many of the features people associate with the lower tier of two-tiered religion. Yet these features would also be found in an integrated religion, even though people may assume that they are incompatible with critical intelligence and rational deliberation.

Let me adduce some features of Chaitanyite Vaishnavism that would lead one to think of it as a lower-tier, non-reflective religion of naive believers.

It is an uncompromisingly devotional tradition. Pure *bhakti*, unalloyed devotional service to God, is at once the means to salvation and salvation itself. Rupa Goswami defines pure devotional service as favorable service to Krishna without endeavor to achieve personal rewards (*karma*) or liberation through mental speculation (*gyan*).[148] The only thing that counts in the end is the purity of one's devotion.

Bhakti is also defined in the *Narada-pancharatra* as "engaging the senses in the service of the Master of the senses (i.e. God)."[149] As a consequence, a salient characteristic of Vaishnava devotional life is an unabashed utilization of the concrete and the sensual. Temples are equipped with lavishly decorated altars bearing opulently dressed images of God; devotees dress in distinctive garb and mark their bodies with sacred signs; much attention is given to the preparation and consumption of elaborate offerings of sanctified vegetarian foodstuffs; long, loud, and colorful public festivals such as the Ratha-yatra are executed with much enthusiasm; and, of course, devotees constantly hear and recite the names, qualities, and activities of Krishna. All these practices are meant to focus the senses and mind of the devotees on God.

Correlative to such devotional activity is a theology which develops and defends the idea of God as someone a person can *really* name, describe, and worship as an image in the temple. Vaishnava theology understands God to be concretely personal, to possess spiritual name, form, qualities, and activities. The descriptions of the persons of Krishna, Rama, Vishnu, etc., in the *Puranas* are not to be taken as allegorical or symbolic.

The distinctive feature, of course, of Chaitanyite Vaishnavism is the emphasis placed on chanting the Hare Krishna *maha-mantra*. Chaitanya taught that chanting God's names was the *yuga-dharma*, the only means of salvation in this age.[150] Chanting is considered to be especially efficacious in the form of *sankirtan*, congregational chanting, in which the *mantra* is sung responsively to the accompaniment of percussion instruments and dancing.[151] Moreover, *sankirtan* is frequently performed in public to attract people to the movement, for Chaitanya's movement was highly evangelistic. Chaitanya himself dispatched followers to preach from door to door, and he personally toured throughout India to propagate his *sankirtan* movement. He held that everyone was eligible for salvation through chanting; caste, sex, race, or learning were irrelevant, and his movement gained many adherents from the socially marginal and disenfranchised.

Chaitanya's attitude is made clear from this story recounted in the *Chaitanya Charitamrita*.[152] While touring South India, Chaitanya encountered a certain brahmin in the temple of Ranga-kshetra. This man daily sat in the temple turning over the pages of the *Bhagavad-gita*, but his constant mispronunciation of the Sanskrit made him the object of general mirth and derision. Chaitanya, however, observed signs of genuine spiritual ecstasy on the brahmin's body, and he asked him what he read in the *Gita* to induce such ecstasy. The brahmin replied that he didn't read anything. He was illiterate and could not understand Sanskrit. Nevertheless, his *guru* had ordered him to read the *Gita* daily, and he complied as best he could. He simply pictured Krishna and Arjuna together on the chariot, and this image of Krishna's merciful dealings with his devotee caused this ecstasy. Chaitanya embraced the brahmin and declared that he was an "authority on reading the *Bhagavad-gita*." The point of the story is that the illiterate brahmin had achieved pure *bhakti* simply because of his fidelity to his *guru's* order, and the commentators cite a verse in this connection from the *Shvetashvatara Upanishad*: "Only unto those great souls who have implicit faith (*para bhakti*) in the Lord and in the *guru* are the imports of the *Vedas* revealed."[153]

Chaitanya himself was quite well-educated. He was born in Nadiya (Navadvip), at the time a center of Sanskrit learning and the seat of Nyaya philosophy.[154] In his youth, Chaitanya himself taught Sanskrit grammar, and he was reputed to be skilled in rhetoric and logic. The change in his behavior after he took initiation from Ishvara Puri, a Vaishnava *sannyasi*, in Gaya, is described by Bhaktivinode Thakur:

> Upon His return to Nadiya, Nimai Pandit (Chaitanya) turned out a religious preacher, and His religious nature became so strongly represented that Adwaita Prabhu, Shrivas, and others...were astonished at the change in the young man. He was then no more a contending *Naiyaik*, a wrangling *Smarta* and a criticising rhetorician. He swooned at the name of Krishna and behaved as an inspired man under the influence of His religious sentiments. . . . It was at this time that He opened a nocturnal school of *kirtan* in the compound of Shrivas Pandit with His sincere followers. There He preached, there He sang, there He danced, and there He expressed all sorts of religious feelings.[155]

These features of Chaitanya and his movement have been the basis for the judgment that it neglects or even disparages the intellect. Since Chaitanyite Vaishnavism grew up in a milieu dominated by a two-tiered religion—I mean the Adwaita Vedanta of Shankara and the *smarta* system he established—that judgment was expressed early on. The *Chaitanya Charitamrita* recounts the meeting between Chaitanya, who was by then a *sannyasi*, and Prakashananda Saraswati, the leader of the Shankarite monks in Benares. Prakashananda Saraswati said to Chaitanya:

> You are a *sannyasi*. Why then do you indulge in chanting and dancing, engaging in your *sankirtan* in the company of fanatics? The sole duties of a *sannyasi* are meditation and the study of Vedanta; why have you abandoned them to dance with fanatics? You look as brilliant as if you were Narayana Himself. Will you explain why you have adopted the behavior of low-class people?[156]

But there was another side to Chaitanya and his movement. The *Chaitanya Charitamrita* recounts two occasions when Chaitanya orally delivered an exacting, sophisticated theistic reading of the *Vedanta-sutras*. One such discourse was offered in answer to Prakashananda Saraswati's criticisms. The other was delivered at Jagannath Puri to Vasudev Sarvabhauma Bhattacharya, a Shankarite and eminent professor of the *navya-nyaya*, who subsequently became Chaitanya's follower.[157]

Moreover, Chaitanya assigned some of his intimate followers to establish *krishna-bhakti* as he preached it, and the *sankirtan* movement itself, on a solid, scholarly and theological foundation. The leaders of this task were Sanatan Goswami and Rupa Goswami, two brothers who quit high ministerial posts in the government of the Nawab Hussain Shah to become disciples of Chaitanya. After taking instruction from Chaitanya, they were dispatched with a large collection of manuscripts to Vrindavan. They were later joined by four other *sannyasi* followers of Chaitanya. The six Goswamis of Vrindavan, as they are called, founded what was in effect a college or school of divinity. They are also responsible for establishing, at Chaitanya's request, Vrindavan as a place of pilgrimage. At that time the place of Krishna's early *lila* was practically wilderness, and the six Goswamis located and restored the sites of Krishna's various pastimes and caused temples to be constructed.

Sanatan, Rupa, and their nephew Jiva were the most prolific writers among the six Goswamis, being credited with four, seventeen, and over twenty works respectively.[158] These include commentaries, devotional verse and dramas, as well as treatises on grammar, systematic theology, and devotional practices and rituals. Rupa Goswami's *Bhakti-rasamrita-sindhu* has become a classic of Indian spirituality. It delineates the proper execution of the techniques and practices of *bhakti-yoga*, and systematically describes the successive stages in spiritual advancement. The work also provides an analytic discussion of spiritual ecstasies and emotions (*bhava*) and shows how to distinguish the genuine from the spurious. Rupa Goswami also adopts the methods and categories of Sanskrit poetics to classify and analyze the spiritual feelings that arise in various relationships between Krishna and his devotees (*rasa*-theology). Thus do emotion and feeling attain a rational, intelligible structure. Rupa Goswami's *Bhakti-rasamrita-sindhu* demonstrates that emotion and even ecstasy can be melded with ordered analytical reflection on that ecstasy.

Jiva Goswami's major contribution is a systematic development, in his *Sat-sandarbha*, of Chaitanya's theology. He also composed a grammar, the *Harinamamrita-vyakarana*, in which the grammatical terms are formed from various names of Krishna.

The intellectual foundation laid by the six Goswamis was built upon by later teachers. We can mention their disciple Krishnadas Kaviraj Goswami, whose Bengali biography of Chaitanya, written probably between 1550 and 1612, is also a compendium of Chaitanyite theology; and, in the eighteenth century, Vishvanath Chakravarti and Baladev Vidyabhushan. The former is noted especially for his *Shrimad Bhagavatam* commentary; the latter, for his *Govinda-bhashya* commentary on the *Vedanta-sutras*. He also wrote commentaries on the *Bhagavad-gita*, the *Shrimad Bhagavatam*, and Jiva Goswami's *Sat-sandarbha*.[159] And in the nineteenth century there was Bhaktivinode Thakur, the author of over one hundred works. He had received a British education and was the first Chaitanya *acharya* to write in English. Bhaktivinode Thakur revitalized Chaitanyite Vaishnavism as a preaching movement and planned its propagation in the West.

When Shrila Prabhupada began to establish Chaitanyite Vaishnavism in America in 1966, the intellectual heritage of the movement was at first not much evident, either to outside observers or to Prabhupada's followers themselves. Most outsiders saw it as just another manifestation of hippiedom, not realizing that while ISKCON may have been *in* the counterculture it most emphatically was not *of* it. For Prabhupada's first disciples the emphasis was on chanting the *maha-mantra,* eating vast quantities of Krishna *prasad*, and getting free from attachment to drugs, sex and rock 'n' roll. Prabhupada's lectures were simple and dwelt on the themes, "human life is meant for self-realization, not sense gratification," and "you are not your body." But as his disciples became more and more purified, Prabhupada introduced more and more elements of Vaishnava culture, and his followers found themselves eventually absorbing a formidable body of teaching.

Prabhupada saw books as the foundation of his movement,[160] and as soon as possible he organized ISKCON into an instrument for producing, publishing, and distributing books. He informed his disciples that the more efficiently they could publish and distribute his books, the more he would write. By studying his books, disciples all over the world could have the association of their spiritual master, and he informed his students that association with him through his books was better than his personal association. By distributing books, Krishna consciousness could be spread efficiently and effectively, for, as Prabhupada's *guru*, Bhaktisiddhanta Saraswati, had said, the printing press was the *brihat-mridanga,* the great drum. The *mridanga* drum used in *sankirtan* could be heard for one street; the printing press could be heard around the world. Furthermore, books demonstrated to the world the authenticity and authority of the Hare Krishna movement; it was not sentimental or contrived, but based on ancient scripture, deep philosophy, and a long and venerable heritage.

This heritage Prabhupada transmitted through his translations and commentaries on the *Bhagavad-gita*, the *Shrimad Bhagavatam*, and the *Chaitanya Charitamrita*, as well as other works such as his "summary study" of Rupa Goswami's *Bhakti-rasamrita-sindhu*, also known as *The Nectar of Devotion*. His commentary on the *Bhagavad-gita* closely follows that of Baladev Vidyabhushan, and his commentary on the *Shrimad Bhagavatam* is indebted to those of Sanatan Goswami, Jiva Goswami, Vishvanath Chakravarti and Baladev Vidyabhushan.

Shrila Prabhupada's books have become widely appreciated in the scholarly community, particularly for their combination of devotion and scholarship. For example, Dr. J. Bruce Long, of the Department of Asian Studies, Cornell University, reviewing *Shri Chaitanya Charitamrita*, remarks:

> Anyone who bothers to give a close reading to the commentary will sense that here, as in his other works, Shrila Bhaktivedanta Swami has combined a healthy mixture of the fervent devotion and aesthetic sensitivity of a devotee and the intellectual rigor of a textual scholar. At no point does he allow the intended meaning of the text to be eclipsed by the promotion of a particular doctrinal persuasion. At the same time, he establishes his doctrinal point of view clearly and convincingly.... [161]

Prabhupada had instituted daily classes on the *Bhagavad-gita* and the *Shrimad Bhagavatam* in ISKCON temples, and he was disturbed by a report in the *Los Angeles Times* (January 11, 1970) that Professor J. F. Staal of Berkeley had rejected an experimental course proposed by devotees on the grounds that ISKCON members "spend too much time chanting to develop a philosophy." Prabhupada answered Staal in a letter to the *Times*, and a scholarly debate ensued between them, by correspondence, over the scriptural validity of chanting. At one point Staal mentioned to Prabhupada that his conversations with ISKCON members had been unsatisfactory, but with Prabhupada, discussion was proceeding on a higher level.[162] Prabhupada found this disturbing, and when he discovered that class attendance and individual study had become slack in many temples, a wave of reform went through the movement. Prabhupada made it clear that it was the duty of his disciples to master the literary and philosophical heritage he was transmitting to them.[163]

Critics of ISKCON have interpreted the injunction against "mental speculation" as intended to make devotees mindless by banishing thought. Prabhupada's actual position was this:

> There is no use in presenting dry speculative theories for sense gratification. Philosophy and science should be engaged to establish the glory of the Lord. Advanced people are eager to understand the Absolute Truth through the medium of science, and therefore a great scientist should endeavor to prove the existence of the Lord on a scientific basis. Similarly, philosophical speculations should be utilized to establish the Supreme Truth as sentient and all-powerful. . . . Scientific knowledge engaged in the service of the Lord and all similar activities are all factually *hari-kirtan,* or glorification of the Lord.[164]

Rupa Goswami had laid down the principle that true renunciation means not rejecting any physical or intellectual facility but engaging it in Krishna's service. Then it counts as *bhakti.*

By 1974 Prabhupada had attracted a number of disciples who had or were in the process of getting doctorate degrees in mathematics, chemistry, economics, Sanskrit, and religion. He had them meet together to form an institute, which the devotees named "Bhaktivedanta Institute," for propagating Krishna consciousness among intellectuals and academics. Prabhupada surprised many devotees by the importance he attached to this endeavor. He called his institute the most important arm in ISKCON, and told its members "the next phase is yours."

It is interesting to note how Prabhupada's actions in establishing the Krishna consciousness movement in the West parallel those of Chaitanya in founding it in India. The *Chaitanya Charitamrita* notes that Chaitanya exhibited "spiritual potencies" in propagating *sankirtan* in South India which he did not exhibit in his native Navadvip. Prabhupada comments that preaching should be done where people are receptive, and because Chaitanya found Navadvip full of unresponsive *smartas,* he went outside his native land to preach. In a similar way, Prabhupada says, he found his native India unresponsive to his attempts to spread Krishna consciousness: "the people of India, being absorbed in political thoughts, did not take to it." Therefore, he took it to the West.[165] And in the same way that Chaitanya in India established Vrindaban as a place of pilgrimage, Prabhupada in America established a "New Vrindaban" as a place of pilgrimage. And in the same way that Chaitanya directed his educated disciples to establish his movement according to the scholarly standards of that time and place, Prabhupada formed his own educated disciples in a body to do the same in the West.

Prabhupada's institute has some further purposes. It is to continue the work of Prabhupada by bringing over from India more and more of the Vaishnava intellectual heritage, and it is to provide higher education to the many academically gifted children now moving up through ISKCON'S school system, where they are already being taught Sanskrit from Jiva Goswami's grammar. In 1975, Prabhupada outlined to me a plan for what he called "ISKCON Bhagavat College"—a university for ISKCON. One feature of this college would be a library housing a complete collection of texts from all the Vaishnava *sampradayas*.

The work of Prabhupada's institute has been inhibited by the necessary period of readjustment ISKCON has gone through after Prabhupada's passing away. In the scientific department, things were somewhat held up by a debate over whether the Christian creationists were a model to be imitated or eschewed. But ISKCON scientists are now breaking new ground, and those who like their science rigorous should appreciate *Mechanistic and Nonmechanistic Science: An Investigation into the Nature of Consciousness and Form*[166] by Richard L. Thompson (Sadaputa Das), who holds a doctorate in mathematics from Cornell.

Those of us working in religious studies and Sanskrit have found at least one common cause with academic scholars of Hinduism, and we have begun a micro-photography project in India to collect, conserve, and make available Vaishnava texts. The project is going on right now and is turning out quite successfully.

What contribution can devotee-scholars make to the field of religious studies? One contribution is simply to present and represent articulately a major religious tradition in the way only those committed to it can, in thought enlivened by feeling. The field of religious studies has learned to be sensitive to the voices of those within a tradition and has recognized that they know their religion in a way no one else can.

And there is possibly another contribution. I mentioned in the beginning that I believe Chaitanyite Vaishnavism provides for a kind of integration of thought and feeling that is rarely seen nowadays. When I first encountered it, this wholeness forcefully struck me. It was highly attractive, and I remember thinking: this is what Christianity must have been like in the Middle Ages.

But we do not live in the Middle Ages, and if what we see today is mostly disintegrated two-tiered religion, it is because religion in the West has had to pass through a Renaissance and an Industrial Revolution and now lives uneasily in a secular culture dominated by naturalism and scientism. All this has left its mark on religion, on the spiritual condition of Western people. We may recognize all too well our disintegration and have seen the truth in Yeats' description—"The best lack all conviction, while the worst/ Are full of passionate intensity." We know our malaise. "This world is too much with us," declared Wordsworth in anguish; "We have given our hearts away," and so he exclaimed that he would "rather be/ A pagan, suckled in a creed outworn." We know what he means, but we can't go back: the past is not available and besides, we know too much.

That's what I thought. But then I encountered Chaitanya's movement. Tucked away in some corner of India, it seemed to have eluded the historical processes going on in the West, to appear suddenly in America in the midst of the twentieth century, whole and integrated—like some living fossil that unaccountably survived a devastation. Something was now available that had not been available before.

But the momentous issue is: If Chaitanyite Vaishnavism had remained whole by not encountering those forces which had broken down Western religion, there was no way, having come West, it could avoid them now. Prabhupada clearly recognized this. He knew that if his tradition were to become established in the West, his disciples in his institute would have to come to grips with those intellectual forces that had led to disintegrated religion in the West—and come out successfully. He believed that he had given us the resources to do so.

It is our task to show that we have reasonable grounds for our convictions. If we have embraced Chaitanya's movement merely out of Romantic nostalgia or Wordsworthian longing or even out of sheer idealistic hope, it will not last. But I believe that we have accepted it because there are the best and most reasonable grounds for doing so. If we are successful in the intellectual task Prabhupada has given us, then we will come out whole. The danger is that Chaitanyite Vaishnavism in the West will gradually disintegrate into a two-tiered religion. No doubt success or failure are each instructive, but success will be the far greater contribution.

William H. Deadwyler, III (Ravindra Swarup Das) has been a member of the In-

ternational Society for Krishna Consciousness since 1971. He received his B.A. in Philosophy from the University of Pennsylvania (1966) and his Ph.D. in Religion from Temple University (1981).

REFERENCES

1. In the following pages, Lord Chaitanya is variously referred to as Nimai, Vishvambhar, Gaur, Mahaprabhu and Chaitanya Mahaprabhu.

2. Since orthodox Vaishnavas, devotees of Krishna, consider Chaitanya Mahaprabhu to be the Supreme Lord Himself, the first letter of all nouns and pronouns referring to Him will be capitalized.

3. His Divine Grace A. C. Bhaktivedanta Swami Prabhupada (trans.), *Shri Chaitanya Charitamrita*, 17 volumes (Los Angeles, Bhaktivedanta Book Trust, 1975), *Adi-lila* 1, ch. 5, text 147, p. 474.

4. Ibid., *Adi-lila* 3, ch. 13, text 1, p. 56.

5. Ibid.

6. Ibid., *Adi-lila* 2, ch. 9, text 5, p.216.

7. M. Hafiz Syed, *Hadith*, trans., *Thus Spake Mohammed* (Madras, Amra Press, 1962), p. 24.

8. *Chaitanya Charitamrita,* op. cit., *Adi-lila* 3, ch. 13, text 42, p. 75.

9. Ibid.

10. Ibid.

11. O.B.L. Kapoor, *The Philosophy and Religion of Sri Caitanya* (Delhi, Munshiram Manoharlal, 1977), p. 6.

12. Ibid.

13. Ibid. It should also be noted that Alvar Kulashekhar Maharaj's realization of devotion (*bhakti*) was so developed that His Divine Grace A. C. Bhaktivedanta Swami Prabhupada, who represented a different disciplic line of teachers, wrote a translation and commentary on his *Mukunda-mala-stotra* entitled "Prayers of King Kulashekhar." This work, however, is as yet unpublished.

14. While Ballabha (who is generally aligned with the Rudra Sampradaya) was philosophically very close to Shankara (the impersonalist), he did acknowledge the worship of Radha and Krishna. For this reason, his doctrine is sometimes considered similar to that of Lord Chaitanya. Nimbarka (who is generally aligned with the Kumara Sampradaya), however, is philosophically still closer to Lord Chaitanya, and he also approved of Radha-Krishna worship.

15. Pandit Rajmani Tigunait, *Seven Systems of Indian Philosophy* (Honesdale, PA., Himalayan Pub., 1983), pp. 4-5.

16. Ibid.

17. Ibid.

18. Dilip Kumar Mukherjee, *Chaitanya* (New Delhi, National Book Trust, 1970), pp. 1-2.

19. Ibid.

20. E. Alan Morinis, *Pilgrimage in the Hindu Tradition: A Case Study of West Bengal* (Delhi, Oxford University Press, 1984), p. 122.

21. Francis Gladwin (trans.), *Ayeen Akbery of Abul Fazl Allami* (Calcutta, The Indian Publishing Soc., 1783), pp. 310-11.

22. Ibid., pp. 310-11.

23. Debnarayan Acharyya, *The Life and Times of Sri Krishna Chaitanya* (Calcutta, Firma KLM Private, 1984), p. 147.

24. Ravindra Swarupa Dasa, "Lord Chaitanya and the Renaissance of Devotion," *Back to Godhead*, Vol. 19, No 4., April 1984.

25. The present town of Navadvip is not the same as old Navadvip (Mayapur) and is consequently not the birthplace of Lord Chaitanya. The Navadvip where Lord Chaitanya was born, now called Shri Mayapur, was rediscovered in the mid-nineteenth century by Shrila Bhaktivinode Thakur and is situated approximately two miles above the confluence of the Bhagirathi and Jalangi Rivers. It should also be noted that the findings of Bhaktivinode Thakur were substanti-

References 175

ated by an archaeological expedition conducted by Sir John Anderson, the then Governor of Bengal.

26. See Bhakti Pradip Tirtha Maharaj, *Sri Chaitanya Mahaprabhu* (Calcutta, Gaudiya Mission, 1947), p. 14. This information was given by Shrila Bhaktivinode Thakur and is considered authoritative. Scholarly differences are based as much on dating techniques as poor scholarship. Dr. B. B. Majumdar suggests that Mahaprabhu was born on February 18 according to the Julian calendar and on February 27 according to the Gregorian calendar. Also, the corresponding *Shaka* Era was 1407, the Bengali Era 892, and the *Sambat* Era was 1542. This information naturally caused some confusion among academics.

27. Upendra Mishra, Lord Chaitanya's grandfather on His father's side, lived at Gupta Vrindavan (also known as Dacca Dhakeen) in Sylhet. Previously known as Shri Hatta, this Sylhet district in northern Bangladesh is where Mahaprabhu's family lineage originates. Today, a devotee named Radhavinode Mishra is the last surviving family descendant of the Mishra clan.

28. Sanskrit *nimba*, the *Azadirachta indica*. Scientists have now extracted the active antiseptic principle of the neem tree, which is called margosic acid.

29. See Sambidananda Das, *Sri Chaitanya Mahaprabhu* (Madras, Sree Gaudiya Math, 1972 reprint), p. 4.

30. Ibid.

31. *Chaitanya Charitamrita*, op. cit., *Adi-lila* 3, ch. 14, texts 14-15, pp. 137-138.

32. Ibid.

33. O. B. L. Kapoor, op. cit., p. 35.

34. *Chaitanya Charitamrita*, op. cit., *Adi-lila* 3, ch. 13, texts 84-86, pp. 98-100.

35. Quoted by Gopinath Acharya in *Chaitanya Charitamrita*, op. cit., *Madhya* 2, ch. 6, text 104, p. 249.

36. Deities of Lord Chaitanya are today worshiped all over Bengal and Orissa, and many of them were installed during the Lord's lifetime. Shrimati Vishnupriya, for instance, began worshipping His Deity form when He left home to take *sannyasa*; this Deity is still in Nadiya. There is also a Deity worshiped in Katwa that was installed by Gadadhar. There are many other examples as well. See O.B.L. Kapoor, op. cit., p. 17.

37. Shrivas Thakur once saw Mahaprabhu manifest His Vishnu form (*Chaitanya Bhagavat* 2.2.256-258). Similarly, the Lord appeared as Varaha Avatar to Murari

Gupta (Ch. B., 2.3) and as Ramachandra as well (Ch. B., 2.10). He appeared in His original form as Krishna to Shridhar (Ch. B., 2.9) and Sachidevi (Ch. B., 2.8). And He also revealed His special six-armed form (*shad-bhuj-murti*) to Nityananda (Ch. B., 2.5), Sarvabhauma Bhattacharya (Ch. B., 2.6), and King Prataparudra (*Kadacha* of Murari Gupta, 3.16.13). He appeared as Govinda to Adwaita Acharya (Ch. B., 2.6), who also saw Mahaprabhu's Universal Form (*Vishvarup*) on one occasion (Ch. B., 2.24).

38. Bhaktivinode Thakur, *Shri Chaitanya Mahaprabhu: His Life and Precepts* (Madras, Sree Gaudiya Math, 1896; reprint, 1984), pp. 60-61.

39. See Krishna Balaram Swami, *Ekadashi: The Day Of Lord Hari* (San Francisco, the Bhaktivedanta Institute, 1986).

40. Not to be confused with the famous Ballabha Acharya of the Rudra Sampradaya.

41. *Chaitanya Charitamrita*, op. cit., *Adi-lila* 3, ch. 15, text 5, p. 185 (purport).

42. Bhaktivinode Thakur, op. cit., p. 6.

43. Ibid., p. 7.

44. There are four recognized lines of disciplic descent: the Shri, Kumara, Rudra, and Brahma *sampradayas*. According to the Vedic literature, anyone who wants genuine spiritual knowledge must search out a qualified teacher in one of these four *sampradayas*.

45. Sambidananda Das, op. cit., p. 23.

46. Bhaktivinode Thakur, op. cit., pp. 7-9.

47. Ibid.

48. Sambidananda Das, op. cit., p. 25.

49. Bhakti Pradip Tirtha Maharaj, op. cit., p. 36.

50. Sambidananda Das, op. cit., p. 26.

51. A. K. Majumdar, *Chaitanya: His Life and Movement* (Bombay, Bharatiya Vidya Bhavan, 1969), p. 137.

52. *Chaitanya Bhagavat*, 1.12.49.

53. *Sampradaya vihina ye, mantras te nishphala matah*. This is stated in the *Padma Purana*.

References

54. Sambidananda Das, op. cit., p. 29.

55. Bhakti Pradip Tirtha Maharaj, op. cit., p.40.

56. *Chaitanya Charitamrita*, op. cit., *Adi-lila* 3, ch. 13, text 74, p. 93 (purport).

57. Ibid., p. 263.

58. O.B.L. Kapoor, op. cit., p. 23.

59. Ibid.

60. Ibid.

61. *Chaitanya Upanishad* (12). By the 1800s, the *Chaitanya Upanishad*, which is appended to the *Atharva Veda*, had become quite rare. In fact, Shrila Bhaktivinode Thakur searched all over Bengal to procure a copy, but he was unsuccessful. When the great devotee Pandit Madhusudana Maharaj had heard of the Thakur's dilemma, he managed to get an ancient hand-written copy of the *Upanishad* and sent it to him. Shrila Bhaktivinode soon wrote a Sanskrit commentary on this work called *Chaitanya Charanamrita*, which was first printed in Calcutta by the Shri Chaitanya Press in 1887. The original *Upanishad* is now available in English: Kushakrata Dasa, *The Glories of Shri Chaitanya Mahaprabhu* (New York, Bala Books, 1984).

62. Jagai and Madhai were actually Jai and Vijai, two great devotees of the Lord who were cursed to take three demonic births before returning to their rightful position in the spiritual world. First, they took birth as Hiranyaksha and Hiranyakashipu. Then, as Ravana and Kumbhakarna. And finally as Shishupal and Dantavakra. After these three incarnations, however, they again took a special birth in the material world. This time as Jagai and Madhai. And in this way they were blessed to take part in Lord Chaitanya's pastimes.

63. It was in Navadvip, too, just after the Jagai and Madhai episode, that Lord Chaitanya popularized religious dramatic performance within the Vaishnava community. The first play to be enacted by Mahaprabhu and His followers was Krishna's marriage to Princess Rukmini, and Lord Chaitanya Himself played the Princess. The performance took place in the house of Chandrashekhar Acharya, and Sadashiva Buddhimanta Khan, a wealthy follower of the *sankirtan* mission, supplied the appropriate costumes. In the months that followed, many such plays, based on the Vedic scriptures, were performed by the devotees of Lord Chaitanya.

64. The Kazi was harassing the devotees for their street chanting. Mahaprabhu could have thus used His confrontation with the Kazi to give an exposition on the theology of the holy name. Instead, however, the Lord chose to discuss meat-eating as the epitome of irreligion. His choice is undoubtedly based on the

Shrimad Bhagavatam (10.1.4), which clearly states that until one gives up the merciless killing of animals, as in the eating of meat, one cannot proceed to more advanced subjects. His Divine Grace A. C. Bhaktivedanta Swami Prabhupada scrupulously followed this example whenever he engaged in interreligious dialogue, for he felt that one could never understand God's mercy if one is not himself merciful to others.

65. This has been more fully explained in my *Food for the Spirit: Vegetarianism and the World Religions* (New York, Bala Books, 1987).

66. Vaishnava tradition recognizes the Old Testament, the New Testament, and the Koran as divine revelations, but only for a particular time, place, and circumstance. Their compilation has a history within this world and thus they are not eternal. Absolute knowledge, however, is found in the *Vedas*, which cannot be traced to one particular prophet at a given point in history. Also see *Chaitanya Charitamrita*, op. cit., *Adi-lila* 3, ch. 17, text 169, p. 347 (purport).

67. Sambidananda Das, op. cit., p. 48.

68. Ibid., p. 50.

69. Usually, *sannyasis* of the impersonalist school receive names such as "Puri" or "Bharati." But *"Krishna Chaitanya"* is not a name traditionally given to the impersonalists. Actually, the name secretly prophesied that Mahaprabhu would spread "consciousness" (*chaitanya*) of Krishna across the land.

Also, it is sometimes said that "Krishna Chaitanya" was the Lord's *brahmachari* name as well. At *sannyasa* initiation the name of a *brahmachari* is customarily changed. Thus, in not changing the Lord's name, Keshava Bharati was perhaps giving further indication that he was not in actuality initiating the Lord into the impersonalist school. (See His Divine Grace A. C. Bhaktivedanta Swami Prabhupada, "The Teachings of Lord Chaitanya," *Back to Godhead,* No. 43, p. 8.)

70. For specific details of the Sakshi Gopal miracle, see *Chaitanya Charitamrita*, op. cit., *Madhya-lila* 2, chapter 5.

71. Jagannath Suta Dasa and Damodar Dasa, "Puri: City of Jagannath, Lord of the Universe," *Back to Godhead*, Vol. 11, No. 6, June 1976, p. 17.

72. Ibid., p. 18.

73. Sambidananda Das, op. cit., p. 88.

74. *Chaitanya Charitamrita*, op. cit., *Madhya-lila* 6, ch. 15, text 278, p. 146.

75. Ibid., *Adi-lila* 3, ch. 17, text 229, p. 375.

References

76. J. Stillson Judah, *Hare Krishna and the Counterculture* (New York, John Wiley & Sons, 1974), pp. 8-9.

77. One may wonder why a *shudra* (laborer) was employed as the governor of Rajahmundry, which is normally a job for a *kshatriya* (administrator). Actually, Ramananda Roy belonged to the "Kayastha" *shudra* class, a special group of *shudras* who were often employed as lawyers and politicians as well as laborers.

78. He was a disciple of Raghavendra Puri, who in turn was a disciple of Madhavendra Puri (Mahaprabhu's grand spiritual master).

79. Once, a priest named Pradyumna Mishra came to Mahaprabhu and desired to hear about Krishna from His lips. But the Lord humbly responded that He knew next to nothing about Krishna and that Pradyumna should instead go to Shri Ramananda, who was expert in the subject of Krishna consciousness. Pradyumna wanted to comply but was reluctant because he had seen Shri Ramananda teaching song and dance to the *devi-dasis*, dancing girls, of the Jagannath temple, and these girls were sometimes considered to be of questionable character. Mahaprabhu, however, assured Pradyumna Mishra: "You go to Ramananda Roy! He is completely in control of his senses. And no one knows Krishna in the way that he does!" In fact, Pradyumna went back to Shri Ramananda and studied under his able tutelage, marveling at the sage's love of God.

80. *Chaitanya Charitamrita*, op. cit., *Antya-lila* 5, ch. 18, text 18, p. 127.

81. Sambidananda Das, op. cit., p. 95.

82. Ibid.

83. Jagat-guru Swami and Bhavananda Raya Dasa, "Visit to Shri Rangam," *Back to Godhead*, Vol. 20, No. 11, November 1985, pp. 32-35.

84. *Chaitanya Charitamrita*, op. cit., *Madhya-lila* 6, ch. 16, text 84, p. 203.

85. See Kavi Karnapur's *Chaitanya Chandrodaya Natakam* (Act 7).

86. Bhaktisiddhanta Sarasvati, *Rai Ramananda* (Madras, Shree Gaudiya Math, 1932; reprint, 1975), p. 27.

87. Most of the information in this chapter is elaborately dealt with in Miles Davis, *Vraja Mandala Darshana: Touring the Land of Krishna* (El Cerrito, CA., International Institute of Indology, 1984), pp. 23-27.

88. *Chaitanya Charitamrita*, op. cit., *Madhya-lila* 7, ch. 17, texts 226 & 227, pp. 124-125.

89. Shrila Bhaktivinode Thakur listed the advent and ascension dates of all six Goswamis in his journal "Sajjana-toshani," Vol. 2, 1882. Also see Bhakti Pradip Tirtha Maharaj, op. cit., p. 98.

90. *Chaitanya Charitamrita*, op. cit., *Madhya-lila* 7, ch. 19, text 40, p. 266.

91. According to one's desire and *karma* (the law of action and reaction) an entity incarnates in one particular body or another. If one acts like an animal, the *Vedas* explain, there are suitable bodies to facilitate such activities. Similarly, if one is interested in spiritual pursuits, there are bodies that are best suited for this as well.

92. *Chaitanya Charitamrita*, op. cit., *Madhya-lila* 1, ch. 1, text 258, p. 150.

93. Murari Gupta's *Kadacha*, ch. 25, text 160. Also see Sambidananda Das, op. cit., p. 185.

94. M. A. Sherring, *The Sacred City of the Hindu: An Account of Benares in Ancient and Modern Times* (London, Trubner & Co., 1868), p. 7.

95. Mark Twain, *Following the Equator: A Journey Around the World* (Hartford, The American Pub. Co., 1898), p. 480.

96. Count Hermann Keyserling, *Indian Travel Diary of a Philosopher* (Bombay, Bharatiya Vidya Bhavan, 1969), pp. 118-22.

97. Shiva is distinct among the demigods, and in a very conditional sense he is considered the Supreme Being. He is not Supreme, however, for that is Krishna's role. Still, according to Vaishnava tradition, he is the best servant of the Supreme, as is confirmed in the *Puranas* ("*vaisnavanam yatah shambhu*"). He is also the master of the mode of ignorance and is in charge of universal destruction.

98. Diana Eck, *Benares: City of Light* (Princeton, Princeton University Press, 1982), p. 210.

99. It might at this point be mentioned that Sanatan Goswami also had a severe case of eczema and sometimes would bleed from sores on his body. Everytime Mahaprabhu saw him, however, He embraced the Goswami, indifferent to the blood that would ooze from his sores onto the Lord's sacred body. Yet Sanatan found this to be intolerable. And he begged the Lord not to embrace him anymore. He threatened to commit suicide, in fact, if the Lord were to again touch him while he was bleeding in this way. Mahaprabhu then chastised Sanatan: "Don't you know that you have surrendered your body to Krishna?" the Lord asked him. "If your life is Krishna's, then you have no right to end it. That is up to Him." See *Letters from Shrila Prabhupada*, Vol. II (Culver City, CA., The Vaishnava Institute, 1987), p. 731.

References

100. *Chaitanya Charitamrita*, op. cit., *Madhya-lila* 8, p. 1.

101. Cited in the *Brihan-naradiya Purana*.

102. *Chaitanya Charitamrita*, op. cit., *Madhya-lila* 9, ch. 25, text 176, p. 395.

103. Previously, the Lord had converted large numbers of Buddhists and Muslims to Vaishnavism. In addition, He had preached to many impersonalists, including Sarvabhauma Bhattacharya, and they too came to be convinced of the Lord's perspective. But when Mahaprabhu persuaded Prakashananda Saraswati of Benares to become a Vaishnava, He became more widely renowned than ever before. This was due to the fact that Prakashananda was the major impersonalist philosopher of India at that time.

104. A. N. Chatterjee, *Shri Krishna Chaitanya: A Historical Study on Gaudiya Vaishnavism* (New Delhi, Associated Publishing, 1983), pp. 27-28.

105. Ibid.

106. Shridhar Swami (circa, 1350-1450) was an eminent scholar of Benares and author of many books. His historic commentary on *Shrimad Bhagavatam*, called the *Bhavartha Dipika*, is greatly respected by the Vaishnava community and is even accepted as divinely inspired by Mahaprabhu.

107. *Chaitanya Charitamrita*, op. cit., *Antya-lila* 3, ch. 7, texts 115-20, pp. 56-58.

108. Ibid., text 171, p. 81.

109. Being influenced by immediate followers of Mahaprabhu, other famous personalities were moved by His teaching, including the Maharastran saint Tukaram (1608-1650) and even the great Muslim Emperor Akbar (1556-1605). Tukaram refers to three Krishna worshippers as his teachers (see *The Poems of Tukaram*, ed. J. Nelson Fraser, Vol. 1, No. 80, p. 31). Shrila Prabhupada, however, says that Tukaram was initiated by Mahaprabhu Himself (which would mean that the traditional biographical dates ascribed to Tukaram are off by at least one hundred years). There is a tradition in Maharastra that attempts to resolve this conflict by positing that Tukaram was initiated by Mahaprabhu in a dream.

Nonetheless, it is certain that Akbar, being influenced by Jiva Goswami, composed a beautiful poem about Lord Chaitanya:

> "Hail Thee O Chaitanya—the victor of my heart,
> Mark the rhythm of his mystic dance
> In lofty ecstasy quite alone.
> Merrily sounds the tabor
> And the cymbals' notes keep time.
> The joyous band following him
> Sing and Dance, merrily, merrily.

> He steps a pace or two onwards
> In his dancing gait, and knows no rest.
> For he is intoxicated
> With his own overflowing joy.
> O, my heart's Lord, how can I express
> The love I have for thee?
> Shah Akbar craves a drop
> From the sea of thy love and piety."

Also see Dinesh Chandra Sen, *Chaitanya and His Age* (Calcutta, Univ. of Calcutta, 1922).

110. Ganda Singh, "Guru Nanak at Puri with Sri Chaitanya and His Followers," *The Punjab Past and Present*, Vol. III, Parts 1 and 2 (Patiala, Punjabi University Press, 1969), pp. 334-39.

111. Trilochan Singh, *Guru Nanak: Founder of Sikhism* (Delhi, Gurdwara Parbandhak Committee, 1969), pp. 232-42.

112. *Journal of Sikh Studies Vol. III*, No. 2 (Amritsar, Guru Nanak Dev University, August, 1976), pp. 158-72.

113. According to Vedic tradition, apart from actually having sex, there are seven kinds of sexual subtleties that must be avoided by one who is truly celibate: one should not dally with, look lustfully at, think about or talk about the opposite sex. Nor should one talk *to* a member of the opposite sex or even plan to engage in sex. Finally, one should not make any endeavor which can possibly lead to sexual activity. (See *Shrimad Bhagavatam*, 6.1.14, purport)

114. Chota Haridas is not to be confused with Haridas Thakur.

115. *Chaitanya Charitamrita*, op. cit., *Antya-lila* 4, ch. 13, text 85, p. 157.

116. Ibid., ch. 12, text 59, p. 77.

117. Ibid. *Antya-lila* 1, ch. 2, text 118, p. 180.

118. See A. N. Chatterjee, op. cit., pp. 27-28.

119. *Chaitanya Charitamrita*, op. cit., *Antya-lila* 4, ch. 14, texts 24-30, pp. 198-201.

120. A. N. Chatterjee, op. cit., p. 28.

121. Ibid.

122. *Chaitanya Charitamrita*, op. cit., *Antya-lila* 5, ch. 16, text 49, p. 27.

123. Ibid., text 74, p. 38.

References

124. Previously, Shiva had initiated Mayadevi into the chanting of Rama's holy name. But now Haridas Thakur was formally initiating her into the chanting of Krishna's name, which she says is superior. "The holy name of Rama gives liberation," she says, "but the holy name of Krishna alone brings one to love of God." (See C.C., *Antya-lila* 1, ch. 3, texts 256-57, p. 339.)

125. I have included numbers to distinguish all seven effects of the chanting process.

126. Bhakti Pradip Tirtha Maharaj, op. cit., p. 43 (Appendix II, footnote).

127. I have numbered these symptoms for the readers' convenience.

128. Dilip Kumar Mukherjee, op. cit., p. 56.

129. *Chaitanya Charitamrita*, op. cit., *Antya-lila* 5, ch. 18, pp. 119-77.

130. Bhaktisiddhanta Sarasvati, op. cit., p. 28.

131. Dinesh Chandra Sen, for instance.

132. See Bhaktivinode Thakur, *Sri Chaitanya Mahaprabhu: His Life and Precepts*, published as a prologue to His Divine Grace A. C. Bhaktivedanta Swami Prabhupada, *Teachings of Lord Chaitanya* (Culver City, CA., Bhaktivedanta Book Trust, 1974 reprint), p. *xxii*.

133. Bhaktisiddhanta Sarasvati, op. cit., p. 28.

134. Recorded conversation of His Divine Grace A. C. Bhaktivedanta Swami Prabhupada and disciple, Hayagriva Dasa, "Outline of Lord Chaitanya Play," San Francisco, April 5 & 6, 1967. Available from the Bhaktivedanta Tape Ministry, Culver City, California.

135. *Jagannath Charitamrita* 7; for more details see Prabhat Mukherjee, *The History of Medieval Vaishnavism in Orissa* (New Delhi, Asian Educational Services, 1981).

136. Traditionally, Gaudiya Vaishnavas prefer to be aware of the disappearance stories without "dwelling" upon them. Naturally, such pastimes tend to evoke a sense of tragedy in the heart of a loving devotee. Therefore, in a sense, I may be accused of departing from tradition. Simultaneously, however, the tradition gives details of Lord Krishna's disappearance and that of great Vaishnavas as well. The central point, then, is not so much to avoid meditating upon the disappearance of the Lord as such. Rather, one should avoid meditating on it as a mundane event. Under proper guidance in disciplic succession, moreover, it is one's duty to learn how to see the Lord's disappearance as one of His transcendental activities.

137. F S. Growse, *Mathura: A District Memoir*, part 1 (Mathura, Northwestern Provinces and Oudh Government Press, 1883), p. 122.

138. Ibid.

139. Ibid., p. 123.

140. Gosvami Nabhaji, *Bhaktamal* (Hindi edition, with notes by Priyadaji, Lucknow, fifth edition, 1961), p. 612. Also see A. N. Chatterjee, op. cit., p. 96.

141. Narahari Chakravarti, *Bhakti-ratnakar*, ed. Nandulal Vidyasagar (Calcutta, second edition, 1940), ch. 2, pp. 60-61.

142. Prabhat Mukherjee, op. cit., p. 168.

143. Mahaprabhu did not previously write a commentary on Vyasadev's *Vedanta Sutra* because He considered *Shrimad Bhagavatam* the "natural" commentary, having been written by Vyasadev himself.

144. Prabhat Mukherjee, op. cit., p. 168.

145. *Chaitanya Bhagavat, Antya-lila*, chapter 4, text 126: *pritivite ache yata nagaradi gram, sarvatra prachar haibe mora nama*: "In every town and village of the world, the chanting of My name will be heard." Also see *Chaitanya Charitamrita*, op. cit., *Adi-lila* 2, ch. 9, texts 34-36, pp. 232-33.

146. This article was originally published as "The Scholarly Tradition in Chaitanyite Vaishnavism: India and America" in *ISKCON Review*, Vol. 1, No. 1 (Philadelphia, PA., Bhaktivedanta Institute of Religion and Culture, 1985), pp. 15-23.

147. His Divine Grace A. C. Bhaktivedanta Swami Prabhupada, *Bhagavad-gita As It Is* (New York, Macmillan Publishing Co., 1972), p. 164.

148. Rupa Goswami, *Bhakti-rasamrita-sindhu*, 1.1.11.

149. *Hrishikena hrishikesha-sevanam bhaktir uchyate*. Quoted in Rupa Goswami's *Bhakti-rasamrita-sindhu*, 1.1.2.

150. He frequently quoted this text from the *Brihan-naradiya Purana* (38.126): "In this Kali-yuga there is no alternative, no alternative, no alternative for spiritual progress than the name of Hari, the name of Hari, the name of Hari."

151. Lord Chaitanya wrote eight verses, called *Shikshashtaka*; this being His only composition. *Sankirtan* is especially glorified in the first of these eight verses. For more details see Chapter Fifteen of this work.

References

152. *Chaitanya Charitamrita*, op. cit., *Madhya-lila* 9, 93-107.

153. *Shvetashvatara Upanishad*, 6.23.

154. Nyaya is one of the six schools of orthodox Hindu philosophy. It deals with the science of correct reasoning, i.e. logic.

155. Bhaktivinode Thakur, op. cit., pp. 5-6.

156. *Chaitanya Charitamrita*, op. cit., *Adi-lila* 2, pp. 51-53.

157. Shri Chaitanya's meeting with Prakashananda Saraswati is found in *Chaitanya Charitamrita*, *Adi-lila*, Chapter Seven. His meeting with (Vasudeva) Sarvabhauma Bhattacharya occurs in *Madhya-lila*, Chapter Six.

158. S. K. De, *Early History of the Vaisnava Faith and Movement in Bengal*, Second Edition (Calcutta, Firma K. L. Mukhopadhyay, 1961), pp. 151-159, gives a list.

159. See Surendranath Dasgupta, *A History of Indian Philosophy*, Vol. 4 (Delhi, Motilal Banarsidass, 1975); Chapter Thirty-three describes the philosophy of Jiva Goswami and Baladev Vidyabhushan.

160. He once summed up ISKCON with the slogan: "Books are the basis; preaching, the essence; utility, the principle; and purity, the force."

161. *The Krishna Consciousness Movement is Authorized* (Los Angeles, Bhaktivedanta Book Trust, 1975), p. 16.

162. See the entire exchange in A. C. Bhaktivedanta Swami Prabhupada, *The Science of Self Realization* (Los Angeles, Bhaktivedanta Book Trust, 1977), pp. 90-104.

163. Shrila Prabhupada wrote many letters concerning the vital necessity for all devotees to study his books. Two of these important letters are quoted verbatim by Satsvarupa Das Goswami in *Vaishnava Behavior* (Port Royal, PA., Gitanagari Press, 1983), pp. 61-62.

164. *Shrimad Bhagavatam*, First Canto, Vol. 1, p. 269.

165. *Chaitanya Charitamrita*, op. cit., *Madhya-lila* 3, p. 54.

166. Lynbrook, New York, Bala Books, 1981.

INDEX

Abhidheya, 121, 122
Absolute Truth, 118, 120
  See also Realization, levels of
Achintya-bhedabheda-tattva, 8, 9
Achyutananda, 143
Adoration, neutral position of passive, 81
Adwaita Acharya, 16, 42, 43, 58, 64, 129
Akbar, Emperor, 148, 181*n*.109
Alexander the Great, 9
Allahabad, 104
Alvar Kulashekhar Maharaj, 174*n*.13
Alvars, 5-6
Ananta-samhita, 20
Andal, 6
Aring (Aritagram), 105
Arjuna, 79
Atmarama verse, 71-72
Atma ("self"), 51
Avesha, 121, 122

Balabhadra, 104, 109-10
Baladev Vidyabhushan, 148-49, 153, 157, 166, 167
Balaram, manifestation of, 41-42
Ballabha, 8, 27, 174*n*.14
Ballabhacharya, 127-28
Bangladesh, journey to, 34-35
Benares, 104, 115-16
  association with Shiva, 116-17
  Mahaprabhu in, 117
  Sanatan Goswami at, 117
  sankirtan movement in, 124-25
Bhagavad-gita, 3, 4, 80, 81, 145, 161, 163, 167
Bhagavan Acharya, 129, 130
Bhagavan realization, 119, 120
Bhakta, 119
Bhakti, 168
  Alvars and, 6
  defined, 162-63
  electrical devotion, 41
  path of devotion, 63
  renaissance, 12
Bhakti-rasamrita-sindhu, 113, 165, 167
Bhaktiratnakar (Narahari Chakravarti), 143
Bhaktisiddhanta Sarasvati, Shrila, iii-iv, 2, 37, 40, 85, 143, 166
Bhaktivinode Thakur, Shrila, 2, 21, 28, 34, 59, 117, 136, 142, 149, 150, 164, 166, 177*n*.61
Bhakti-yoga (devotional service to God), ii, 47, 55, 61, 81, 165
Bhandarkar, R.G., 6
Bharginadi river, 65
Bhavananda Roy, 129
Bhavartha Dipika (Shridhar Swami), 181*n*.106
Bhirabhadra, 149
Bhubaneshwar, Museum of, 157
Bilvamangal Thakur, 4
Biographies, authorized, 17-18

Bipin Bihari Das Gupta, 130
Bodily symptoms of divinity, 16–17
Brahma, Lord, 43
Brahmajyoti, 118
Brahma-Madhva Sampradaya, 3
Brahmanas, 56
Brahmanda Purana, 46
Brahman realization, 117–18, 120
Brahma-samhita, 4
Brahma-yamala, 19–20
Brishabhanu, King, 43
British, Ratha-yatra festival and, 152–54
Buchanan, Claudius, 153
Buddha, 7
Buddhists, conversion of, 90–91

Caste system, 79–80
Celibacy, 182n.113
Chadoganga Deva, King, 156
Chaitanya, Lord
  achievements, iii
  on *atmarama* verse, 71–72
  aversion to opulence, 93–94
  Ballabhacharya and, 127–28
  at Bangladesh, 34–35
  in Benares, 117
  birth, 15–16
  conversations with Vyenkata Bhatta, 87–88
  conversion of Buddhists, 90–91
  conversion of Chand Kazi by, 53–59
  Dabir Khas and, 100–102
  defeat of Keshava Kashmiri, 31–36
  on devotional service, 112
  on devotional sweetness, 112–13
  disappearance of, 141–45, 183n.136
  divinity of, 16–21, 25–26
  education of, 164
  encounter with *pathans* (Muslim soldiers), 109–10
  at Gambhira Lila, 136–38
  as God, 144–45
  Gopalaji and, 106
  at Govardhan Hill, 105–6
  as greatest scholar, 34
  Guru Nanak and, 128
  Haridas Thakur and, 133–35
  ideal asceticism of, 129–32
  illiterate Brahmana and, 88–90
  infancy and youth, 23–30
  initiation in Gaya, 37–44
  instruction on *Vedanta Sutra*, 69–70
  Jagannath of, 88
  Kalidas and, 132
  Kavi Karnapur and, 132–33
  at Khadiravana, 106
  at Khelanavana, 106–7
  King Prataparudra and, 93–102
  manifestations of, 175n.37
  marriage, 29
  at Mathura, 104–5
  miracles of, 76–78
  at Nandagram, 106
  as Nimai the scholar, 28–29
  Nityananda Prabhu's breaking the Lord's staff, 65–66
  in Orissa, 93
  Prakashananda Saraswati and, 122–25
  at Radha kunda, 105
  Ramananda Roy and, 73, 76, 78–85, 95–98, 129, 136, 138, 179n.77
  Ratha-yatra festival and, 151, 158–59
  reasons for appearance in this world, 83
  renunciation, 61–66
  return to Puri, 127–39
  Rupa Goswami and, 109–14
  Sakara Mallik and, 100–102
  Sarvabhauma Bhattacharya and, 67–73
  at Sheshashai, 106
  Shikshashtakam prayers, 138–39
  at Shri Rangam, 87–91
  at Shyama kunda, 105
  on the soul, 111–12
  teachings in West, 149–50
  tricked by Nityananda, 64–65
  on Vedanta, 124
  on *Vedanta-sutra*, 70–71
  visual description, 17
  at Vrindavan, 103–8
  on women, 130–31
Chaitanya Bhagavat, 63
Chaitanya Bhagavat (Ishvara Das), 128, 143
Chaitanya Bhagavat (Vrindavandas Thakur), 17, 18, 33–34
Chaitanya Charanamrita (Bhaktivinode Thakur), 177n.61
Chaitanya Charitamrita, iv, ix, x, 141, 163, 164–65, 167, 168
Chaitanya Mangala (Jayananda), 18, 142
Chaitanya Mangala (Lochandas), 18
Chaitanya Upanishad, 177n.61
Chandidas, 5
Chand Kazi, conversion of, 53–59

Index

Chandrashekhar, 37, 63
Chandrashekhar Vaidya, 117
Chanting, 163
   three stages of, 49
   ways of, 45–46
   See also Hare Krishna *maha-mantra*
Chota ("junior") Haridas, 130
Clay/pot philosophy, 25
Confidential knowledge, 83
Conjugal relationship, 82
Consciousness, Krishna, 82

Dabir Khas, 100–102
Danda-bhanga, Nityananda Prabhu's historic act of, 65–66
Danda-bhanga-nadi (river), 65
Dashashvamedha Ghat, 111
Dasya-rasa, 113
da Vinci, L., 12
De, S.K., 125
Death, natural, 142
Debate, Sanskrit, 31
Deity worship, 154–55
Delusions of love, 84–86
Desires, material, 112
Devotional service, 112
Devotion and reflection in Gaudiya Vaishnava tradition, 161–71
Disappearance stories, 141–45, 183n.136
Disciplic succession, iii, xii
Divakara Das, 143
Divine madness, 39–40
Divinity of Lord Chaitanya, 16–21
   revelation to *brahmana*, 25–26
Dramatic performance, religious, 177n.63
Drowning at sea, 141–42
Dung, cow, 70–71
Dvaita, doctrine of, 8

Eck, Diana, 116
Ekadashi Day, 26
Electrical devotion (*bhakti*), 41
Europe, Renaissance in, 1–2, 12
Evidence of divinity, scriptural, 18–21

Festival of the Chariots. *See* Ratha-yatra festival
Francis, St., 1
Fraternal relationship with Krishna, 82

Gadadhar Pandit, 42–43, 63, 129

Gambhira Lila, 136–38
Ganda Singh, 128
Gangadas Pandit, 28
Ganges
   bathing in, 27–28
   glorification of, 32
Gaudiya Vaishnavism, 3
Gauranga-stava-kalpavriksha, 137
Gaya, initiation in, 37–44
Ghosh, Mrinal K., 130
Gita-govinda (Jayadeva), 5
Gitavali, 59
Gopalaji, Deity of, 106
Gopal Bhatta, 88, 89, 129, 147
   See also Goswamis of Vrindavan, six
Gopal Guru, 128
Gopinath Acharya, 29, 69, 75, 76, 130, 149
Gopis, spiritual love of, 82
Goswamis, 147–48
Goswamis of Vrindavan, six, 89, 129, 165
   See also Gopal Bhatta
Govardhan Hill (Giriraj), 105–6
Govinda, 136
Govinda-bhashya (Baladev Vidyabhushan), 166
Gundicha Temple, 155, 157, 158
Guru (spiritual master), 47, 49
   sannyasa, 62–63
Guru Nanak, 128
Gyan, 63
Gyan-yoga, 118

Hadai Pandit, 42
Hare Krishna *maha-mantra*, 45–52, 163
   defined, 46
   inverted mantra, 48
   name and shadow, 48–49
   science of sound and, 47
   ten offenses, 49–50
   three stages of chanting, 49
   ultimate goal of, 51–52
   ways of chanting, 45–46
Haridas Thakur, 43–44, 54, 129, 133–35, 142, 183n.124
   passing of, 135–36
Harinamamrita-vyakarana (Jiva Goswami), 165–66
Hinduism, misconceptions surrounding, 9–10
Hridai Chaitanya, 149
Humanism, 1–2

Hussain Shah, Nawab, 53, 57, 68

Idol worship, 154–55
Impersonalist school, 178n.69
India
   devotional renaissance in, 2
   foreign invaders of, 10–11
   map of, 14
   origin of name, 9
Indradyumna, 155
Initiation in Gaya, 37–44
Intellectual side of Chaitanyite Vaishnavism, 162, 165–71
International Society for Krishna Consciousness, iii, 3, 159, 161, 166, 167–68, 169
Inverted mantra, 48
Ishvara Das, 128, 143
Ishvara Puri, Shri, 29–30, 38, 39–40, 164
ISKCON. *See* International Society for Krishna Consciousness

Jagadananda Pandit, 129
Jagai, 54–55, 128, 177n.61
Jagannath, Lord
   festival of, 151–59
   merging with, 143–44
   story of, 155–56
   temple of, 67–73
Jagannath Charitamrita (Divakara Das), 143
Jagannath Das Babaji, 149
Jagannath Mutt, Shri, 88
Jagannath (Purandara) Mishra (father), 15, 25, 26, 28, 29
Jagannath Puri, 64, 65, 66, 156–57
   Ratha-yatra festival in, 152
   See also Puri
Jahnavidevi, 149
Jaiyada Nrisingha, 78
Jangli, 128
Janma Bhumi, 104
Jayadeva Goswami, 5
Jayananda, 18, 142
Jesus Christ, 3–4
Jiva, 129
Jiva Goswami, Shri, 19, 147–48, 149, 165–66
Judah, J. Stillson, 77

Kalidas, 129, 132
Kalisantarana Upanishad, 46, 48
Kanai, temple of, 40

Kanair Natshala, visit to, 40
Kapoor, O.B.L., iii–iv
Kapoteshvar temple, 65
Karabhajana Muni, 19
Karma, 180n.91
Kashi. *See* Benares
Kasi Mishra, 129, 136, 142
Kavi Karnapur, 17–18, 91, 132–33, 141
Keshava Bharati, 62–63, 178n.69
Keshavadev, Deity of, 104
Keshava Kashmiri, defeat of, 31–36
Keyserling, Count Hermann, 116
Khadiravana, 106
Khelanavana, 106–7
Kirtan, 45, 128
Knowledge, confidential, 83
Krishna, Lord, 52, 151
   childhood pastimes, 106–7
   conjugal relationship with, 82
   departure of, 144, 145
   expansions of, 120–22
   fraternal relationship with, 82
   as nondifferent from His name, 46–47
Krishna, meaning of, 46
Krishna consciousness, 9, 82
Krishnadas, 75, 109–10
Krishnadas Kaviraj Goswami, Shrila, v, vi, ix, x, 18, 34, 83, 91, 107, 114, 124–25, 125, 138, 141, 142, 166
Krishna Karnamrita (Bilvamangal Thakur), 4
Krishna Lilamrita (Ishvara Puri), 30
Krishna-yamala, 20
Kulashekhar, Maharaj, Alvar, 6, 174n.13
Kurmadev, temple of, 76

Lakshahira, 133
Lakshman Sen, 10, 11
Lakshmidevi (wife), 27–28, 29
   passing of, 35–36
Lalitadevi, 78
Lalita-madhava, 114
Lochandas, 18
Long, J. Bruce, 167
Lord Chaitanya: His Life and Precepts (Bhaktivinode Thakur), 149, 150
Love, delusions of, 84–86
Luther, Martin, 1

Madan Mohan, temple of, 148
Madhai, 54–55, 128, 177n.61
Madhava Mishra, 42

Index

Madhavidevi, 129, 130
Madhurya-rasa, 6, 113
Madhusudana, Deity of Shri, 37
Madhvacharya, 8
Madhva Sampradaya, 8
Madness, divine, 39-40
Mahabharata, 20
Mahabhava prakash, 58-59
Maha-mantra, Hare Krishna, 45-52, 83-84, 163
 defined, 46
 inverted mantra, 48
 name and shadow, 48-49
 "Pancha-tattwa," 51-52
 science of sound and, 47
 ten offenses, 49-50
 three stages of chanting, 49
 ultimate goal of, 51-52
 ways of chanting, 45-46
Mahamaya (illusory energy), 27
Mahaprabhu. *See* Chaitanya, Lord
Maho purusha lakshanas, 16-17
Majumdar, A. K., 125
Majumdar, B. B., 125, 130
Man Singh of Amber, King, 148
Mantra
 divine madness and, 39-40
 inverted, 48
Marriage of Lord Chaitanya, 29
Material pleasure, insufficiency of, 50-51
Mathura, city of, 104-5
Mathura Mahatmya (Rupa & Sanatan), 147
Maulana Sirajuddin Khan (Chand Kazi), 53-59
Mayadevi, 183*n*.124
Mayavadis, 122-24
Miracles, 76-78
Muhammed Bakhtiar Khilji, 11
Mujahphara Khan, 53
Mukunda Dutt, 63
Murari Gupta, vii, 17, 35, 45, 141
Muslim soldiers, Lord Chaitanya's encounter with, 109-10

Nagar Purushottama, 128
Nandagram, 106
Nanda Maharaj, 106
Narada Muni, 43
Narada-pancharatra, 162
Narahari Chakravarti, 143, 148
Narottam Das Thakur, 148

Navadvip, 11-12, 174*n*.14
Nava-Kishor Krishna, 40
Navya-nyaya, 11, 68
Nilambar Chakravarti, 15, 16
Nimai, Shri, 16-17, 28-29
 See also Chaitanya, Lord
Nimbarka, 174*n*.14
Nityananda Prabhu, 41-42, 54-55, 58, 63, 64-65, 75, 91, 95, 128, 129, 149

Odoric, Friar, 153
Offenses, ten, 49-50
Opulence, aversion to, 93-94

Padma Purana, 47
"Pancha-tattwa" *maha-mantra*, 43, 51-52
Paramananda Puri, 63, 90
Paramananda Sen. *See* Kavi Karnapur
Paramatma realization, 118-19, 120
Parashuram, 52
Pathans, 109-10
Path of devotion (*bhakti*), 63
Path of knowledge (*gyan*), 63
Pinda-dan (*shraddha*), 37, 38
Pleasure, insufficiency of material, 50-51
Prabandham, 6
Prabhodananda Saraswati, 87, 88
Prabhupada, A.C. Bhaktivedanta Swami, i, iii, iv, vi, ix, x, 2-3, 20, 77, 125, 143, 150, 159, 161, 166-70, 174*n*.13, 178*n*.64
Pradyumna Mishra, 179*n*.79
Prahlad Maharaj, 43
Prakashananda Saraswati, 122-25, 164, 165, 181*n*.103
 conversion of, 124-25
Prapatti (self-surrender), 6
Prataparudra, King, 93-102
 Lord Chaitanya's garment and, 95
 meeting with the Lord, 98-99
 petititon to the Lord, 94-95
 service to the Lord, 99-100
 son of, 97-98
 sweeping of road, 98
Prayag (Allahabad), 104
Prayojana, 121, 122
Prema-bhakti, 81
Prema Tarangini (Sadananda Kavisurya Brahma), 143
Prema-vilasa-vivarta, 84-85, 137
Pundarik Vidyanidhi, 43
Puri, 67, 93, 147, 156-57

devotees's coming to, 129
Lord Chaitanya's return to, 127-39
See also Jagannath Puri
Puridas. *See* Kavi Karnapur

Radha Kanta Math, 136
Radha kunda, 105
Radharani, Shrimati, 43, 46, 82, 83-84, 151, 152, 158
  manifestation of, 43
Raghava Pandit, 129
Raghunath Bhatta Goswami, 35, 129, 147
Raghunath Das Goswami, 129, 137, 147
Rajahmundry, governor of, 78-79
  See also Ramananda Roy
Rama, meaning of, 46
Ramachandra, Lord, 52
Ramachandra Khan, 133
Ramadas, 110
Ramananda Gaudiya Math (monastery), 85-86
Ramananda Roy, 73, 76, 78-85, 95-98, 129, 136, 138, 179n.77
Ramanuja, 6, 7, 8
Ramanuja (Shri) Sampradaya, 8
Ranga-kshetra, temple of, 163
Ranganath Swami, 90
  temple of, 87-88
Rangaraj Bhatta, 90
Rasa (relationship with God), 6, 82
Rasikananda, 149
Ratha-yatra festival, 100, 151-54, 157-59
  British Imperialists and, 152-54
  confidential theme of, 152
Ravindra Swarup Das, 12
Realization, levels of, 117-19
  analogy clarifying, 119-20
Religious pursuit, ultimate perfection of, 108
Renaissance
  devotional, 2
  European, 1-2, 12
  spiritual, 12-13
Renunciation (*sannyasa*), 61-66, 81
Rupa Goswami, Shrila, 19, 47, 52, 109-14, 128, 147, 162, 165, 168
  prayers of, 110-11
Rupanugas, 113-14

Sachidevi (mother), 15, 26, 27, 28-29, 58, 62, 131
Sacrifice, greatest, 51

Sadananda Kavisurya Brahma, 143
Sadashiva. *See* Adwaita Acharya
Sakara Mallik, 100-102
Sakhya (friendly love), 6
Sakhya-rasa, 113
Samadhi, 127
Sambandha, 121, 122
Sanatan, 128, 147
Sanatan dharma (eternal function of the soul), 3, 10
Sanatan Goswami, Shri, 19, 115-25, 142, 165, 180n.99
  at Benares, 117
  instructions to, 117
Sanatan Mishra, 35
Sankirtan, 88
Sankirtan movement, 12, 19, 20, 35, 53, 115, 163
  beginning of, 41
  in Benares, 124-25
Sankirtan-yagya, 51
Sannyasa, 61-66
Sannyasa guru, 62-63
Sanskrit debate, 31
Sarang, 128
Saraswati (goddess of learning), 32, 33-34
Sarvabhauma Bhattacharya, 67-73, 75, 76, 91, 93-94, 96-97, 129, 165
  conversion of, 72-73
Sata-prahariya bhava, 59
Sat-sandarbha (Jiva Goswami), 165, 166
Science of sound, 47
Scriptural evidence of divinity, 18-21
Sen Dynasty, 11
Service, devotional, 112
Shabda brahman, 47
Shad-bhuj-murti, 58
Shankara, 7, 174n.14
Shankaracharya, 8, 62, 70
Shanta-rasa, 113
Sherring, Rev. M.A., 116
Sheshashai, 106
Shikshashtakam prayers, 138-39
Shiva, 116-17, 180n.97, 183n.124
Shivananda Sen, 129
Shri Chaitanya-chandrodaya (Kavi Karnapur), 18
Shri Chaitanya Charitamrita (Krishnadas Kaviraj Goswami), v, vi, 18, 20, 34
Shridhar Swami, 106n.181
Shri Krishna Chaitanya-charitamrita (Murari Gupta), 17

Index

Shrimad Bhagavatam, vii, 4, 18–19, 84, 144, 166, 167
"Shri Mandir" (temple), 156
Shri Mayapur, 174*n*.25
Shrinivas Acharya, 148
Shri Nrisingha-chalam (Jaiyada Nrisingha), 78
Shripad Shankaracharya, 25
Shri Rangam, 87–91
Shri Shri Kishor-Kishori, vi
Shri Shri Radha-Damodar, vi
Shri Shri Radha-Govinda, vi
Shrivas Thakur, 43, 45, 58, 76, 129, 142
Shuddhadvaita (pure non-dualism), 8
Shukadev Goswami, 84
Shunya Samhita (Achyutananda), 143
Shvetashvatara Upanishad, 164
Shyama kunda, 105
Shyamananda, 148, 148–49
Sikhi Mahiti, 129
Sindhu River, 9
Sitadevi, abduction of, 90
Sitadevi Thakurani, 16, 131
Six Goswamis of Vrindavan, 129, 165
Society, *Vedas* divisions of, 79–80
Soul, 111–12, 119
Sound, science of, 47
Spiritual renaissance, 12–13
Staal, J. F., 167
Staff, Nityananda Prabhu's breaking of the, 65–66
Sthayibhava, 112–13
Subhadra, 153, 157
Sudarshan, 28
Sufis, 110
Supersoul, 119
Svamsha, 121–22
Svayam-rupa, 120–22
Swarup Damodar, vii, 129, 136, 137, 138

Tad-ekatma, 120–22
Tapan Mishra, 35, 104, 117
Tattvavadis, 8
Teachings of Lord Chaitanya, The (Prabhupada), ii
Ten offenses, 49–50
Thompson, Richard L., 169
Tiruppana, 6
Tondaradippodi, 6
Tota Gopinath Deity, merging into, 142–43
Tridanda philosophy, 65

Trilochan Singh, 128
Truth
  Absolute, 118, 120
  higher, 80–81
  See also Realization, levels of
Tukaram, 181*n*.109
Twain, Mark, 116

Ujjvala-nilamani, 113–14
Uttar Pradesh, 48

Vaibhava, 121–22
Vakreshvara Pandit, 129, 136
Vallabha (Anupama) Goswami, 111
Varanasi. *See* Benares
Varnashram Dharma, 79–80
Vatsalya (parental love), 6
Vayu Purana, 19
Vedanta Sutra, 69–71, 149
Vedas, iii, iv, 3–4, 56, 154
  social divisions in, 79–80
  spiritual orders in, 80
Vedic literature, 3–4, 154
  Shrimati Radharani in, 84
Vegetarianism, 56–57
Vidagdha-madhava, 113
Vidyapati, 5
Vijuli Khan, 110
Vilas, 121–22
Vishaka, 79
Vishishtadvaita philosophy, 7
Vishnu, 28, 116–17
Vishnupriya Devi, Shri, 35–36, 62
Vishnu Purana, 79
Vishram Ghat, 104
Vishvakarma, 155
Vishvambar Mishra. *See* Chaitanya, Lord
Vishvanath Chakravarti Thakur, 108, 149, 166, 167
Vishvarup, 15–16
Vivekachudamani (Shripad Shankaracharya), 25
Vrindavan, 102, 103–8, 147
  devotees in, 148
  six Goswamis of, 129, 165
Vrindavandas Thakur, Shrila, 17, 33–34, 38, 125, 141
Vyasadev, 124
Vyenkata Bhatta, 87–88, 89

Women, Lord Chaitanya on, 130–31

Wordsworth, William, 170
Worship
  deity, 154–55
  idol, 154–55

Yamunacharya, 6
Yamuna (river), 64
Yashoda, Mother, 106
Yogamaya, 27
Yuga-avatars, 19
Yuga-dharma, 19, 163

F O L K B O O K S

FOLK art is, indeed, the oldest of the aristocracies of thought, and because it refuses what is passing and trivial, the merely clever and pretty, as certainly as the vulgar and insincere, and because it has gathered into itself the simplest and most unforgettable thoughts of the generations, it is the soil where all great art is rooted. Wherever it is spoken by the fireside, or sung by the roadside, or carved upon the lintel, appreciation of the arts that a single mind gives unity and design to, spreads quickly when its hour is come.

— *W.B. Yeats*